Ariel Feldman

The Dead Sea Scrolls Rewriting Samuel and Kings:
Texts and Commentary

Beihefte zur Zeitschrift für die alttestamentliche Wissenschaft

Edited by
John Barton, Ronald Hendel,
Reinhard G. Kratz and Markus Witte

Volume 469

Ariel Feldman

The Dead Sea Scrolls Rewriting Samuel and Kings

—

Texts and Commentary

DE GRUYTER

G

ISBN 978-3-11-033811-9
e-ISBN (PDF) 978-3-11-033929-1
e-ISBN (EPUB) 978-3-11-038949-4
ISSN 0934-2575

Library of Congress Cataloging-in-Publication Data
A CIP catalog record for this book has been applied for at the Library of Congress.

Bibliographic information published by the Deutsche Nationalbibliothek
The Deutsche Nationalbibliothek lists this publication in the Deutsche Nationalbibliografie;
detailed bibliographic data are available in the Internet at http://dnb.dnb.de.

© 2015 Walter de Gruyter GmbH, Berlin/Boston
Typesetting: Dörlemann Satz GmbH & Co. KG, Lemförde
Printing and binding: CPI books GmbH, Leck
♾ Printed on acid-free paper
Printed in Germany

www.degruyter.com

MIX
Papier aus verantwor-
tungsvollen Quellen
FSC
www.fsc.org   FSC® C083411

Contents

Abbreviations

Periodicals and Serials

AB	The Anchor Bible
AGJU	Arbeiten zur Geschichte des antiken Judentums und des Urchristentums
BETL	Bibliotheca ephemeridum theologicarum lovaniensium
BN	Biblische Notizen
BZAW	Beihefte zur Zeitschrift für die alttestamentliche Wissenschaft
CBQ	Catholic Biblical Quarterly
DJD	Discoveries in the Judaean Desert
DSD	Dead Sea Discoveries
HTR	Harvard Theological Review
HUCA	Hebrew Union College Annual
JAJ	Journal of Ancient Judaism
JAJSup	Journal of Ancient Judaism Supplement Series
JBL	Journal of Biblical Literature
JJS	Journal of Jewish Studies
JSJ	Journal for the Study of Judaism
JSJSup	Journal for the Study of Judaism Supplement Series
JSNT	Journal for the Study of the New Testament
JSP	Journal for the Study of the Pseudepigrapha
LCL	Loeb Classical Library
OLP	Orientalia lovaniensia periodica
RevQ	Revue de Qumrân
SJOT	Scandinavian Journal of the Old Testament
STDJ	Studies on the Texts of the Desert of Judah
SubBi	Subsidia biblica
SVT	Supplements to Vetus Testamentum
SVTP	Studia in Veteris Testamenti pseudepigraphica
TSAJ	Texte und Studien zum antiken Judentum

Frequently Cited Works

ABD   *Anchor Bible Dictionary.* Edited by D. N. Freedman. New York: Doubleday, 1992, 6 vols.

BDB   F. Brown, S. R. Driver, C. A. Briggs, *Hebrew and English Lexicon of the
Old Testament.* Oxford: Clarendon Press, 1975.

Davis, "Elijah"
     C. J.P. Davis, "4Q382, Elijah and the Dead Sea Scrolls." M. A. thes.,
Trinity Western University, 2002.

DSSR   *The Dead Sea Scrolls Reader.* Edited by D. W. Parry, E. Tov. Leiden:
Brill, 2004–2005, 6 vols.

EDEJ   *The Eerdmans Dictionary of Early Judaism.* Edited by J. J. Collins, D. C.
Harlow. Grand Rapids, Michigan, Cambridge, UK: Eerdmans, 2010.

EDSS   *The Encyclopedia of the Dead Sea Scrolls.* Edited by L. H. Schiffman,
J. C. VanderKam. New York: Oxford University Press, 2000, 2 vols.

García Martínez, Tigchelaar, *Study Edition*
     F. García Martínez, E. J.C. Tigchelaar, *The Dead Sea Scrolls Study
Edition.* Leiden: Brill, 1997–1998, 2 vols.

HALOT   L. Koehler, W. Baumgartner, *The Hebrew and Aramaic Lexicon of
the Old Testament.* Edited and translated by M. E.J. Richardson et al.
Leiden: Brill, 1994–2000, 5 vols.

Jacobson, *Commentary*
     H. Jacobson, *A Commentary on Pseudo-Philo's Liber Antiquitatum
Biblicarum.* AGJU 31; Leiden: Brill, 1996, 2 vols.

Jastrow, *Dictionary*
     M. Jastrow, *A Dictionary of the Targumim, the Talmud Bavli and
Yerushalmi, and the Midrashic Literature.* New York: Judaica Press,
1982.

Joüon-Muraoka, *Grammar*
     P. Joüon, *A Grammar of Biblical Hebrew.* Translated and revised by
T. Muraoka. SubBi 14/II; Rome: Editrice Pontifico Instituto Biblico,
1996.

NETS   *A New English Translation of the Septuagint.* Edited by A. Pietersma,
B. G. Wright. New York, Oxford: Oxford University Press, 2007.

OTP   *The Old Testament Pseudepigrapha.* Edited by J. H. Charlesworth.
Garden City: Doubleday, 1983, 2 vols.

Outside the Bible
     Outside the Bible. Edited by L. H. Feldman et al. Philadelphia: The
Jewish Publication Sociey, 2013, 3 vols.

Preliminary Concordance
R. E. Brown et al., *Preliminary Concordance to the Hebrew and Aramaic Fragments from Qumran II-X*. Published privately, Göttingen, 1988, 4 vols.

PTSDSSP   *Princeton Theological Seminary Dead Sea Scrolls Project*. Edited by J. H. Charlesworth. Tübingen/Louisville: J. C.B. Mohr/Westminster John Knox, 1994–2011, 7 vols.

Qimron, *Hebrew of the Dead Sea Scrolls*
E. Qimron, *The Hebrew of the Dead Sea Scrolls*. HSS 29; Atlanta: Scholars Press, 1986.

Qimron, *Hebrew Writings*
E. Qimron, *The Dead Sea Scrolls: The Hebrew Writings*. Between Bible and Mishnah; Jerusalem: Yad Ben-Zvi Press, 2010–2014, 3 vols.

Schürer, *History*
E. Schürer, *The History of the Jewish People in the Age of Jesus Christ (175 BC – AD 135)*. New English Version Revised and Edited by G. Vermes, F. Millar, and M. Black. Edinburgh: T & T Clark, 1973–87, 4 vols.

Tov, *Scribal Practices*
E. Tov, *Scribal Practices and Approaches Reflected in the Texts Found in the Judean Desert*. STDJ 54; Leiden: Brill, 2004.

Tov, *Textual Criticism*
E. Tov, *Textual Criticism of the Hebrew Bible: Third Edition Revised and Expanded*. Minneapolis: Fortress Press, 2012.

Wacholder-Abegg, *Preliminary Edition*
B. Z. Wacholder, M. G. Abegg, *A Preliminary Edition of the Unpublished Dead Sea Scrolls*. Washington, D. C.: Biblical Archaeology Society, 1991–1995, 3 vols.

Wise et al., *Dead Sea Scrolls*
M. Wise, M. Abegg, E. Cook, *The Dead Sea Scrolls. A New Translation*. Revised Edition. New York: HarperCollins, 2005.

DJD Volumes

DJD 1   D. Barthélemy, J. T. Milik, *Qumran Cave 1*. DJD 1; Oxford: Clarendon Press, 1955.

DJD 3   M. Baillet et al., *Les 'petites grottes' de Qumrân*. DJD 3; Oxford: Clarendon Press, 1962, 2 vols.

DJD 5   J. M. Allegro with A. A. Anderson, *Qumrân Cave 4.I (4Q158–4Q186)*. DJD 5; Oxford: Clarendon Press, 1968.

DJD 10   E. Qimron, J. Strugnell, *Qumran Cave 4.V: Miqṣat Maʻaśe ha-Torah*. DJD 10; Oxford: Clarendon Press, 1994.

DJD 13   H. Attridge et al., *Qumran Cave 4.VIII: Parabiblical Texts, Part 1*. DJD 13; Oxford: Clarendon Press, 1994.

DJD 14   E. Ulrich et al., *Qumran Cave 4.IX: Deuteronomy, Joshua, Judges, Kings*. DJD 14; Oxford: Clarendon, 1995.

DJD 17   F. M. Cross et al., *Qumran Cave 4.XII: 1–2 Samuel*. DJD 17; Oxford: Clarendon Press, 2005.

DJD 19   M. Broshi et al., *Qumran Cave 4.XIV: Parabiblical Texts, Part 2*. DJD 19; Oxford: Clarendon Press, 1995.

DJD 22   G. J. Brooke et al., *Qumran Cave 4.XVII: Parabiblical Texts, Part 3*. DJD 22; Oxford: Clarendon Press, 1996.

DJD 23   F. García Martínez et al., *Qumran Cave 11.II: 11Q2–18, 11Q20–31*. DJD 23; Oxford: Clarendon Press, 1998.

DJD 25   É. Puech., *Qumran Cave 4.XVIII: Textes hébreux (4Q521–4Q528, 4Q576–4Q579)*. DJD 25; Oxford: Clarendon Press, 1998.

DJD 27   H. Cotton, A. Yardeni, *Aramaic, Hebrew and Greek Documentary Texts from Naḥal Ḥever and Other Sites*. DJD 27; Oxford: Clarendon Press, 1997.

DJD 28   D. M. Gropp, M. J. Bernstein, *Wadi Daliyeh II: The Samaria Papyri from Wadi Daliyeh and Qumran Cave 4.XXVIII: Miscellanea, Part 2*. DJD 28; Oxford: Clarendon Press, 2001.

DJD 29   E. Chazon et al., *Qumran Cave 4.XX: Poetical and Liturgical Texts, Part 2*. DJD 29; Oxford: Clarendon Press, 1999.

DJD 30   D. Dimant, *Qumran Cave 4.XXI: Parabiblical Texts, Part 4: Pseudo-Prophetic Texts*. DJD 30; Oxford: Clarendon Press, 2001.

DJD 36   S. J. Pfann et al., *Qumran Cave 4.XXVI: Cryptic Texts; Miscellanea, Part 1*. DJD 36; Oxford: Clarendon Press, 2000.

DJD 37   É. Puech, *Qumran Cave 4.XXVII: Textes arameens, deuxieme partie: 4Q550–575*. DJD 37; Oxford: Clarendon Press, 2008.

DJD 39   *The Text from the Judaean Desert: Indices and an Introduction to the Discoveries in the Judaean Desert Series*. Edited by E. Tov. DJD 39; Oxford: Clarendon Press, 2002.

Preface

The editing of the Dead Sea Scrolls is frequently compared to putting together a puzzle. The present attempt to re-edit the scrolls rewriting Samuel and Kings fits that description very well. The "pieces" of this "puzzle" are small and the task of making sense out of them is daunting. I am indebted to those who trained me to rise to this challenge. Prof. Devorah Dimant, who saw the need for a new edition of the Dead Sea Scrolls rewriting the Scripture, guided me as I worked on the fragmentary Dead Sea Scrolls rewriting the Torah (now available in *Scripture and Interpretation,* de Gruyter 2014). Prof. George J. Brooke lead me through yet another textual "puzzle," the rewritten Joshua scrolls from Qumran (published as *Rewritten Joshua Scrolls from Qumran,* de Gruyter 2013). As to the monograph at hand, several mentors, colleagues, and friends offered me advice and critique. Prof. Warren Carter encouraged me to turn this project into a book. Dr. Kipp Davis sent me a copy of his work on 4Q382. Prof. Elisha Qimron graciously reviewed my edition of 4Q382 and shared with me drafts of his own forthcoming edition of 4Q160 and 4Q382. While his final edition of the scrolls re-edited here was published after the completion of this volume, I was still able to incorporate most of his new readings and reconstructions. Dr. Noam Mizrahi, as always, generously lent his linguistic expertise. Dr. Joe McDonald skillfully proofread the entire manuscript. Profs. Reinhard Kratz, John Barton, Ronald Hendel, and Markus Witte, the editors of the BZAW series, kindly agreed to accept this volume for publication in their distinguished series.

This research began with a grant from the Orion Center for the Study of the Dead Sea Scrolls and was later supported by the Newton International Fellowships Alumni Funding. A semester-long research leave granted by Brite Divinity School allowed me to complete the work on this book. I am grateful to all these organizations.

I dedicate this volume to my wife and best friend, Faina, who, true to her name, is the light of my life.

Brite Divinity School
January 2015

Introduction

Samuel and Kings captivate their readers, both modern and ancient. A vivid testimony to this is a vast body of exegetical traditions, Jewish, Christian, Samaritan, and Muslim, concerned with Samuel-Kings.[1] Some of these traditions have been adequately studied, while others await detailed inquiry. The present monograph explores one admittedly very limited stratum of this multi-story exegetical edifice: the interpretation of Samuel-Kings in the Dead Sea Scrolls, and particularly in the scrolls rewriting these books. Preserved in their original language and dated to the last century BCE, these rewritings are among our earliest extant witnesses to the transmission and interpretation of Samuel-Kings, which underlines their importance for reconstructing the reception history of these books.

The Dead Sea Scrolls rewriting Samuel-Kings belong with a larger body of previously unknown ancient Jewish texts rewriting the Hebrew Bible that emerged from the caves of Qumran. The precise scope of this corpus is yet to be clarified, as the criteria for identifying a rewritten Bible/Scripture text remain a matter of a lively scholarly discussion.[2] Yet if one is willing to include within it not only rewritings of biblical narratives but also texts reworking legal, prophetic, and sapiential materials,[3] it would appear that rewritten Scripture literature from Qumran as a

---

1 For an overview of the Jewish and Christian exegesis of Sam-Kgs, see L. Ginzberg, *Legends of the Jews* (Philadelphia: The Jewish Publication Society, 2003), 2:887–1109; J.R. Franke (ed.), *Ancient Christian Commentary on Scripture: Old Testament IV: Joshua, Judges, Ruth, 1–2 Samuel* (Downers Grove, Illinois: InterVarsity Press, 2005); M. Conti (ed.), *Ancient Christian Commentary on Scripture: Old Testament V: 1–2 Kings, 1–2 Chronicles, Ezra, Nehemiah, Esther* (Downers Grove, Illinois: InterVarsity Press, 2008). Some of the key Samaritan texts are discussed in P. Stenhouse, "Samaritan Chronicles," in *The Samaritans* (ed. A.D. Crown; Tübingen: J.C.B. Mohr, 1989), 219–264. For Islamic lore, see the relevant entries in P.J. Bearman et al., (eds.), *The Encyclopedia of Islam* (2nd ed.; Leiden: Brill, 1960–2005), 12 vols. For a sample of studies on the reception history of Sam-Kgs across these traditions, see D. McLain Carr, *From D to Q: A Study of Early Jewish Interpretations of Solomon's Dream at Gibeon* (SBL Monograph Series; Atlanta, Georgia: Scholars Press, 1991); P. Torijano, *Solomon the Esoteric King: From King to Magus: Development of a Tradition* (JSJSup 73; Leiden: Brill, 2002); J. Verheyden, *The Figure of Solomon in Jewish, Christian and Islamic Tradition: King, Sage and Architect* (Themes in Biblical Narrative; Leiden: Brill, 2013).

2 For a critical overview of the recent scholarship on the rewritten Scripture, see D. Machiela, "Once More, with Feeling: Rewritten Scripture in Ancient Judaism—A Review of Recent Developments," *JJS* 61 (2010): 308–320. Some of the main issues pertaining to the rewritten Scripture are discussed afresh in J. Zsengellér, K. Gáspár (eds.), *Rewritten Bible after Fifty Years: A Last Dialogue with Geza Vermes* (JSJSup 166; Leiden: Brill, 2014).

3 As argued, among others, by G.J. Brooke, "Rewritten Bible," EDSS, 777–781.

corpus is dominated by the rewritings of the Torah,[4] whereas among the non-Penateuchal rewritings, the pride of place belongs to those of the Former Prophets.[5] Although there is no scroll rewriting the book of Judges,[6] Joshua is reworked in five scrolls,[7] whereas Samuel and Kings are rewritten in another three or four: 4Q160, 4Q382, 4Q481a, and 6Q9.[8] Yet, while the reworked Joshua scrolls have received considerable scholarly attention, the texts rewriting Samuel and Kings have been mostly neglected. To a large extent, this is a result of their poor state of preservation and, in the case of 4Q160 and 4Q382, inadequate first editions. The present study, bringing all four scrolls under one cover for the first time, hopes to fill this gap.

This monograph proceeds as follows. Its first chapter "sets the stage" by surveying Second Temple texts concerned with Samuel-Kings. Chapters 2–5 analyze the scrolls 4Q160, 4Q382, 4Q481a, and 6Q9. Each chapter offers a revised text of the manuscript, a commentary, and, where applicable, a discussion of wider issues posed by the scroll. Utilizing the insights gained from the examination of all four scrolls, the concluding chapter, Chapter 6, outlines the contribution of the Dead Sea Scrolls rewriting Samuel-Kings to the study of the transmission and interpretation of these biblical books in Second Temple times.

---

4 For a recent re-edition and discussion of some of these, see A. Feldman, L. Goldman, *Scripture and Interpretation: Qumran Texts that Rework the Bible* (ed. D. Dimant; BZAW 449; Berlin: de Gruyter, 2014).

5 The Latter Prophets are represented by the rewritings of Jeremiah (4QapocrJer A [4Q383]; 4QapocrJer B? [4Q384]; 4QapocrJer C[a-f] [4Q385a, 387, 387a, 388a, 389–390]; M. Smith, DJD 19:137–152; D. Dimant, DJD 30:91–260) and Ezekiel (4QpsEzek[a-e] [4Q385, 386, 385b, 388, 391; see also 4Q385c]; M. Smith, DJD 19:153–194; D. Dimant, DJD 30:1–88). The precise number of works found in these manuscripts remains unclear. See E. Tigchelaar, "Classifications of the Collection of Dead Sea Scrolls and the Case of Apocryphon of Jeremiah C," *JSJ* 43 (2012): 533; Qimron, *Hebrew Writings*, 2:84, 94; K. Davis, *The Cave 4 Apocryphon of Jeremiah and The Qumran Jeremianic Traditions* (STDJ 111; Leiden, Boston: Brill, 2014). As to the Writings, see the recent discussion of 11QPs[a] as a rewriting of Psalter in D. A. Teeter, "Torah, Wisdom, and the Composition of Rewritten Scripture: Jubilees and and 11QPs[a] in Comparative Perspective," in *Wisdom and Torah: The Reception of 'Torah' in the Wisdom Literature of the Second Temple Period* (ed. B. U. Schipper, D. A. Teeter; JSJSup 163; Leiden: Brill, 2013), 260. On the rewriting of Prov 1–9 in 4Q525 (and the related 5Q16 and 4Q184), see E. Uusimäki, "Use of Scriptures in 4QBeatitudes: A Torah-Adjustment to Proverbs 1–9," *DSD* 20 (2013): 71–97.

6 The scroll 4Q522 reworks Judges 1 (frg. 8) along with passages from Joshua. See A. Feldman, *The Rewritten Joshua Scrolls from Qumran* (BZAW 438; Berlin: de Gruyter, 2014), 128–167.

7 These are 4Q123, 4Q378, 4Q379, 4Q522, and 5Q9. Although they are frequently assumed to be copies of the same literary work, "Apocryphon of Joshua," these scrolls do not overlap and should be viewed as separate rewritings of Joshua (Feldman, ibid., 187–193). A scroll from Masada, Mas 1039–211, is often listed as another copy of the "Apocryphon of Joshua." However, a close study indicates that this scroll does not rewrite the book of Joshua (Feldman, ibid., 182–186).

8 On the possibility that 4Q160 and 4Q382 are copies of the same composition, see Chapter 6.

Chapter 1: Samuel and Kings in Second Temple Literature

This survey of the use of Samuel and Kings in Second Temple literature pursues two goals.[9] First, it maps the literary and exegetical landscape in which the Qumran rewritings of Samuel-Kings ought to be situated. Second, it assesses the contribution of other Dead Sea Scrolls to the study of the transmission and interpretation of Samuel-Kings.[10] To keep this overview within manageable limits, writings that came to be a part of the Jewish canon, as well as those composed after 70 CE, are excluded from it.[11] Two notable exceptions are 1–2 Chronicles and Josephus's *Jewish Antiquities*, vital for any study of the rewritings of Samuel-Kings.[12] This chapter begins with a brief analysis of the Qumran copies of Samuel and Kings. A survey of Second Temple writings alluding to, quoting from, and expanding on these books follows. To make sure the "forest is seen for the trees," these texts are grouped according to the way they use Samuel-Kings.[13] First, instances of expositional use are scrutinized.[14] Next come compositional uses of

---

9 This survey does not aim at being exhaustive, but rather representative. The reader is referred to more detailed studies elaborated in the footnotes. Unless otherwise noted, all translations of the biblical texts in this book are from the new JPS translation.

10 For earlier surveys of the Qumran materials pertaining to Sam-Kgs, see F. Polak, "Samuel, First and Second Books of," EDSS, 2:819–823; J. Trebolle Barrera, "Kings, First and Second Books of," ibid., 1:467–468; idem, "Qumran Fragments of the Books of Kings," in *The Books of Kings: Sources, Composition, Historiography and Reception* (ed. A. Lemaire, B. Halpern; SVT 129; Leiden, Boston: Brill, 2010), 19–39.

11 Among the works excluded from this overview because of their late date are 2 Baruch, 4 Ezra, Martyrdom and Ascension of Isaiah, Testament of Solomon, and the Lives of the Prophets. Some scholars argue also for a post-destruction date for Pseudo-Philo's Biblical Antiquities, yet this issue remains unresolved (see, for instance, F. J. Murphy, "Biblical Antiquities [Pseudo-Philo]," EDEJ, 440). As one of the early rewritings of Samuel, it is included here, as are the New Testament writings, though some of them are dated after 70 CE.

12 Writings relying on Chronicles, rather than on Sam-Kgs, e.g., 1 Esdras, are excluded from this discussion. However, those instances where it is difficult to determine whether a given Second Temple text relies on Sam-Kgs or on a parallel passage from 1–2 Chr (or, for that matter, Isaiah or Jeremiah) are included. See further E. Ben Zvi, "The Authority of 1–2 Chronicles in the Late Second Temple Period," in idem, *History, Literature and Theology in the Book of Chronicles* (London, Oakville: Equinox, 2006), 243–268; I. Kalimi, *The Retelling of Chronicles in Jewish Tradition and Literature: A Historical Journey* (Winona Lake, IN: Eisenbrauns, 2009), 34–121.

13 I have used the typology proposed by D. Dimant, "Use and Interpretation of Mikra in the Apocrypha and Pseudepigrapha," in *Mikra* (ed. M. Mulder; Peabody, Massachusetts: Hendrickson, 2004), 379–419.

14 As Dimant, ibid., 382, remarks, when the Scripture is used expositionally, "the divine word is

Samuel-Kings, including allusions, references to figures and events, pseudepigraphy, and rewritings. The discussion of each type of use begins with texts that were known prior to the discovery of the Dead Sea Scrolls, and then proceeds with writings that have emerged from the caves of Qumran.

The Qumran Copies of Samuel and Kings

Before the Dead Sea Scrolls came to light, the scholarly quest for the early textual history of Samuel-Kings focused on meticulous comparison of medieval copies of the Masoretic Text (henceforth: MT) with ancient translations. However, since the Hebrew texts underlying the Aramaic Targum, Latin Vulgate, and Syriac Peshitta seem to be close to the MT, they reveal little about the time before it emerged as the dominant textual tradition.[15] Even the contribution of the earlier Septuagint (henceforth: LXX) version of Samuel-Kings (1–4 Kingdoms/Reigns) is limited,[16] for in 2 Sam 11:2–1 Kgs 2:11 and 1 Kgs 22—2 Kgs 1–25 the LXX features the so-called kaige revision of the Old Greek toward a Hebrew text also close to the MT.[17] Still, the Old Greek sections of Samuel-Kings, limited as they are, yield valuable data. In the case of Samuel, several passages of the non-kaige Greek differ considerably from the MT. Some of the best known deviations are found in the Song of Hannah (1 Sam 2) and the account of David's combat with Goliath (1 Sam 16–18). Since these divergences appear to originate with the translator's Hebrew text, this putative Hebrew *Vorlage* of the Old Greek Samuel is considered to be a different, earlier (in comparison to the MT), edition of this book.[18] No less

---

introduced in order to interpret it as such," whereas in a compositional use "the biblical element is subservient to the independent aim and structure of its new context."

15 See E. Tov, "The Aramaic, Syriac, and Latin Translations of Hebrew Scripture vis-à-vis the Masoretic Text," in *Eukarpa, homage à Gilles Dorival* (ed. M. Loubet, D. Pralon; Paris: Cerf, 2011), 173–185; idem, *Textual Criticism*, 149, 152, 153. To be sure, some of the exegetical traditions embedded in these translations may go back to Second Temple times. See, for instance, Y. Maori, *The Peshitta Version of the Pentateuch and Early Jewish Exegesis* (Jerusalem: Magnes Press, 1995; Hebrew).

16 For an overview of LXX Sam-Kgs, see B. A. Taylor, NETS, 244–248. On the date and provenance of the Greek translations of the Former Prophets, see E. Tov, "Reflections on the Septuagint with Special Attention Paid to the Post-Pentateuchal Translations," in *Die Septuaginta–Texte, Theologien, Einflüsse* (ed. W. Kraus, M. Karrer; WUNT 252; Tübingen: Mohr Siebeck, 2010), 3–22.

17 See D. Barthélemy, *Les devanciers d'Aquila* (SVT 10; Leiden: Brill, 1963).

18 See discussion and pertinent bibliography in Tov, *Textual Criticism*, 301–303. On the use of the term "edition" to describe different stages of the literary growth of certain books included in the Hebrew Bible, see recently G. J. Brooke, "What Is a Variant Edition? Perspectives from the

significant is the evidence offered by the Old Greek of 1 Kgs 2:12–21:43, featuring diverse textual phenomena absent from the MT, e.g., duplications, alternative accounts, re-arrangements, and theme summaries. Again, rather than reflecting the translator's tampering with the text, these seem to have been found in his *Vorlage*, which, according to some scholars, is a rewriting of an MT-like text.[19] As to the kaige sections of Samuel-Kings, the closest attainable approximation of the Old Greek translation thereof seems to be preserved in the Antiochene or proto-Lucianic manuscripts, as well as in the Vetus Latina translation made from the Greek. In the case of Kings, the analysis of these witnesses may also indicate a different literary edition of this book, likely to be dated earlier than the MT.[20]

The copies of Samuel and Kings from Qumran shed further light on the textual histories of these books in late Second Temple times.[21] Four manuscripts of Samuel were identified among the Dead Sea Scrolls:[22]

– 1QSam (1Q7), extant in seven fragments dated to the early Herodian period, preserves 1 Sam 18:17–18; 2 Sam 20:6–10; 21:16–18; 23:9–12.[23]
– 4QSam[a] (4Q51), dated to 50–25 BCE, is comprised of eleven partially preserved columns, some 165 fragments with identified contents, and multiple uni-

---

Qumran Scrolls," in *In the Footsteps of Sherlock Holmes: Studies in the Biblical Text in Honour of Anneli Aejmelaeus* (ed. by K. De Troyer et al.; Leuven, Paris, Walpole, MA: Peeters, 2014), 607–622.

19 See the recent studies by G. Darshan, "The Long Additions in LXX 1 Kgs (3 Kgdms) 2 (35a–k; 46a–l) and their Importance for the Question of the Literary History of 1 Kgs 1–11," *Tarbiz* 75 (2006): 5–50 (Hebrew); E. Tov, "Three Strange Books of the LXX: 1 Kings, Esther, and Daniel Compared with Similar Rewritten Compositions from Qumran and Elsewhere," in idem, *Hebrew Bible, Greek Bible and Qumran: Collected Essays* (TSAJ 121; Tübingen: Mohr Siebeck, 2008), 283–308; Z. Talshir, "The Miscellanies in 2 Reigns 2:35a-o, 46a-l and the Composition of the Book of Kings/Reigns," in *XIV Congress of the International Organization for Septuagint and Cognate Studies: Helsinki 2010* (ed. M. K.H. Peters; Septuagint and Cognate Studies 59; Atlanta: Society of Biblical Literature, 2013), 155–174. For a survey of earlier scholarship, see P. S.F. van Keulen, *Two Versions of the Solomon Narrative* (SVT 104; Leiden, Boston: Brill, 2005), 1–25.

20 See Tov, *Textual Criticism*, 306–308; A. Schenker, "The Septuagint in the Text History of 1–2 Kings," in *The Books of Kings: Sources, Composition, Historiography and Reception* (ed. A. Lemaire, B. Halpern; SVT 129; Leiden, Boston: Brill, 2010), 3–15.

21 To be sure, the very notion of different textual forms/editions of a given scriptural book is by and large a result of the impact that the Scrolls, not least the copies of Samuel, had on biblical studies. Thus, the foregoing discussion of the textual evidence on Samuel-Kings available prior to the discovery of Qumran is already informed by the Dead Sea Scrolls. Also, as Trebolle Barrera, "Qumran Fragments," 33, points out, the identification of the kaige revision is a result of the discovery of the Minor Prophets scroll from Naḥal Ḥever (8ḤevXIIgr).

22 For an overview and bibliography, see A. Lange, *Handbuch der Textfunde vom Toten Meer: Band 1: Die Handschriften biblischer Bücher von Qumran und den anderen Fundorten* (Tübingen: Mohr Siebeck, 2009), 213–253.

23 See D. Barthélemy, DJD 1:64–65. The dating of the scroll is according to Lange, ibid., 214.

dentified fragments. These contain 1 Sam 1:9, 11–13, 17–18, 22–26, 28; 2:1–10, 16–3:4; 3:18–21; 4:3–4, 9–10, 12; 5:8–6:13, 16–18; 6:20–7:1; 8:7, 9–14, 16–20; 9:6–8, 10–12, 16–24; 10:3–12, 14, 16, 18; 10:24–11:2, 7–12; 12:7–8, 10–19; 14:24–25, 28–34, 47–51; 15:20–21, 24–32; 17:3–8, 40–41; 18:4–5; 20:37–40; 22:10–11; 24:3–5, 8–10, 14–23; 25:3–12, 20–21, 25–27, 38–40; 26:9–12, 21–24; 27:1–2; 27:8–28:3; 28:22–29:1; 30:22–31; 31:1–4; 2 Sam 1:4–5, 10–13; 2:5–16, 25–28; 2:29–3:15; 3:17, 21; 3:23–4:4; 4:9–5:3, 6–16, 18–19; 6:2–18; 7:6–7, 22–29; 8:1–8; 9:8–10; 10:4–5, 6–7, 18–19; 11:2–12, 15–20; 12:1, 3, 4–6, 8–9, 13–14, 14–20; 12:29–13:6; 13:13–34, 36–14:3; 14:14, 18–19, 33; 15:1–7, 20–23, 26–31, 37–16:2; 16:6–8, 10–13, 17–18, 20–23; 17:2–3, 23–25; 17:28–18:11; 18:28–29; 19:6–12, 14–16; 19:25, 27–29, 38; 20:1–2, 4, 9–14, 19, 21–25; 21:1, 3–6, 8–9, 12, 15–17; 22:17, 19, 21, 24, 26–28, 30–31; 22:33–23:6; 23:14–16, 21–22, 37–39; 24:16–22.[24]

- 4QSam[b] (4Q52), preserved in twenty three fragments, is dated to around 250 BCE. It contains 1 Sam 12:3, 5–6; 14:41–42; 15:16–18; 16:1–11; 19:10–13, 15–17; 20:26–21:3, 5–10; 22:8–9; 23:8–23.[25]
- 4QSam[c] (4Q53), dated approximately to 100–75 BCE, survives in three partially preserved columns and four small fragments. The following passages are extant: 1 Sam 25:30–32; 2 Sam 14:7–21, 22–15:15.[26]

Of these four manuscripts, 1QSam seems to be the closest to MT Samuel. Yet, this description must be qualified: the scroll is highly fragmentary and its meager remains at times disagree with the MT. For instance, its wording of 2 Sam 20:8 is significantly shorter than that of the MT and other textual witnesses. 4QSam[b] shares several readings with the putative Hebrew *Vorlage* of the Old Greek, yet also contains multiple unique readings.[27] 4QSam[c] features an array of variants, some supported by the Old Greek, some unique to this scroll.[28] The largest manuscript, 4QSam[a], preserves a significant number of variant readings, some of which are quite extensive. Since its publication, several approaches to this scroll have emerged. One of these highlights the readings that 4QSam[a] shares with the presumed *Vorlage* of the Old Greek of Samuel and places this scroll within the

---

24 F. M. Cross, D. W. Parry, R. J. Saley, DJD 17:1–216.

25 F. M. Cross, D. W. Parry, R. J. Saley, DJD 17:219–246; É. Puech, "4QSamuel[a] (4Q51): notes épigraphiques et nouvelles identifications," in *Florilegium Lovaniense: Studies in Septuagint and Textual Criticism in Honour of Florentino García Martínez* (ed. H. Ausloos et al.; BETL 224; Leuven: Peters, 2008), 373–386.

26 E. Ulrich, DJD 17:247–267.

27 F. M. Cross, D. W. Parry, R. J. Saley, DJD 17:221–224.

28 E. Ulrich, DJD 17:252–54.

same textual tradition.[29] Another approach emphasizes its multiple secondary readings reflecting exegetical techniques common to the rewritten Scripture. Among these are the nomistic reading of Eli's sons' misconduct, Hannah's vow for Samuel to become a Nazirite, the story of Nahash the eye-gouger, the account of the plague at the census, which employs phraseology found in Chronicles, and the story of David's transfer of the Ark, which aggrandizes sacrifices offered at that occasion. According to the chief proponent of this approach, the preponderance of such "midrashic" elements suggests that 4QSam[a] is an early commentary on Samuel, rather than a copy thereof.[30] To be sure, there are also several middle-course opinions accounting for the aspects of 4QSam[a] highlighted by these two approaches. One such view considers the similarities and divergences between the MT, LXX, and 4QSam[a] to be the outcome of scribal mishandling of the text (in the case of MT) and its expansion with midrashic elements (in the case of LXX and, to a greater extent, 4QSam[a]).[31] Another scholar describes 4QSam[a] as an attempt "to produce a perfect manuscript" by an amplification of the base text, which was closer to the *Vorlage* of the LXX, with materials originating in all kinds of sources, including Chronicles.[32] Yet another view classifies 4QSam[a] as a *codex mixtus* including some readings that are in agreement with the Old Greek, as well as previously unknown developments.[33] All in all, the prevalent scholarly opinion is that this manuscript contains a third edition of the book of Samuel, along with the MT and the Hebrew *Vorlage* of the Old Greek.[34]

The Books of Kings are extant at Qumran in three manuscripts:

---

29 For a recent presentation of the arguments, see F. M. Cross, R. J. Saley, "A Statistical Analysis of the Textual Character of 4QSamuel[a] (4Q51)," *DSD* 13 (2006): 46–54; idem, "Singular Readings in 4QSamuel[a] and the Question of Rewritten Scripture," *DSD* 20 (2013): 1–16.

30 Thus A. Rofé in his multiple articles. See, for instance, his "Midrashic Traits in 4Q51 (So-Called 4QSam[a])," in *Archaeology of the Books of Samuel* (ed. P. Hugo, A. Schenker; SVT 132; Leiden, Boston: Brill, 2010), 75–90.

31 Z. Talshir, "Biblical Text from the Judaean Desert," in *The Qumran Scrolls and Their World* (ed. M. Kister; Between Bible and Mishnah; Jerusalem: Yad Ben-Zvi, 2009), 1:127 (Hebrew).

32 A. Aejmelaeus, "Hannah's Psalm in 4QSam[a]," in *Archaeology of the Books of Samuel* (ed. P. Hugo, A. Schenker; SVT 132; Leiden, Boston: Brill, 2010), 37.

33 P. Hugo, "The History of the Book of Samuel: An Assessment of the Recent Research," in *Archaeology of the Books of Samuel* (ed. P. Hugo, A. Schenker; SVT 132; Leiden, Boston: Brill, 2010), 4.

34 See, for instance, Aejmelaeus, "Hannah's Psalm in 4QSam[a]," 37; Z. Talshir, "Textual Criticism at the Service of the Literary Criticism and the Question of an Eclectic Edition of the Hebrew Bible," in *After Qumran: Old and Modern Editions of the Biblical Texts–The Historical Books* (ed. H. Ausloos et. al.; BETL 246; Leuven, Paris, Walpole, MA: Peters, 2012), 34–60.

- 4QKgs (4Q54) survives in nine fragments, seven identified and two non-iden-tified, dated to the middle of the first century BCE.[35] The fragments preserve 1 Kgs 7:20–21, 25–27, 29–42, 50–8:9, 16–18.
- 5QKgs (5Q2) is extant in three fragments inscribed in a Hasmonean hand.[36] Belonging with the first column of the scroll, they contain 1 Kgs 1:1, 16–17, 27–37.
- 6QpapKgs (6Q4) is preserved in some seventy-five fragments of papyrus dated to the second half of the second century BCE.[37] Its extant fragments feature 1 Kgs 3:12–14, 28–31; 22:28–31; 2 Kgs 5:26; 6:32; 7:8–10, 20–8:5; 9:1–2, 10, 19, 21.

The extant text of 5QKgs agrees with the MT, including the point of division of Kings into two books.[38] The text of 4QKgs is also quite close to the MT,[39] with some variations in the use of prepositions, the definite article, and plural/singu-lar forms. More importantly, frg. 7 1–2, containing 1 Kgs 8:16–18, features phrases that are missing from the MT (probably due to homoioteleuton), yet are found in the parallel text of 2 Chr 6:5–6 (and, partially, in the LXX Kgs). 6QpapKgs attests to several variant readings, including instances of shorter and longer text (1 Kgs 22:30; 2 Kgs 7:20, 8:2, 3). Some of these are supported by the LXX (1 Kgs 22:31; 2 Kgs 8:3).

Samuel-Kings in Second Temple Literature: Expositional Uses

Prior to the discovery of the Dead Sea Scrolls, instances of an expositional use of Samuel-Kings in Second Temple literature were found exclusively in the allegori-cal works of Philo.[40] A prolific exegete, Philo engages Samuel-Kings only a few

---

35 J. Trebolle Barrera, DJD 14:171–183. According to the editor, one of the two unidentified frag-ments, frg. 8, may well belong with another scroll.

36 J. T. Milik, DJD 3.1:171–172.

37 M. Baillet, DJD 3.1:107–112.

38 Unlike the LXX, placing 1 Kgs 1:1–2:11 with 2 Sam. See J. Trebolle Barrera, "Samuel/Kings and Chronicles: Book Division and Text Composition," in *Studies in the Hebrew Bible, Qumran, and the Septuagint* (ed. P. W. Flint et al.; SVT 101; Leiden, Boston: Brill, 2006), 96–108; idem, "Qumran Fragments," 24.

39 J. Trebolle Barrera, DJD 14:183.

40 For a detailed discussion see N. G. Cohen, *Philo's Scriptures: Citations from the Prophets and Writings* (JSJSup 123; Leiden: Brill, 2007), 117–136. Philo's works are cited from the LCL edition by F. H. Colson and G. H. Whitaker.

times in his voliminous writings.[41] He expounds on Hannah's vow (1 Sam 1:11; *Somn.* 1.254),[42] her prayer (1 Sam 2:5; *Deus* 10–15; *Mut.* 143–144),[43] Samuel's life-long abstention from wine (deduced from 1 Sam 1:11 LXX;[44] *Ebr.* 143–152), Saul's hiding in the baggage (1 Sam 10:22; *Migr.* 196–197), and the widow of Zarephath (1 Kgs 17:10, 18; *Deus* 136–139).[45] For him, Hannah, whose name means "grace" (*Somn.* 1.254; *Deus* 5; *Ebr.* 143–144; *Mut.* 143–144), is "the gift of the wisdom of God" (*Deus* 5), whereas Samuel, "appointed or ordered to God" (reading שמואל as שְׁמוֹ אל; *Somn.* 1.254; *Ebr.* 144), is "a mind which rejoices in the service and worship of God and that only" (*Ebr.* 143–152; cf. also *Migr.* 196; *Somn.* 1.254).

The Dead Sea Scrolls yield another instance of an expositional use of Samuel (not Kings). Dubbed by scholars as 4QFlorilegium, Midrash Shemuel, Escha-tological Midrash, and, most recently, 4QEschatological Commentary A,[46] the scroll 4Q174, most likely a sectarian work, quotes and expounds on 2 Sam 7:10–14 (=1 Chr 17:9–12). The passage in question (frgs. 1–2, 21 i 1–13) is comprised of three sections. The first one takes up 2 Sam 7:10–11a and interprets it as referring to an eschatological temple, citing Exod 15:17–18 to prove that it will be established by God and paraphrasing Deut 23:3–4 to justify the ban of non-Israelites from the future sanctuary:[47]

---

41 In fact, both "God's psalmist David" and Solomon are mentioned in his extant works only once (*Conf.* 149; *Prelim. Studies* 177). On the paucity of references to Sam-Kgs in Philo's writ-ings, see Y. Amir, "Authority and Interpretation of Scripture in the Writings of Philo," in *Mikra* (ed. M. Mulder; Peabody, Massachusetts: Hendrickson, 2004), 422–423.

42 Philo deals with 1 Sam 1:11, 28 also in *Deus* 5–6. Highlighting Hannah's willingness to give her child to God, he presents her as "a disciple and successor" of Abraham.

43 See further V. Nikiprowetzky, "Στεῖρα, Στερρα, Πολλη et l'exégèse de 1 Sam. 2, 5, ches Philon d'Alexandrie," *Sileno* 3 (1977): 149–185.

44 1 Sam 1:11 (MT) does not mention Samuel's abstention from wine, yet the LXX, which Philo relies on, and, perhaps, 4QSam[a] (as reconstructed by F. M. Cross, D. W. Parry, R. J. Saley, DJD 17:29–30) do. In what follows, Philo quotes 1 Sam 1:14, which he puts, as does the LXX, in the mouth of Eli's servant.

45 See also the allusions to 1 Sam 9:8–9 in *Migr.* 38; *Her.* 78; *QG* 4.138.

46 The latter title was recently proposed by G. J. Brooke in his "From Florilegium or Midrash to Commentary: The Problem of Re-naming an Adopted Manuscript," in *The Mermaid and the Partridge* (ed. G. J. Brooke, J. Høgenhaven; STDJ 96; Leiden, Boston: Brill, 2011), 129–150. For an overview of scholarship on 4Q174, see J. G. Campbell, *The Exegetical Texts* (Companion to the Qumran Scrolls; London, New York: T & T Clark, 2004), 33–44.

47 The translation is based on the recent re-editions of the Hebrew text by D. Dimant, "4QFlori-legium and the Idea of the Community as a Temple," in idem, *History, Ideology and Bible Inter-pretation in the Dead Sea Scrolls: Collected Studies* (FAT 90; Tübingen: Mohr Siebeck, 2014), 270, and Qimron, *Hebrew Writings*, 2:289.

Quotation
"I will establish a place for my people Israel and no] enemy [will oppress him any]more[48] [neither will] a son of wickedness [afflict] him anymore as formerly and as from the day that [I commanded judges to be] over my people Israel."

Exposition
This is the house which [he will establish] for h[im] in the latter days, as it is written in the book of [Moses: [Exod 15:17–18]"The sanctuary] of YHWH which your hands have established; YHWH will reign forever and ever."[49]

This is the house to which [Deut 23:3–4]shall not come [the uncircumcised in heart and the uncir-cumcised in fl]esh[for]ever, nor Ammonite, nor Moabite nor bastard nor foreigner nor pros-elyte forever.[50] For his holy ones(?) there he [will] rev[e]al,[51] [and his glory fo]rever, always, will appear upon it.[52] And foreigners shall not make it desolate again, as they have deso-lated formerly the sanctuar[y of Is]rael because of their sin.[53] And he commanded to build for him מקדש אדם ("a sanctuary built by men" or "a sanctuary of men") so that they may offer in it (as incense) for him, before him, works of Law (or "thanksgiving").[54]

The last clause seems to expound on 2 Sam 7:13a: "He shall build a house for my name," yet the precise intent of the phrase מקדש אדם is debated.[55] Some suggest that it stands for the sectarian community functioning as a "temple of men."

---

48 The scroll seems to borrow the phrase "[and no] enemy [will oppress him any]more" from Ps 89:23, as suggested by J. Strugnell, "Notes en marge du volume V des 'Discoveries in the Ju-daean Desert of Jordan'," *RevQ* 7 (1970): 220.

49 G. J. Brooke, *Exegesis at Qumran: 4QFlorilegium in Its Jewish Context* (Sheffield: JSOT, 1985), 134, observes that the association of 2 Sam 7:10 with Exod 15:17 might have been suggested by the passages' use of the verb נטע.

50 Identifying קהל יהוה of Deut 23:3 with the "house" (Brooke, ibid., 136), the scroll expands the Deuteronomic list with at least two additional groups, foreigners and proselytes. See further J. M. Baumgarten, "The Exclusion of Nethinim and Proselytes in 4QFlorilegium," in idem, *Stud-ies in Qumran Law* (Leiden: Brill, 1977), 75–87; K. Berthelot, "La notion de גר dans les textes de Qumrân," *RevQ* 19 (1999): 195–198.

51 Reading קדושׁו with Dimant, "4QFlorilegium," 272, as referring to angels, קדושׁ(י)ו. Qimron, *Hebrew Writings*, 2:289, suggests that this is a divine title.

52 Reconstructing with Qimron, ibid., ולכבודו ל[עולם תמיד עליו יראה]. Dimant, ibid., 270, 271, re-stores [עולם תמיד עליו יראה וכבוד] and translates "[and] eternal [glory]will continually appear upon it."

53 Interpreting 2 Sam 7:10–11 as applying to the destruction of the First Temple.

54 The last word can be read either as תורה, "Law," or as תודה, "thanksgiving." See discussion in Dimant, "4QFlorilegium," 273–274.

55 For an overview of scholarly opinions, see M. Wise, *Thunder in Gemini and Other Essays on the History, Language and Literature of Second Temple Palestine* (JSPSup 15; Sheffield: Sheffield Academic Press, 1994), 152–185.

Others read it as a reference to the First Temple, which, unlike the divinely established eschatological sanctuary, was built by men.[56]

The second section of this exegetical unit features an actualizing interpretation of 2 Sam 7:11b, applying the divine promise to David to the exegete's community:

Quotation
And as for what He said to David: "And [I shall give] you [re]st from all your enemies,"

Exposition
that means that he will give rest to them from a[ll] the sons of Belial who cause them to stumble in order to destroy [them through] their [wickedness] just as they came with the plot of [Be]l[i]al to cause to stumble the so[ns of] lig[ht] and in order to devise against them evil plots s[o] that they [might be tr]apped by Belial through a guilty error.

Its final section offers an eschatological interpretation of 2 Sam 7:11b-14 with a sectarian twist:

Quotation
[And] the Lord [de]clares to you that he will build you a house. "And I will raise up your seed after you, and I shall establish the throne of his kingdom [for ev]er. I will be to him as a father, and he will be to me as a son."

Exposition
He is the shoot of David who stands with the Interpreter of the Torah, whom [he will raise] in Zi[on at the] end of days, as it is written: ^Amos 9:11^"And I will raise up the booth of David which has fallen." It is the booth of David which has fall[en w]ho will be raised up to save Israel.

Interpreting the "seed" of 2 Sam 7 as a messianic figure, the "shoot of David," the scroll envisions him standing at the end of days with the "Interpreter of the Torah," a figure mentioned in several sectarian writings.[57] It then relates this sce-

---

56 Kister suggests that the two temples mentioned here, the eschatological one and that of Solomon, correspond to the two houses of 2 Sam 7: the one that God will establish (v. 11b; reading this verse as referring to a temple, rather than to a dynasty) and the one that Solomon will build (v. 13). The Second Temple seems to be completely ignored here, which, as Kister observes, suits well an address to David. See M. Kister, "Jerusalem and the Temple in the Writings from Qumran," in *The Qumran Scrolls and Their World* (ed. M. Kister; Between Bible and Mishnah; Jerusalem: Yad Ben-Zvi, 2009), 2:489–490 (Hebrew).
57 This is a non-biblical locution, pointing, apparently, to Jer 23:5. Note the use of the same verbal form, והקמתי, in both 1 Sam 7:12 and Jer 23:5. Amos 9:11, cited further on, also utilizes a Hifil of קום, אקים.

nario to the prophecy from Amos 9:11, identifying the "shoot of David" with the "booth of David which has fallen," only to be raised by God to deliver Israel.

Samuel-Kings in Second Temple Literature: Compositional Uses

Literary Models. Several Second Temple texts utilize passages, events, and figures from Samuel-Kings as literary models. For instance, the accounts of military campaigns in Samuel could have served as models for the descriptions of Maccabean battles in 1 Maccabees.[58] The depiction of Simon's rule in 1 Macc 14:4–15 seems to be modeled on that of Solomon.[59] Pseudo-Solomon's petition in Wis 9 imitates Solomon's prayers from 1 Kgs 3:6–9 and 8:15–21.[60] Hannah's song (1 Sam 2:1–10) is a model for the Magnificat (Luke 1:46–55),[61] just as Elijah and Elisha are for the "two witnesses" of Rev 11.[62]

The Psalms Scroll from Qumran supplies yet another example—a catalogue of David's literary works (11QPs[a] XXVII, 2–11). Presenting David as shining like the sun and walking blamelessly before God and men,[63] the so-called "David's Compositions" credits him with 4,050 psalms and songs.[64] All these are said to

58 U. Rappaport, "A Note on the Use of the Bible in 1 Maccabees," in *Biblical Perspectives: Early Use and Interpretation of the Bible in Light of the Dead Sea Scrolls* (ed. M. E. Stone; STDJ 28; Leiden: Brill, 1998), 175–179. For a list of parallels between 1 Macc and Sam-Kgs see J. A. Goldstein, *2 Maccabees* (AB; Garden City, N. Y.: Doubleday, 1983), 31–32.

59 J. A. Goldstein, *1 Maccabees* (AB; Garden City, N. Y.: Doubleday, 1974), 490.

60 See J. H. Newman, "The Democratization of Kingship in Wisdom of Solomon," in *The Idea of Biblical Interpretation* (ed. H. Najman, J. H. Newman; JSJSup 83; Leiden: Brill, 2004), 309–28.

61 See M. E. Gordley, *Teaching through Song in Antiquity* (WUNT 2 302; Tübingen, Mohr Siebeck, 2011), 307.

62 See M. Zetterholm, "The Books of Kings in the New Testament and the Apostolic Fathers," in *The Books of Kings: Sources, Composition, Historiography and Reception* (ed. A. Lemaire, B. Halpern; SVT 129; Leiden, Boston: Brill, 2010), 561–2.

63 These epithets, along with the reference to a calendar of 364 days, may point to a sectarian provenance for this composition, as was pointed out by N. Mizrahi, "A Comparison of the List of David's Compositions" (11QPs[a] 27:2–11) to the Characterization of David and Solomon in Kings and Chronicles," *Meghillot* 5–6 (2007): 181 (Hebrew).

64 Of these, 3600 are psalms, 364 are songs for the daily burnt sacrifices, implying a calendar of 364 days, 52 are songs for Sabbaths, and 30 are songs for the new moons and festivals. There are also 4 songs for the "stricken ones," i.e., those possessed by demons. For a recent attempt to explain the number 3600 as pointing to 2 Chr 2:1, see N. Mizrahi, "David's Compositions in 11QPs[a] and the Semantics of נצח," *Studies in Language (Meḥkarim Balashon)* 11–12 (2008): 199–212 (Hebrew). On other numbers utilized here, see J. C. VanderKam, "Studies on 'David's Composition'

have been composed by David "under the spirit of prophecy."[65] While this text's emphasis on David's cultic activities seems to be influenced by 1 Chr 16–17,[66] the catalogue of his writings is modeled on 1 Kgs 5:12.[67]

Quotations and Allusions. Rare outside of writings treating Samuel-Kings expositionally (see above),[68] an explicit quotation from Samuel occurs in the legal section of the Damascus Document (CD) 9:8–10 (=4Q267 9 i 4–5):[69]

> Concerning oaths: as to that which he said, "*Let not your hand help you* (לא תושיעך ידך לך)": a man who causes (another) to swear in the open field that is not in the presence of the judges or by their bidding has let his hand help him.[70]

This prohibition against taking an oath in the absence of judges (or without their consent) cites as a proof-text Abigail's words to David from 1 Sam 25:26, "and taking vengeance with your own hand" (RSV; והושע ידך לך), introducing its modified wording with a formula "as to that which he said."[71]

Second Temple writings feature multiple implicit quotations and allusions to Samuel-Kings.[72] Thus, Simon's address to the people of Jerusalem in the face of the imminent assault of Tryphon (1 Macc 13:4) points to Elijah's cry to God at Mt. Horeb (1 Kgs 19:10, 14). Luke's description of the young Jesus (Luke 2:52) borrows the language of 1 Sam 2:26, whereas his account of the Jesus's instructions to his

---

(11QPs^a 27:2–11)," *Eretz Israel* 26 (1999): 212*-220*; V. Noam, "The Origin of the List of David's Songs in 'David's Compositions'," *DSD* 13 (2006): 134–149.

65 On David as a prophet in Second Temple writings, see J. L. Kugel, "David the Prophet," in *Poetry and Prophecy: The Beginnings of a Literary Tradition* (ed. J. L. Kugel; Ithaca, NY: Cornell University Press, 1990), 45–55; P. W. Flint, "The Prophet David at Qumran," in *Biblical Interpretation at Qumran* (ed. M. Henze; Studies in the Dead Sea Scrolls and Related Literature; Grand Rapids: Eerdmans, 2005), 158–167.

66 Mizrahi, "Comparison," 189–195.

67 Mizrahi, ibid., 172–174, 178–181.

68 Another explicit quotation may have originally been found in the Damascus Document (CD) VIII, 20–21, ascribing to Elisha a certain "word" to "Gehazi his servant." Its wording is missing from the Geniza manuscripts of CD and is not extant in its Qumran copies. S. Hultgren, *From the Damascus Covenant to the Covenant of the Community* (STDJ 66; Leiden: Brill, 2007), 55, suggests that this "word" might have to do with a disciple's betrayal of his master.

69 Explicit quotations are usually identified by an introductory formula. See Dimant, "Use," 385.

70 J. M. Baumgarten, D. R. Schwartz, PTSDSSP, 2:43. Italics are mine.

71 See further J. M. Baumgarten, "A 'Scriptural' Citation in 4QFragments of the Damascus Document," *JJS* 43 (1992): 97; A. P. Jassen, *Scripture and Law in the Dead Sea Scrolls* (Cambridge, MA: Cambridge University Press, 2014), 222–224.

72 Since the criteria for distinguishing between an implicit quotation and an allusion remain unclear, these are treated here together.

disciples (Luke 10:4) may allude to 2 Kgs 4:29. The scribe's reply to Jesus in Mark 12:33 is reminiscent of 1 Sam 15:22. Paul's speech on the Areopagus in Acts 17:24 and the description of the heavenly temple in Rev 15:8 seem to depend on 1 Kgs 8:27, 10–11.[73]

More allusions to Samuel-Kings are found in the Dead Sea Scrolls. The interpretation of Gen 49:10 in 4QCommentary on Genesis A (4Q252 V 1–4) alludes to the Davidic promise as formulated in 1 Kgs 2:4 (line 2) and in 2 Sam 7:12–13 (line 4).[74] The description of David as "wise" in 11QPs[a] XXVII, 2 may point to 2 Sam 14:20, while his capacity of "understanding" alludes to 1 Sam 16:18. An allusion to David's combat with Goliath is found in 4Q373 1 3, 6–7 (with parallels in 2Q22 i and 4Q372 19 4).[75] The description of the temple's furnishings and courts in 11QTemple[a] III–XIII, XXX–XLVI blends together the Exodus account of the Tabernacle with the relevant passages pertaining to Solomon's Temple from Kings and Chronicles.[76] The "Law of the King" embedded in the same scroll (LVIII, 20–21; LIX, 16–18) alludes to Samuel's warnings regarding royal power (1 Sam 8:14) and to the divine promises to Solomon (1 Kgs 6:12; 9:5).[77]

In several cases there is a generic correlation between the alluding text and its scriptural antecedent. Thus, allusions to prayers and psalms found in Samuel and Kings often occur in liturgical contexts. For instance, Tobit's prayer (Tobit 13:2) alludes to Hannah's song (1 Sam 2:6). A thanksgiving hymn in 4QBarkhi Nafshi (4Q437 2 i 14–15) features a series of allusions to 1 Sam 2:1.[78] Another allusion to 1 Sam 2:2–3 is found in the praise of God, apparently by Joshua, in one of the rewritten Joshua scrolls (4Q379 22 i 5–6).[79] Allusions to a psalm embedded in both 2 Sam 22 and Ps 18 appear in a *hodayah* from 1QH[a] XVII, 28–29 and in

---

73 For more allusions/quotations from Sam-Kgs in Second Temple literature, see "Loci citati vel allegati," in *Novum Testamentum Graece* (ed. E. Nestle et al.; 27th edition; Stuttgart: Deutsche Bibelgesellschaft, 1993), 894; S. Delamarter, *A Scripture Index to Charlesworth's The Old Testament Pseudepigrapha* (London: Sheffield Academic Press, 2002), 18–20, 73–77; A. Lange, M. Weigold, *Biblical Quotations and Allusions in Second Temple Jewish Literature* (JAJS 5; Göttingen: Vandenhoeck & Ruprecht, 2011), 115–126.

74 See W. M. Schniedewind, *Society and the Promise to David* (New York: Oxford University Press, 1999), 163–164.

75 It has been suggested that this is a reference to Moses' destruction of Og, employing language borrowed from 1 Sam 17 (see M. Bernstein, E. Schuller, DJD 28:199–204).

76 See Y. Yadin, *The Temple Scroll* (Jerusalem: The Israel Exploration Society, 1983), 1:179–180, 226.

77 See Yadin, ibid., 2:268–270; Schniedewind, *Society and the Promise*, 161–163.

78 See M. Weinfeld, D. Seely, DJD 29:317–318.

79 See Feldman, *Rewritten Joshua*, 98–99.

a prayer included in XHev/Se 6 1 3–4 (2 Sam 22:2–3=Ps 18:3).[80] The priests' plea for divine vengeance on Nikanor in 1 Macc 7:37 is indebted to Solomon's prayer at the dedication of the temple (1 Kgs 8:27), as is the High Priest's supplication in 3 Macc 2:10 (1 Kgs 8:33–34, 48–50). In a similar fashion, allusions to passages perceived as rulings tend to appear in legal/halakhic contexts. For instance, the rules pertaining to war booty in 11QTemple[a] LVIII, 11–15 harmonize the regulations given in Num 31:27–30 with 1 Sam 8:15, 17 and 1 Sam 30:24 (without utilizing the wording of the latter).[81] The legislation proscribing the lame and the blind from the Temple city, the eschatological army, and the eschatological *Yaḥad* (11QT[a] XLV, 12–14; 1QM VII, 4–5; 1QSa II, 3–11) hearkens back to 2 Sam 5:8.[82]

The Dead Sea Scrolls also yield instances of allusions to Samuel-Kings that incorporate an actualizing exegesis of a scriptural passage.[83] A cluster of such implicit *pesharim*, as they are dubbed by scholars, is found in the Damascus Document (CD) III, 19–20:[84]

> So He built for them a faithful house (בית נאמן) in Israel, like none that had ever appeared before and until now.[85]

Since the immediate context deals with the appointment of the true priesthood, CD most likely alludes here to the prophecy to Eli in 1 Sam 2:35: "And I will raise up for myself a faithful priest (כהן נאמן) ... and I will build for him an enduring

---

80 The word משגבי, missing from Ps 18, yet present in 1QH[a], suggests a familiarity with the version of the psalm as found in 2 Sam. The wording of 2 Sam 22:32=Ps 18:32 is also employed in a speech concerned with the role of Moses at Sinai in 4Q377 2 ii 8. Yet there the use of the divine epithet אלוה (as in Ps 18), rather than אל (as in 2 Sam 22), suggests the influence of Ps 18. For more instances of similar ambiguity, see K. De Troyer, "The Septuagint and the New Testament: Another Look at the Samuel-Kings Quotations and Allusions in the New Testament," in *The Reception of the Hebrew Bible in the Septuagint and The New Testament* (ed. D. J.A. Clines, J. C. Exum; Sheffield: Sheffield Phoenix Press, 2013), 49–55.
81 See Yadin, *The Temple Scroll*, 1:360–362; D. Swanson, *The Temple Scroll and the Bible: The Methodology of 11QT* (STDJ 14; Leiden: E. J. Brill, 1995), 146–148; L. H. Schiffman, "The Laws of War in the Temple Scroll," in idem, *The Courtyards of the House of the Lord* (STDJ 75; Leiden: Brill, 2008), 510–512.
82 Yadin, ibid., 2:289–291. See further S. M. Olyan, *Social Inequality in the World of the Text: The Significance of Ritual and Social Distinctions in the Hebrew Bible* (JAJSup 4; Göttingen: Vandenhoeck & Ruprecht, 2011), 129–140.
83 On actualizing interpretation in the Dead Sea Scrolls in general and in the Damascus Document in particular, see L. Goldman, "Biblical Exegesis and Pesher Interpretation in the Damascus Document" (PhD. diss., University of Haifa, 2007), 10–21 (Hebrew).
84 The following discussion is based on Goldman, ibid., 42 ff.
85 J. M. Baumgarten, D. R. Schwartz, PTSDSSP, 2:17.

house (בית נאמן)." Yet, the allusion is not to the plain meaning of the verse, but to its actualizing interpretation, reading "house" as referring to the sectarian community, rather than to a dynasty, with נאמן understood as both "faithful" and "enduring." Assuming CD's familiarity with the notion of a community as a temple, it may also allude to the divine promise to David in 2 Sam 7:16: "Your house and your kingship shall ever be secure before you (ונאמן ביתך)," read to mean that the establishment and the function of the community are akin to those of the Temple. The reference to Israel may point to yet another verse containing the phrase בית נאמן, 1 Kgs 11:38: "and I will build for you a lasting dynasty (בית נאמן) as I did for David. I hereby give Israel to you," interpreted once again as referring not to a dynasty, but to a community. These allusions to actualizing interpretations of 1 Sam 2:35, 2 Sam 7:16, and 1 Kgs 11:38 describe the sectarians as a priestly community chosen from within Israel.

Another instance of an allusion incorporating an actualizing interpretation, this time of 2 Sam 7:10 (ולא יסיפו בני עולה לענותו; "Evil men shall not oppress them any more"), seems to be found in Pseudo-Ezekiel (4Q386 1 ii 3): "And YHWH said, 'A son of Belial will scheme to oppress my people / but I will not allow him (ויאמר יהוה בן בליעל יחשב לענות את עמי / ולא אניח לו)'." It has been suggested that this scroll applies the divine promise from 2 Sam 7:10 to Antiochus IV.[86]

References to Biblical Figures and Events. References to figures and events from Samuel-Kings occur in a variety of contexts.

Liturgy. The prayers of Judas Maccabeus in 1–2 Maccabees evoke God's deliverance of David in the combat with Goliath, Jonathan's overpowering the Philistine camp (1 Macc 4:30), and the divine intervention during Sennacherib's invasion (1 Macc 7:40–41; 2 Macc 8:19; 15:22). A prayer embedded in the War Scroll recalls David's trust in God's name when he fought Goliath, as well as his victories over the Philistines, also by God's holy name (1QM XI, 1–3). A liturgy included in the Words of the Luminaries (4Q504 XVII, 8) refers to God's establishing a covenant with David, whereas 4QEschatological Hymn (4Q457b 2) speaks of "David rejoicing to bring back," perhaps a reference to the bringing of the Ark to Jerusalem.[87]

Legal/halakhic argumentation.[88] Calling for a celebration of the recently introduced Festival of Hanukkah, the second festival letter embedded in 2 Macc

---

86 D. Dimant, DJD 30:56.

87 E. Chazon, DJD 29:417–418.

88 On the use of non-Pentateuch passages to derive or to support halakhic rulings in the Dead Sea Scrolls, see M. J. Bernstein, Sh. A. Koyfman, "The Interpretation of Biblical Law in the Dead Sea Scrolls: Forms and Methods," in *Biblical Interpretation at Qumran* (ed. M. Henze; Studies in the Dead Sea Scrolls and Related Literature; Grand Rapids: Eerdmans, 2005), 73–74; Jassen, *Scripture and Law*, 216–246.

1:10–2:18 places Judas Maccabeus alongside scriptural figures who dedicated sanctuaries, such as Moses, Solomon, and Nehemiah.[89] As a biblical precedent for the new eight-day celebration, this letter notes that Solomon's dedication of the Temple lasted for eight days (2:9–12).[90] In the gospels, when the Pharisees find fault with the hungry disciples' plucking heads of grain on the Sabbath (Matt 12:1–4; Mark 2:25–26; Luke 6:3, 4), Jesus is reported to cite the story of David and his men eating the sacred bread permitted to the priests alone (1 Sam 21:6). Among the Dead Sea Scrolls, the Damascus Document (CD) IV, 20-V, 6 (=4Q269 3 2; 6Q15 1 1–3), arguing against polygamy, cites the Deuteronomic prohibition of a king taking many wives (Deut 17:17). Anticipating the counter-argument that the exemplary King David took several wives and was never condemned for doing so, CD presents his acts as a result of an ignorance of the Torah regulations on this matter. It claims that the Torah was hidden in the Ark of the Covenant since the days of Joshua and the elders, until the High Priest Zadok arose.[91] Only then was the Book of the Law consulted. As a result, "the deeds of David rose up (ויעלו[92])", except the blood of Uriah, and God left (i.e., forgave) them to him." The exegete distinguishes here between David's polygamy and "the blood of Uriah."[93] For

---

89 For scholarly opinions regarding the authenticity, date, and provenance of this letter, see R. M. Doran, *2 Maccabees* (Hermeneia; Augsburg: Fortress Press, 2012), 14–17.

90 It has been suggested that the letter follows Chr here, rather than Kgs, as the heavenly fire is mentioned in 2 Chr 7:1, 3 alone. The reference to the duration of Solomon's dedication might have originated either in 1 Kgs 8:65–66 or in 2 Chr 7:8–9. However, none of the biblical accounts reports Solomon's request that "the glory of the Lord and the cloud will be seen" (2:8). See Goldstein, *2 Maccabees*, 186; J. C. VanderKam, "Hanukkah: Its Timing and Significance according to 1 and 2 Maccabees," *JSP* 1 (1987): 33.

91 On the timing of Zadok's coming to prominence in CD, apparently during Absalom's rebellion, see Ch. Milikowsky, "'Until Tzadoq Arose' in the Damascus Document: Tzadoq and His Appointment as High Priest in Early Jewish Interpretation," in *Shoshannat Yaakov: Jewish and Iranian Studies in Honor of Yaakov Elman* (ed. Sh. Secunda, S. Fine; Leiden, Boston: Brill, 2012), 285–299.

92 The precise meaning of ויעלו is somewhat unclear. Several renditions, based on the uses of עלה in both biblical and post-biblical Hebrew, have been proposed, e.g., "rose up" (Vermes), "were excellent" (Ginzberg), "were reckoned <as inadvertent sins>" (Rabin), "were accepted" (Baumgarten and Schwartz). G. Vermes, *The Complete Dead Sea Scrolls in English* (London: Penguin, 2004), 132; L. Ginzberg, *An Unknown Jewish Sect* (New York: Jewish Theological Seminary of America, 1970) 22; Ch. Rabin, The *Zadokite Documents* (Oxford: Clarendon Press, 1958), 18; J. M. Baumgarten, D. R. Schwartz, PTSDSSP, 2:21. J. C.R. de Roo, "David's Deeds in the Dead Sea Scrolls," *DSD* 6 (1999): 44–65, suggests that this passage should be read in light of the notion of a community as a temple in which righteous deeds are offered as sacrifices. Yet it is unlikely that CD assumes this notion here and even more unlikely that it applies it anachronistically to David.

93 CD apparently alludes here to 1 Kgs 15:5.

him, the former was the result of ignorance, whereas the latter was a willful transgression of the explicit divine prohibition in Gen 9:5–6, the so-called Noahide Laws, and therefore did not require a knowledge of the Mosaic Law.

Perhaps one should also mention here the references to figures and events from Samuel-Kings in the epilogue of the halakhic letter 4QMMT.[94] Unlike the foregoing texts, these are not evoked to support its halakhic views, but rather to motivate one to accept them. Referring to the Deuteronomic covenantal blessings and curses, 4QMMT names Solomon, apparently suggesting that the foretold blessings came to pass in his days, and notes that the curses befell Israel "from the days of [Jero]boam the son of Nebat and until the ex[i]le of Jerusalem and Zedekiah King of Jud[ah]" (C 18–19 [=4Q398 11–13 1–2]). With these in mind, it implores the addressee(s) to "remember the kings of Israe[l] and contemplate their deeds" (C 23–25 [=4Q398 11–13 6–7, 14–17 ii 1]),[95] singling out David, "a man of pious deeds," who "was delivered from many troubles and was forgiven" (C 25–26 [=4Q398 14–17 ii 1–2]).[96]

Vaticinia ex eventu. The visionary in Sibylline Oracles 11:80–105 foresees the appearance of a great king, clearly Solomon, who will build the Temple and cast down the idols.[97] In the rewritten version of Judges in LAB 26:12 God announces to the first judge, Kenaz, the appearance of Jahel (apparently, Solomon), who will build a house in his name.[98] The scroll 4Q522 (4QapocrJoshua^c 9 ii) depicts Joshua foretelling the birth of David, the capture of Zion, preparations for the building of

---

94 The precise placement of the fragment in question is unclear. The editors situated it between 4Q398 14–17 i and 14–17 ii (E. Qimron, J. Strugnell DJD 10:201–202). H. von Weissenberg, *4QMMT: Reevaluating the Text, the Function, and the Meaning of the Epilogue* (STDJ 82; Leiden: Brill, 2009), 70–71, 85–90, believes that it belongs with the beginning of the epilogue of 4QMMT (i.e., the beginning of DJD's section C). The translation here follows that of DJD 10 with slight alterations accounting for suggestions by von Weissenberg, ibid., 102–103, and Qimron, *Hebrew Writings*, 1:211.
95 The phrase "kings of Israe[l]" stands for all the kings of Israel and Judah together, a usage attested in Chr (e.g., 2 Chr 28:27, 33:18), rather than in Sam-Kgs, as observed by M. J. Bernstein, "The Employment and Interpretation of Scripture in 4QMMT: Preliminary Observations," in *Reading 4QMMT: New Perspectives on Qumran Law and History* (ed. J. Kampen, M. J. Bernstein; Atlanta, Georgia: Scholars Press, 1996), 50.
96 E. Qimron, J. Strugnell, DJD 10:61, 63. See further G. J. Brooke, "The Significance of the Kings in 4QMMT," in *The Qumran Chronicle: Qumran Cave 4: Special Report: 4QMMT* (ed. Z. J. Kapera; Krakow: Enigma Press, 1991), 109–113.
97 Quoted from J. J. Collins, OTP, 1:436.
98 See Jacobson, *Commentary*, 773–774.

the temple, Solomon's construction thereof, and Zadok's officiating in the sanctuary.[99]

Chronological treatises. The almost completely lost chronological treatise by a certain Demetrius, presumably entitled "Concerning the Kings in Judea," refers to Sennacherib's invasion and estimates the time that lapsed between this event and the Babylonian exile.[100] The Aramaic text from Qumran, 4Q559 (4QpapChronologie biblique ar), dealing in its extant form with the chronology of the Pentateuch, Joshua, and Judges, seems also to mention Samuel (frg. 6 2 [reconstructed]).[101]

Lists. The Aramaic 4Qpseudo-Daniel[c] ar contains two lists of names (4Q245 1 i).[102] One of these records the names of high priests, from Levi and Qahat, through "Zado]k" and Abiathar, to the Hasmoneans Jonathan and Simon. Next to this comes a catalogue of kings, naming David, Solomon, "Ahazia[h," and "Joa]sh."[103] Another Aramaic text, 4Q339 (4QList of False Prophets ar), lists the names of "the false prophets who arose in [Israel]."[104] Opening with "Balaam [son of] Beor" and concluding, according to some, with John Hyrcanus I, it names "[the] Old Man from Bethel" of 1 Kgs 13:11–31 and "[Zede]kiah son of Cha[na]anah" mentioned in 1 Kgs 22:1–28 (cf. 2 Chr 18:1–27).[105]

Pesher-Title. Several sectarian texts from Qumran evoke names of scriptural figures in an exegetical device dubbed a "*pesher*-title."[106] A *pesher*-title utilizing a name of a figure from the book of Samuel occurs in 1QpHab V, 9, expounding

---

99 See Feldman, *Rewritten Joshua*, 142–146. On the influence of Chronicles on this passage see G. J. Brooke, "The Books of Chronicles and the Scrolls from Qumran," in *Reflection and Refraction: Studies in Biblical Historiography in Honour of A. Graeme Auld* (ed. R. Rezetko et al.; SVT 113; Leiden, Boston: Brill, 2007), 44–45.

100 C. R. Holladay, *Fragments from Hellenistic Jewish Authors, Vol. 1: Historians* (SBLTT 20; Pseudepigrapha Series 10; Atlanta: Scholars Press, 1983), 90, points to 2 Kgs 18:9–13 as the source for this calculation.

101 É. Puech, DJD 37:285.

102 J. J. Collins, P. Flint, DJD 22:153–164. See further M. Wise, "4Q245 (PsDan Ar) and the High Priesthood of Judas Maccabaeus," *DSD* 12 (2005): 313–362.

103 J. J. Collins, P. Flint, DJD 22:156–157. Both catalogues may take their cue from the lists found 1 Chr 3:10–16 and 5:27–41.

104 M. Broshi, A. Yardeni, DJD 19:78–79. See further S. J.D. Cohen, "False Prophets (4Q339), Netinim (4Q340), and Hellenism at Qumran," *JGRChJ* 1 (2000): 55–66; A. Lange, "'The False Prophets Who Arose Against Our God' (4Q339 1)," in *Aramaica Qumranica* (ed. K. Berthelot, D. Stökl Ben Ezra; STDJ 94; Leiden, Boston: Brill, 2009), 205–224.

105 The purpose served by this list remains unclear, but it is not impossible that it had a didactic purpose, as was suggested by L. Mazor in a lecture "The List of the False Prophets (4Q339)," presented at the 15th World Congress of Jewish Studies (Jerusalem; August 3, 2009).

106 See Goldman, "Biblical Exegesis," 10–21.

on Hab 1:13: "the House of Absalom and the men of their council who kept silent when the Teacher of Righteousness was rebuked and did not help him against the Man of the Lie." While some have argued that Absalom is a real contemporary figure, others, correctly, take him as a personification of treacherous behavior, a trait which, according to the exegete, is characteristic of the group referred to as the "house (בית) of Absalom."[107]

Miscellaneous. Second Temple sources yield more references to persons and events from Samuel-Kings, e.g., the expulsion of the Canaanite population from Jerusalem by David (J. W. 6.439), David and Solomon's subjugation of the nations (Ag. Ap. 2.132), death and burial of the "patriarch" David (Acts 2:29–30, 34), construction of the temple (J. W. 5.137, 143, 185; 6.269), Solomon's splendor (Matt 6:29; Luke 12:27), the Queen of Sheba's visit to hear Solomon's wisdom (Matt 12:42; Luke 11:31), Shishak's invasion (J. W. 6.436), Elijah's stay with the widow in Zarephath (Luke 4:25–26) and his address to God at Horeb (Rom 11:2–4; James 5:17–18), Elisha's miraculous healing of a water spring (J. W. 4.460), Naaman's healing (Luke 4:27), the captivity of the northern tribes (Tobit 1:2), the death of Sennacherib (Tobit 1:21), and Nebuchadnezzar's sacking of Jerusalem (J. W. 6.439, 442; Ag. Ap. 1.154, 159). To these the Dead Sea Scrolls add the people's request for a king (4Q389 5 2–3) and Saul's defeat of the Amalekites (4Q252 IV, 1–3).[108]

In addition to isolated references to figures and events from Samuel-Kings, Second Temple literature features also so-called catalogues of scriptural examples.[109] These catalogues tend to occur in exhortations and prayers. Thus, Mattathias, admonishing his sons to "remember the deeds of our ancestors" (1 Macc 2:51), mentions David, who for "his piety received ... a royal throne for ages," and Elijah, "taken up as if into heaven" because of "his acts of zeal on behalf of the

---

107 M. A. Collins, The Use of Sobriquets in the Qumran Dead Sea Scrolls (Library of Second Temple Studies 67; London: T&T Clark, 2009), 145–146.

108 The scroll seems to view Saul's deed as a fulfillment of Deut 25:19. See further M. Bernstein, "4Q252: From the Re-Written Bible to Biblical Commentary," JJS 45 (1994): 15–16; J. Saukkonen, "The Story Behind the Text: Scriptural Interpretation in 4Q252" (Ph.D. diss., University of Helsinki, 2005), 34–36. In addition to these texts, a poorly preserved 6Q10 mentions Samuel (frg. 16; the context is unclear). A reference to Saul is found in a single fragment of an unknown work reading: "and] behold Sa[ul" (frg. 54 on PAM 43.691). The scroll 4Q479 (4QText Mentioning Descendants of David) refers to David (frg. 1 5) and the "seed of David" (frg. 1 4, 5). 4Q558 4QpapVision[b] ar 54 4 names Elijah, but it is uncertain whether the reference is to the eschatological Elijah or to an event from the Elijah cycle, as may be the case in frg. 33 5.

109 These catalogues exhibit a more or less consistent pattern: the name of a figure is followed by a succinct reference to his/her characteristic trait or a biblical episode in which this figure was involved. See Dimant, "Use," 392–395.

Torah" (vv. 57–58).[110] The encomium on men and women of faith in Hebr 11:32–39 names David, Samuel, and the "prophets," including Elisha and Elijah,[111] and lists some of their deeds.[112] Put in the mouth of a certain Eleazar, the prayer for divine rescue in 3 Macc 6:4–8 mentions, among other occasions when God made his power manifest, Sennacherib's invasion.[113] Three prayers, apparently of Jewish Hellenistic origin, embedded in the Apostolic Constitutions, also include lists of biblical figures.[114] One of them (*Apos. Con.* 7.37.1–5), pleading with God to accept "the entreaties of the lips" of his people, lists among the righteous who were heard Samuel, David, Solomon, Elijah, Elisha, Jehoshaphat, Hezekiah, Manasseh, and Josiah.[115] Another prayer (7.38.1–8) praises God for his acts of salvation, including "the days of … Elijah and of the Prophets … of David and of the Kings."[116] In yet another prayer (8.5.1–4), Samuel, "a priest and a prophet," is named among those "marked out beforehand, from the beginning, priests for dominion over your people" (vv. 10–16).[117] As far as the Dead Sea Scrolls are concerned, only the admonition in the Damascus Document (CD) III, 8–10 (=4Q266 2 iii 5; 269 2 3–4), surveying faithful and unfaithful of the past, includes a passing reference to figures and events from Samuel-Kings:

---

110 See discussion in T. Hieke, "The Role of the 'Scripture' in the Last Words of Mattathias (1 Macc 2:49–70)," in *The Books of the Maccabees: History, Theology, Ideology* (ed. G. Xeravits, J. Zsengellér; JSJSup 118; Leiden: Brill, 2007), 61–74; R. Egger-Wenzel, "The Testament of Mattathias to His Sons in 1 Macc 2:49–70: A Keyword Composition with the Aim of Justification," in *History and Identity: How Israel's Later Authors Viewed Its Earlier History* (ed. N. Calduch-Benages, J. Liesen; Deuterocanonical and Cognate Literature Yearbook; Berlin: de Gruyter, 2006), 141–149.
111 As suggested by a reference to women receiving "their dead by resurrection."
112 See further H. W. Attridge, *The Epistle to the Hebrews* (Hermeneia; Philadelphia: Fortress Press, 1989), 347–352.
113 The Old Latin version of Addition C in Greek Esther appends to Esther's prayer recalling God's past saving acts a list of figures helped by God, including Hezekiah and Hannah (v. 16). See C. A. Moore, *Daniel, Esther, and Jeremiah: The Additions* (AB; New York: Doubleday, 1977), 210–211.
114 On these prayers see D. A. Fiensy, *Prayers Alleged to Be Jewish: An Examination of the Constituones Apostolorum* (Chico, California: Scholars Press, 1985); P. van der Horst, J. H. Newman, *Early Jewish Prayers in Greek* (Commentaries on Early Jewish Literature; Berlin: de Gruyter, 2008), 83–87.
115 D. A. Fiensy, D. R. Darnell, OTP, 2:684–85
116 Ibid., 2:685.
117 Ibid., 2:687–88.

Rather, they murmured in their tents and God's anger was kindled against their congregation and their sons perished through it (i.e., stubbornness of heart) *and their kings were cut off through it, and through it their heroes perished, and their land became desolate due to it.*[118]

Resisting a clear-cut classification are two texts treating an array of biblical figures, as do the aforementioned catalogues, yet in far greater detail. The first one is 4 Maccabees, presenting David, along with Joseph, Moses, and Jacob, as a man able to rule over his passions. This is deduced from a lengthy paraphrase of 2 Sam 23:13–17 (=1 Chr 11:15–19), reading David's pouring of the water obtained for him at the risk of his soldiers' lives as an example of the supremacy of a temperate mind over desires of the body (3:6–18).[119] The second text is Ben Sira's Praise of the Fathers (Sir 44–49), described as a canonical reflection on the Scripture by means of evoking exemplary figures.[120] From Samuel-Kings Ben Sira selects Samuel, Nathan, David, Solomon, Rehoboam, Jeroboam, Elijah, Elisha, Hezekiah, Isaiah, and Josiah.[121] Based primarily but not exclusively on Samuel-Kings, the portrayals of these characters vary in length, from a brief remark (e.g., Nathan) to an extensive inventory of personal traits and activities (e.g., Samuel).[122] Rehoboam and Jeroboam are presented in a negative light, whereas Samuel, David, Elijah, Elisha, Hezekiah, Isaiah, and Josiah are depicted as exemplary. Solomon's portrayal features both praise and sharp critique.[123] Ben Sira applauds

---

118 J. M. Baumgarten, D. R. Schwartz, PTSDSSP, 17 (italics are mine). Cf. Judith 5:17–18, which depicts the period from the entrance into the Promised Land to the Exile as a time of initial faithfulness to God that was followed by a departure from his ways and subsequent military defeats and captivity.

119 The account in 4 Macc departs from those found in 2 Sam and 1 Chr in several respects. It suggests that the incident occurred after a long day of a battle against the Philistines. David's desire for water located in the enemy's territory (Bethlehem in 2 Sam and 1 Chr) is presented as an unreasonable one. His bodyguards are said to be grumbling at his desire. Two soldiers (in the biblical accounts these are three chieftains) depart and search for the spring through the enemy's encampment.

120 A. Goshen-Gottstein, "Ben Sira's Praise of the Fathers: A Canon-Conscious Reading," in *Ben Sira's God* (ed. R. Egger-Wenzel; Berlin: de Gruyter, 2002), 244–260.

121 For recent discussions of their portrayals, see *Rewriting Biblical History: Essays on Chronicles and Ben Sira* (ed. J. Corley, H. van Grol; Deuterocanonical and Cognate Literature Studies 7; Berlin/New York: de Gruyter, 2011) and the bibliography cited there.

122 Ben Zvi, "Authority," 245–246, notes that David's establishing of the cult (Sir 47:9–10) is indebted to 1 Chr 25, just as Hezekiah's fortification of the city (Sir 48:17) is influenced by 2 Chr 32:5 (or Isa 22:9–11).

123 See, among others, P. C. Beentjes, "'The Countries Marvelled at You': King Solomon in Ben Sira 47:12–22," in idem, *"Happy the One Who Meditates on Wisdom" (Sir. 14,20): Collected Essays on the Book of Ben Sira* (CBET 43; Leuven; Peeters, 2006), 135–144; C. Camp, *Ben Sira and the Men*

young Solomon for his wisdom and love of peace, yet, reading his later life in light of Deut 17:17, seems to accuse him of amassing gold and silver (according to the Hebrew text) and allowing women to rule his body.

Historical summaries also fall under the compositional uses of the Scripture. Some of the summaries dealing with Samuel-Kings are found in exhortations. In his address to the defenders of Jerusalem, Josephus resorts, among other past events, to the recovery of the Ark from the Philistines, the angelic intervention during Sennacherib's invasion, the Babylonian siege, and the imprisonment of Zedekiah (*J. W.* 5.384–388, 391–2, 404). Stephen's speech in Acts 7 refers to David's finding favor with God, his desire to build a dwelling place for him, and Solomon's building of the Temple (7:45–47). Another historical summary embedded in Paul's address in Acts 13:20–22 mentions Samuel, the peoples' request for a king, Saul's forty-year rule, his removal by God, the divine election of David, and the latter's death (13:36).

Historical summaries occur also in apocalyptic texts. Presenting the course of history as comprising ten weeks, the Apocalypse of Weeks (1 En 93:3–10) concludes the fifth week with the construction of the temple, and includes in the next one Elijah's ascent, the destruction of the temple, and Israel's dispersion. More detailed is the Animal Apocalypse (1 En 85–90), spanning events from Samuel to the construction of the temple, followed by Israel's apostasy and the appointment of seventy angelic shepherds under whom Jerusalem is sacked (89:41–67). Another summary embedded in the Testament of Moses (2:3–3:3) depicts the period between the entrance into the Promised Land and the destruction of Jerusalem by Nebuchadnezzar as a sequence of 38 "years." The first 18 years, from the conquest to the division of the kingdom, seem to stand for the fifteen judges of the book of Judges and Israel's first three kings, Saul, David, and Solomon.[124] After the ten tribes "establish for themselves kingdoms according to their own ordinances," the two tribes keep offering sacrifices for 20 "years," which appear to refer to the twenty kings of Judah, from Rehoboam to Zedekiah.[125]

Who Handle Books: Gender and the Rise of Canon-Consciousness (Hebrew Bible Monographs 50; Sheffield: Sheffield Phoenix, 2013), 168–72.

124 R. H. Charles, "Assumption of Moses," in *The Apocrypha and Pseudepigrapha of the Old Testament* (ed. R. H. Charles; Oxford: Clarendon Press, 1913), 2:416. J. Tromp, *The Assumption of Moses: A Critical Edition with Commentary* (Leiden: Brill, 1993), 154–155, views the numbers utilized by this historical resume as a schematic periodization of history with no link to figures mentioned in Sam-Kgs.

125 These are further divided into seven, nine, and, probably, four. Charles, ibid., 2:416, suggests that the seven are Rehoboam, Abijah, Asa, Jehoshaphat, Jehoram, Ahaziah, and Athaliah. The nine are Joash, Amaziah, Uzziah, Jotham, Ahaz, Hezekiah, Manasseh, Amnon, and Josiah.

The texts from Qumran yield more historical summaries engaging figures and events from Samuel-Kings. Thus, 4Q385a 1a-b ii mentions the divine promise from 2 Sam 7:12, 9?, 15 (lines 1–3), David's humility before the Lord (line 4), and Solomon's ascension to the throne (line 5), sacrifice at Gibeon, and dedication of the temple (line 7).[126] The scroll 4Q470 (4QText Mentioning Zedekiah) features a historical summary covering the bondage in Egypt, the Exodus, and the giving of the Torah (frg. 3). It may well be that frg. 1, describing a past (cf. Jer 34:8–22) or a future covenant with Zedekiah, mediated by Michael, also belongs with this summary.[127] The scroll 4Q247 (4QPesher on the Apocalypse of Weeks) offers a succinct overview of history periodized into "weeks," as in the Apocalypse of Weeks.[128] According to the proposed reconstruction, its fifth week begins with the Sinai revelation and ends with the construction of the First Temple. The scroll mentions Solomon, the 480 years of 1 Kgs 6:1, and Zedekiah, implying, perhaps, that the sixth week ends with the destruction of the temple. The Aramaic 4Qpseudo-Daniel incorporates a historical summary, mentioning the Israelites' sacrificing their children to "demons of error" and their being delivered into the hand of Nebuchadnezzar (4Q243 12 2–3; 4Q244 12).[129]

Pseudepigraphy.[130] The Second Temple pseudepigraphic writings ascribed to figures from Samuel-Kings can be broadly divided into those utilizing internal

---

The remaining four are Jehoahaz, Jehoiakim, Jehoiachin, and Zedekiah. For an alternative proposal, see Ben Zvi, "Authority," 247–248.

126 D. Dimant, DJD 30:133–134. For a recently identified textual overlap between 4Q387a 5 (Qimron; disputed by Davis) and 4Q481d 3 (Qimron; Davis), see Qimron, *Hebrew Writings*, 2:101; K. Davis, "4Q481d frg. 3: A New Fragment of 4QApocryphon of Jeremiah C-b (4Q387)," *Semitica* 56 (2014): 213–230.

127 See E. Larson, L. H. Schiffman, J. Strugnell, "4Q470. Preliminary Publication of a Fragment Mentioning Zedekiah," *RevQ* 16 (1993–95): 335–349; E. Larson, "4Q470 and the Angelic Rehabilitation of King Zedekiah," *DSD* 1 (1994): 210–228; E. Larson, L. Schiffman, J. Strugnell, DJD 19:235–244; B. Nitzan, "4Q470 in Light of the Tradition of the Renewal of the Covenant between God and Israel," in *The Scrolls and Biblical Traditions: Proceedings of the Seventh Meeting of the IOQS in Helsinki* (ed. G. J. Brooke et al.; STDJ 103; Leiden: Brill, 2012), 163–176; G. J. Brooke, "Zedekiah and Covenant in the Scrolls from Qumran," in *On Warriors, Prophets, and Kings* (ed. G. J. Brooke, A. Feldman; BZAW 470; Berlin: de Gruyter), forthcoming.

128 M. Broshi, A. Yardeni, DJD 36:189–191, argue that this scroll comments on the Apocalypse of Weeks. However, this proposal finds no support in the text.

129 See P. Flint, J. J. Collins, DJD 22:106–107, 129–130.

130 On pseudonymity and pseudepigraphy in early Jewish literature, see D. Dimant, "Pseudonymity in the Wisdom of Solomon," in *La Septuaginta en la Investigacion Contemporanea* (ed. N. Fernández-Marcos; Madrid: Instituto Arias Montano, 1985), 243–255; M. J. Bernstein, "Pseudepigraphy in the Qumran Scrolls: Categories and Functions," in *Pseudepigraphic Perspectives* (ed. E. G. Chazon et al.; STDJ 31; Leiden, Boston, Köln: Brill, 1999), 1–26; E. Tigchelaar,

pseudonymity and those using external pseudonymity.[131] Whereas the former simply attach a name to a piece, the latter utilize a variety of literary strategies to link a composition to a scriptural figure.

One work utilizing internal pseudonymity is the Wisdom of Solomon.[132] While it never explicitly mentions Solomon, the attribution to him is made clear by several autobiographical notes embedded throughout this work. Thus, the speaker identifies himself as a king (8:15), chosen by God (9:7), and charged with the construction of the temple and the altar (9:8). His prayers in 7:7–12 and 9:1–18 point to Solomon's prayers at Gibeon (1 Kgs 3:6–9) and at the dedication of the temple (1 Kgs 8:15 f).[133] Wisdom presents an ideal Solomon. Not only does he possesses the four cardinal virtues (8:70),[134] but the knowledge revealed to him (7:15–22) transforms him, according to one scholar, into "a model hermetic sage."[135]

Exhibiting internal pseudonymity is also Psalm 151, composed as David's autobiographic recollection of his youth, election by God, anointing by Samuel, and victory over Goliath.[136] Prior to the discovery of Qumran, this psalm was known in Greek, Latin, and Syriac.[137] Yet the Scrolls brought to light a Hebrew version of this psalm, in fact, two psalms, 151A and 151B,[138] diverging signifi-

---

"Forms of Pseudepigraphy in the Dead Sea Scrolls," in *Pseudepigraphie und Verfasserfiktion in frühchristlichen Briefen* (ed. J. Frey et al.; WUNT 246; Tübingen: J. C. B. Mohr [Paul Siebeck], 2009), 85–101.

131 See Dimant, ibid.

132 On the representation of Solomon in Wis, see M. Gilbert, "La figure de Solomon en Sg 7–9," in *Études sur le Judaïsme Helenistique* (ed. R. Kuntzmann, J. Schlosser; Paris: Cerf, 1984), 225–249; Dimant, "Pseudonymity," 243–255; Newman, "The Democratization of Kingship," 309–28; N. La-Coste, "The Exemplary Sage: The Convergence of Hellenistic and Jewish Traditions in the Wisdom of Solomon," *The University of Toronto Journal for Jewish Thought* 1 (2010).

133 Dimant, "Pseudonymity," 248, suggests that the appeal to rulers in Wis 6:1–11 may also be "inspired by the Kings-Chronicles narrative, where Solomon is described as venerated by all the kings of the earth."

134 LaCoste, "Exemplary Sage."

135 Torijano, *Solomon the Esoteric King*, 93–95.

136 For a recent discussion see E. D. Reimond, *New Idioms Within Old: Poetry and Parallelism in the Non-Masoretic Poems of 11Q5(=11QPsᵃ)* (Leiden, Boston: Brill, 2011), 51–74.

137 Another two biographical psalms attributed to David, Pss 152 and 153, appear to have been composed in Syriac, in which they are extant. See H. F. van Roy, *Studies on the Syriac Apocryphal Psalms* (JSSS 7; Oxford: Oxford University Press, 1999), 110–132.

138 What remains of Ps 151 B loosely corresponds to the last verses of the Greek Psalm 151 depicting David's victory over Goliath. Preceded by the superscription "[Dav]id's first mighty d[ee]d after the prophet of God had anointed him," this psalm links David's victory over Goliath to his anointing.

cantly from the previously known one (1QPs^a XXVIII, 3–14). While the precise relations between the two are debated, it is possible that the Greek reflects an earlier Hebrew text of the psalm, while the Qumran text is its expanded version.[139] From an exegetical point of view, both versions elucidate the divine choice of David, highlighting, each in its own way, his musical/poetical gifts as the main reason for it.[140]

One example of a work employing external pseudonymity is the collection of seventeen psalms known as the Psalms of Solomon. While their superscriptions attribute these poems to Solomon, their wording displays no affinity to the scriptural portrayal of the king.[141] This type of pseudepigraphy is also amply attested among the Dead Sea Scrolls.[142] Reflecting a well-known tradition crediting David and Solomon with exorcistic powers, two of the exorcism psalms collected in 11Q11 (11QapocrPs) are ascribed to these kings (II, 2; V, 4).[143] Similarly, non-Masoretic psalms from 4Q381 (4QNon-Canonical Psalms B) bearing superscriptions attributing them to "the Man of G[o]d" (frg. 24 4), understood by several scholars

<hr />

139 See M. Segal, "The Literary Development of Psalm 151: A New Look at the Septuagint Version," *Textus* 21 (2002): 159–174, and the bibliography cited there.
140 On the exegetical aspects of this psalm, see, among others, Y. Zakovitz, "'The Last Words of David': Studies in Psalm 151 from Qumran," in *On a Scroll of a Book* (ed. L. Mazor; Jerusalem: Magnes, 1997), 73–84 (Hebrew); D. Amara, "Psalm 151 from Qumran and its relation to Psalm 151 LXX," *Textus* 19 (1998): 1–35 (Hebrew); N. Fernández-Marcos, "David the Adolescent: On Psalm 151," in *The Old Greek Psalter* (ed. R. J.V. Hiebert et al.; Sheffield: Sheffield Academic Press, 2001), 205–217; H. Debel, "'The Lord Looks at the Heart'" (1 Sam 16,7): 11QPs^a 151A–B as a 'Variant Literary Edition' of Ps 151 LXX," *RevQ* 23 (2008): 459–73. Scriptural sources utilized in Ps 151 are analyzed in M. S. Smith, "How to Write a Poem: The Case of Psalm 151 A (11QPs^a 28.3–12)," in *The Hebrew of the Dead Sea Scrolls and Ben Sira* (ed. T. Muraoka, J. F. Elwolde; STDJ 26; Leiden: Brill, 1997), 182–208.
141 See K. Atkinson, *I Cried to the Lord: A Study of the Psalms of Solomon's Historical Background and Social Setting* (JSJSup 84; Leiden: Brill, 2004).
142 The dating of the so-called "Songs of David" from the Cairo Geniza, as well as their affinity to the Dead Sea Scrolls, is disputed. For an overview of the arguments, see D. M. Steck, *The Geniza Psalms* (Cambridge Geniza Studies 5; Leiden: Brill, 2013), 1–22, who favors the 1st century CE as a possible date of this work.
143 On this scroll see F. García Martínez, E. Tigchelaar, A. S. van der Woude, DJD 23:189, 198. See further K. Berthelot, "Guérison et exorcisme dans les textes de Qumrân et les évangiles," in *Guérisons du corps et de l'âme: Approches pluridisciplinaires* (ed. P. Boulhol et al.; Aix-en-Provence: Publications de l'Université de Provence, 2006), 135–148; I. Fröhlich, "'Invoke at Any Time ...': Apotropaic Texts and Belief in Demons in the Literature of the Qumran Community," *BN* 137 (2008): 41–74; G. Bohak, "From Qumran to Cairo: The Lives and Times of a Jewish Exorcistic Formula (with an Appendix by Shaul Shaked)," in *Ritual Healing: Magic, Ritual and Medical Therapy from Antiquity until the Early Modern Period* (ed. I. Csepregi, C. Burnett; Firenze: Sismel, Edizioni del Galuzzo, 2012), 31–52.

as referring to David,[144] and to "the "[ki]ng of Judah" (frg. 31 4), identified by some with Hezekiah,[145] reveal no affinity to any particular scriptural figure. This is also true of another prayer found in this scroll, a "Prayer of Manasseh, King of Judah, when the King of Assyria imprisoned him" (frg. 33a, b, 35).[146] Just like the Greek Prayer of Manasseh, found in the much later Apostolic Constitutions,[147] this prayer takes its cue from 2 Chr 33:13, 18–19 (unparalleled in 2 Kings), mentioning the repentant king's prayer, yet failing to provide its actual wording.[148]

Two additional works should be mentioned here. First, a sapiential work preserved in 4Q525, 5Q16, and, perhaps, 4Q184 bears close similarities to Proverbs 1–9. According to some, it might have been attributed to Solomon.[149] Second, several features of 11QPs^a suggest that its compiler perceived all the compositions included in it, Masoretic and non-Masoretic, both explicitly ascribed to David and anonymous, as Davidic.[150] For instance, a poem depicting a young man's pursuit

---

144 See E. Schuller, "Qumran Pseudepigraphic Psalms," PTSDSSP, 4A:2; A. P. Jassen, *Mediating the Divine: Prophecy and Revelation in the Dead Sea Scrolls and Second Temple Literature* (STDJ 68; Leiden: Brill, 2007), 119–120.

145 M. S. Pajunen, *The Land to the Elect and Justice for All: Reading Psalms in the Dead Sea Scrolls in Light of 4Q381* (JAJSup; Göttingen: Vandenhoeck & Ruprecht, 2013), 197–198, 214–216. He also suggests that two other psalms found in 4Q381 were ascribed to royal figures, Josiah (frgs. 79, 31) and Jehoiachin (frg. 31; ibid., 236–237, 251–257, 267–269). However, the textual evidence he adduces fails to convince.

146 Pajunen, ibid., 219, 371. See also W. M. Schniedewind, "A Qumran Fragment of the Ancient 'Prayer of Manasseh'?" *ZAW* 108 (1996): 105–107; M. S. Pajunen, "The Prayer of Manasseh in 4Q381 and the Account of Manasseh in 2 Chronicles 33," in *The Scrolls and Biblical Traditions* (ed. G. J. Brooke et al.; STDJ 103; Leiden, Boston: Brill, 2012), 143–161.

147 On this prayer see J. R. Davila, "Is the Prayer of Manasseh a Jewish Work?" in *Heavenly Tablets: Interpretation, Identity and Tradition in Ancient Judaism* (ed. L. LiDonnici, A. Lieber; JSJSup 119; Leiden: Brill, 2007), 75–85; Newman, van der Horst, *Early Jewish Prayers in Greek*, 148–180; E. G. Chazon, "Prayer of Manasseh," in *Outside the Bible*, 2:2143–2147. On the medieval translation of this prayer into Hebrew, see R. Leicht, "A Newly Discovered Hebrew Version of the Apocryphal 'Prayer of Manasseh'," *JSQ* 3 (1996): 359–73.

148 Another non-scriptural psalm, "a praise by Obadiah," is found in a collection of psalm-like compositions in 4Q380 1 ii 8 (4QNon-Canonical Psalms A). Since its wording is not extant, it remains unclear whether this is Obadiah of 2 Kgs 18 or the prophet Obadiah.

149 The former two are copies of the same composition; this might also be the case with the third one, 4Q184. Thus É. Puech, DJD 25:121; E. Qimron, "Improving the Editions of the Dead Sea Scrolls," *Meghillot* 1 (2003):137; idem, *Hebrew Writings*, 2:113; E. J.C. Tigchelaar, "Lady Folly and Her House in Three Qumran Manuscripts: On the Relation between 4Q425 15, 5Q16, and 4Q184 1," *RevQ* 23 (2008): 371–81.

150 On the Davidic features of 4QPs^a, see P. W. Flint, *The Dead Sea Psalms Scrolls and the Book of Psalms* (STDJ 17; Leiden: Brill: 1997), 189–194. On the debate as to whether this scroll is an edition of the book of Psalms or a liturgical collection, see ibid., 172–227. Some of the non-Masoretic

of wisdom in terms of the pursuit of a woman (XXI, 11–17) could be read as yet another Davidic autobiographical psalm, though it bears no resemblance to the scriptural portrayal of David's youth.[151] 11QPs[a] preserves only several lines of this poem. Its complete text in Ben Sira 51, a re-translation from Syriac, differs from the Qumranic version in several details, including the toning down of some of the latter's eroticisms.[152]

Rewritings. Prior to the discovery of the Dead Sea Scrolls, several rewritings of Samuel-Kings were known: 1–2 Chronicles, a work attributed to a certain Eupolemus, Biblical Antiquities (LAB), and Josephus's *Jewish Antiquities*.[153] The earliest of these is, apparently, Chronicles.[154] Its recasting of Samuel, beginning in 1 Chr 10 with a reworked citation from 1 Sam 31:1–13, is aptly summarized by Japhet:

> When the selection from II Samuel is viewed as a whole, a very clear procedure emerges: the Chronicler borrowed all the beginning of the story in II Sam. 5.1–12.31 … and three chapters from the end (II Sam. 21.18–22; 23.8–39; 24). He refrained from citing any part of the comprehensive pericope known as the 'succession narrative' (II Sam. 9; 12.2–25; 13:1–20.23; I Kings 1–2), and passed over a few other sections at the beginning (II Sam. 1–4) and the end (II Sam. 20.23–26; 21.1–17; 22.1–23.7).... Beginning with I Chron. 22 the Chronicler strikes out independently, with a comprehensive presentation of the preparation for the Temple, David's administration, and Solomon's accession.[155]

As to the Chronicler's treatment of Kings, famously focusing on Judah alone, the same study observes:

---

psalms incorporated in it were known before the discovery of Qumran: Pss 151 (discussed above), 154, 155 (these two were available in Syriac), and the poem from Sir 51. The previously unknown compositions found in this scroll are "Apostrophe to Zion," "Plea for Deliverance," "Hymn for the Creator," "Eschatological Psalm," and "David's Compositions" (discussed above).

151 See a recent discussion in Reymond, *New Idioms within Old*, 21–50.

152 On its eroticisms see T. Muraoka, "Sir 51, 13–30: An Erotic Hymn to Wisdom?" *JSJ* 10 (1979): 166–78. On the gradual neutralization of the erotic language as this poem was translated from Hebrew into Greek, into Syriac, and then back into Hebrew, see H. Eshel, "Non-Canonical Psalms from Qumran," in *The Qumran Scrolls and Their World* (ed. M. Kister; Between Bible and Mishnah; Jerusalem: Yad Ben Zvi Press, 2009), 216–222 (Hebrew).

153 Doubts have been expressed as to the legitimacy of placing 1–2 Chr within rewritten Scripture literature. See concerns raised by G. N. Knoppers, *1 Chronicles 1–9* (AB; New York: Doubleday, 2004), 1:129–137, and the counter-arguments by Brooke, "Books of Chronicles," 40–42.

154 While there is no consensus on the matter, it is assumed here with the majority of scholars that 1–2 Chr rewrite Sam-Kgs. For an overview of scholarship on this topic, see Knoppers, ibid., 1:66–68.

155 S. Japhet, *I & II Chronicles: A Commentary* (OTL; Louisville, Ky.: Westminster John Knox, 1993), 16.

The book of Kings ... is differently employed, however, for the description of Solomon's reign and the reigns of the kings of Judah ... Thus, the portrayal of Solomon's reign is very clearly a shortened reformulation of 1 Kings 1–11 ... For the history of the kingdom of Judah the Chronicler borrowed from Kings as much as possible ... The Chronicler's own contribution in this part, however, is characterized by extensive additions, which more than double the scope of the narrative. These include not only literary elaborations of existing narratives and isolated new episodes, but introduction of topics which were not handled in the Deuteronomistic history: the military organization of the kingdom, records of economic achievements, administrative details, a systematic history of the Temple, etc.[156]

Among the many notable features of the Chronicler's rewriting is the penchant for rhetoric, exhibited in multiple speeches, prayers, and dialogues. Some of these are expansions of those found in his sources, others are his creations.[157]

The extant fragments of "Concerning the Kings in Judea," composed by a certain Eupolemus in Greek, retell the events of Israelite history focusing on Solomon's reign, and particularly on the construction of the Temple.[158] Dated around 158–157 BCE,[159] this work expands, omits, summarizes, and re-arranges its scriptural sources, which included, but were not limited to, Samuel-Kings.[160]

---

156 Japhet, *Chronicles*, 17–18.

157 Ibid., 36.

158 For text and translation see Holladay, *Fragments from Hellenistic Jewish Authors*, 93–156. It remains unclear whether the author is identical with Eupolemus of 1 Macc 8:17–20 (cf. also 2 Macc 4:11; *Ant.* 12.415), as many, including Holladay, have argued, or is another person bearing this name. For the latter view see E. S. Gruen, *Heritage and Hellenism* (Berkeley and Los Angeles: University of California Press, 1998), 138–146.

159 Thus Y. Guttman, *The Beginnings of Jewish Hellenistic Literature* (Jerusalem: Mosad Bialik, 1958–1963), 76 (Hebrew); D. Mendels, *The Land of Israel as a Political Concept in Hasmonean Literature* (Tübingen: Mohr, 1987), 28. For an alternative dating, 141 BCE, see F. Clancy, "Eupolemus the Chronographer and 141 BCE," *SJOT* 23 (2009): 274–281. In an attempt to identify this work's *Tendenz*, scholars pointed out that it presents current events in the light of the past, particularly the glorious past of David and Solomon furnishes support for the Hasmonean dynasty, presenting them as the sole rulers of Judea, and promotes the centrality and uniqueness of the Jerusalem Temple. See Guttman, ibid., 75, Mendels, ibid., 30, 34; G. A. Keddie, "Solomon to His Friends: The Role of Epistolarity in Eupolemos," *JSP* 22 (2013): 228–229.

160 On Eupolemus's use of the Hebrew Bible see, among others, A. Spiro, "Manners of Rewriting Biblical History from Chronicles to Pseudo-Philo" (Ph.D. diss., Columbia University, 1953), 63–173; B.-Z. Wacholder, *Eupolemus: A Study of Judaeo-Greek Literature* (Cincinnati: Hebrew Union College-Jewish Institute of Religion, 1974); J. R. Bartlett, *Jews in the Hellenistic World: Volume 1, Part 1: Josephus, Aristeas, The Sibylline Oracles, Eupolemus* (Cambridge Commentaries on Writings of the Jewish and Christian World; London: Cambridge University Press, 1985), 56–71. In several episodes Eupolemus seems to follow Chr, rather than Kgs, e.g., the census episode and Souron's epistle. To be sure, he also utilizes other scriptural sources to create his account of the events, as demonstrated by Wacholder, ibid., 244–245.

Among his expansions are several non-scriptural chronological details (e.g., the duration of Saul's rule), the list of nations conquered by David, aggrandizing this king's expansive politics, and Solomon's correspondence with the Egyptian king Vaphres, depicting Solomon as the latter's superior. Of Eupolemus's omissions, particularly glaring is the absence of the period of the Judges in his description of the succession of the prophets from Joshua to Samuel. David's life is summarized, his sins are completely omitted, and the account of the transition from him to Solomon is greatly abbreviated.

Another rewriting of Samuel is found in Pseudo-Philo's Biblical Antiquities (LAB).[161] Composed either before or after the destruction of the Second Temple,[162] LAB offers an extensive, though highly selective, recasting of Samuel up to the death of Saul. As with Chronicles and Eupolemus, LAB exhibits familiar rewriting techniques, yet its elaborations of the scriptural text are particularly rich.[163] Thus, its version of the events preceding 1 Sam 1 tells of the people's search for a suitable leader after the demise of Phineas. When lots point to Elkanah, he refuses to assume the leadership, which prompts a divine announcement that Elkanah's son from Hannah will lead them (LAB 49). The story of Samuel's call introduces his age, God's soliloquy revealing his reasons for addressing Samuel as a man, and not as God, and Eli's explanation on how to distinguish between God's voice and that of an impure spirit (53).[164] Saul takes pity on Agag because the latter promised to show him hidden treasures (58). Anointed by Samuel, David sings an autobiographical song, and then another one, to make the evil spirit depart from Saul (59–60). Prior to his combat with Goliath, who turns out to be of his kin, David inscribes on his sling's stones the names of Abraham, Isaac, Jacob, Moses, and Aaron (61). The murder of the priests of Nob comes as a punishment for their taking the first fruits of the people (63). The medium from Endor, named Sedecla, happens to be the daughter of the Midianite diviner who led Israel astray (64). Saul is killed by the son of Agag, as was prophesied to him (65). At the same time, LAB is very selective. Among its numberless omissions are the annual travel of Elkanah and Hannah to Shiloh, Hannah's vow, and sacrifices offered while presenting Samuel to Eli (50–51). LAB omits the sexual depravity of Hophni and Phineas, as well as

---

161 For a recent overview of LAB, see H. Jacobson, "Biblical Interpretation in *Liber Antiquitatum Biblicarum*," in *A Companion to Biblical Interpretation in Early Judaism* (ed. M. Henze; Grand Rapids, Michigan/Cambridge, UK: Eerdmans, 2012), 180–199.

162 On the date of LAB see note 11.

163 See, for instance, Spiro, "Manners of Rewriting," 173–248; F. J. Murphy, *Pseudo-Philo: Rewriting the Bible* (New York: Oxford University Press, 1993), 186–219.

164 See H. M. Jackson, "Echoes and Demons in the Pseudo-Philonic *Liber Antiquitatum Biblicarum*," *JSJ* 27 (1996): 1–20.

the visit of the man of God to Eli (52). There is no mention of the episode of Nahash the Ammonite (56), or of Samuel's admonition from 1 Sam 12:6–17, 20–25 (57).

Of the extant early Jewish rewritings of Samuel-Kings, Josephus's *Jewish Antiquities* 5.338–10.185 is the most extensive and detailed.[165] His account of the events utilizes Samuel-Kings along with other relevant scriptural (and non-scriptural) sources:[166]

> *Ant.* 5: 1 Sam 1–4 (for *Ant. 5.338–362*)
> *Ant.* 6: 1 Sam 5–31
> *Ant.* 7: 2 Sam 1–24, 1 Kgs 1–2 with materials from 1 Chr 1–29, and 2 Chr 2
> *Ant.* 8: 1 Kgs 2–22 with materials from 2 Chr 1–18
> *Ant.* 9: 2 Chr 19–31 with materials from 1 Kgs 22, 2 Kgs 1–17, Jonah, Zechariah, and Nahum
> *Ant.* 10: 2 Kgs 18–24, 2 Chr 32–36, Isa 38–39, Ezek 12, and Jer 22–52 (for *Ant. 10.1–185*)

Josephus's rewriting techniques are similar to those of other rewritings: he amplifies, omits, summarizes, and rearranges.[167] Among his correct to numerous additions are the names of David's brothers, Samuel's private talk to David as he anoints him (6.157–168), and Saul's preservation of Agag due to the former's admiration of the latter's beauty and body size (6.131). Expanding on the scriptural account, Josephus fleshes out characterizations of biblical figures. Thus, Hophni and Phineas are accused of rape, seduction, violence, and tyranny (6.32–34). Samuel is a warrior (6.30), a capable organizer (6.31), and a staunch supporter of aristocratic rule (6.36–37). Of his countless omissions notable is the consistent exclusion of scriptural poetic passages, e.g., Hannah's song (5.347) and David's lament of Jonathan (7.5). Yet perhaps the most striking feature of his work, in comparison to other rewritings surveyed here, is that Josephus lets his own voice be

---

165 Of the extensive bibliography on Josephus's rewriting of Sam-Kgs, see, for instance, C. T. Begg, *Josephus' Account of the Early Divided Monarchy (AJ 8,212–420): Rewriting the Bible* (BETL 108. Leuven: Leuven University Press, 1993); idem, *Josephus' Story of the Later Monarchy (AJ 9.1–10.185)* (BETL 145; Leuven: Leuven University Press, 2000); idem, *Judean Antiquities 5–7* (Flavius Josephus: Translation and Commentary 4; Leiden: Brill, 2005); C. T. Begg, P. Spilsbury, *Judean Antiquities 8–10* (Flavius Josephus: Translation and Commentary 5; Leiden: Brill, 2005). For Josephus's treatment of specific figures from Sam-Kgs, see L. H. Feldman, *Josephus's Interpretation of the Bible* (Berkeley: University of California Press, 1998); idem, *Studies in Josephus' Rewritten Bible* (Leiden: Brill, 1998).

166 Adapted from Z. Rodgers, "Josephus' Biblical Interpretation," in *A Companion to Biblical Interpretation in Early Judaism* (ed. M. Henze; Grand Rapids, Michigan/Cambridge, UK: Eerdmans, 2012), 438. On Josephus's use of Chr, see F. G. Downing, "Redaction Criticism: Josephus' Antiquities and the Synoptic Gospels," *JSNT* 8 (1980): 61–64; Kalimi, *Retelling*, 93–97. Among non-biblical sources used by Josephus are the writings of Nicolaus of Damascus (e.g., *Ant.* 7.101).

167 For a recent overview of his rewriting techniques see Rodgers, "Josephus' Biblical Interpretation," 437–455.

heard by the readers, making the audience privy to his thoughts. Thus at the end of Ruth's story, serving as a transition from Judges to Samuel, he points out that God can elevate anyone, as in the case of David, a descendant of Ruth (5.537). Josephus digresses at length on the value of courage in the case of Saul (6.343–350). He also shares his views on human nature, kingship (6.59), aristocracy (6.84–85, 268), generosity (6.340–342), and the corrupting influence of power (7.35).

Samuel-Kings in Second Temple Literature: The Contribution of the Dead Sea Scrolls

This survey sought not only to catalogue the various modes of the use of Samuel-Kings in Second Temple literature, but also to identify the contribution of the previously unknown texts found among the Dead Sea Scrolls to the study of their transmission and interpretation. The insights gleaned from the foregoing discussion can be summarized as follows.

In comparison to many other scriptural books, only a few manuscripts of Samuel and Kings were found among the Dead Sea Scrolls. While the three copies of Kings are poorly preserved, the four Samuel scrolls, along with the MT and the putative *Vorlage* of the Old Greek, offer a glimpse of substantial variation among the copies of this book that might have been in circulation in late Second Temple times. The multiple unique readings of the best preserved manuscript, 4QSam^a, seem to be tantamount to a separate literary edition of Samuel, alongside the MT and the Hebrew text underlying the Old Greek translation.

The Dead Sea Scrolls yield further specimens of the already known modes of use of Samuel-Kings. In light of the previously available evidence, notable are the multiple uses of Samuel-Kings in legal contexts, as well as the preponderance of poetical and liturgical compositions pseudepigraphically ascribed to figures mentioned in these books. Also, the Dead Sea Scrolls feature previously unattested exegetical uses of Samuel-Kings. These are varieties of an actualizing (*pesher*-type) exegesis found predominantly in sectarian texts.

As far as exegetical traditions are concerned, the Dead Sea Scrolls share traditions attested to elsewhere in Second Temple writings (e.g., David as a prophet), yet also preserve unique ones (e.g., David's inability to consult the Torah as a justification of his polygamous marriages, and his authoring a liturgy for a year of 364 days). Perhaps, it is of significance that these otherwise unattested traditions occur in writings bearing marks of sectarian literature.

How do the Dead Sea Scrolls rewriting Samuel and Kings fit into this picture? The next four chapters analyzing the scrolls 4Q160, 4Q382, 4Q481a, and 6Q9 will attempt to answer this question.

Chapter 2: 4Q160

The Manuscript
The *editio princeps* of 4Q160 published by J. M. Allegro in DJD 5 contains 7 fragments.[168] However, on a recent image of this scroll, B-298173 (taken in January 2012), two additional fragments appear.[169] On this photograph they are designated as frgs. 10 (found also on PAM 44.180; 44.191) and 11.[170] Frg. 10 reads ל לֹ[. Frg. 11 is an assemblage of three tiny scraps of leather, two of which seem to contain residues of ink. It remains unknown when these two fragments were assigned to this scroll. While nothing certain can be said about frg. 11, the script of frg. 10 resembles that of 4Q160, classified as an early or a middle Hasmonean hand.[171]

Contents
Frgs. 1 and 7 rework 1 Sam 3:14–18 and 12:2–3 respectively. Frgs. 2+6+10, 3 ii, and 4 i+5 contain prayers. The extant text leaves the identity of the speakers and the circumstances in which these prayers were uttered undetermined.[172]

Textual Overlap between 4Q160 2+6+10 and 4Q382 104 ii
The prayers found in 4Q160 2+6+10 and 4Q382 104 ii overlap. Hence, the two scrolls may be copies of the same composition rewriting both Samuel and Kings (see Chapter 6).[173]

---

168 J. M. Allegro, DJD 5:9–11.
169 Accessible on http://www.deadseascrolls.org.il/explore-the-archive/image/B-298173. This image has 12 fragments. The difference in the number of the fragments between this image and the DJD edition can be explained as following. First, a small fragment (שמואל שׁ[ון]), joined by Allegro to frg. 1, appears on this image separately as frg. 2. Second, frg. 7 of the first edition broke into three fragments numbered on B-298173 as 8, 9, and 12. Third, B-298173 contains two fragments that are missing from all the previous images of this scroll (discussed above).
170 The present edition follows the numbering of the DJD edition. The fragments missing from the *editio princeps* are given the numbers assigned to them on the image B-298173, i.e., 10 and 11.
171 Strugnell, "Notes en marge," 179. F. Polak, "Samuel," EDSS, 2:822, dates it around 100 BCE, while Vermes in Schürer, *History*, 3.1:335, suggests second century BCE.
172 Since Samuel is the chief protagonist mentioned in the extant fragments of this scroll, several scholars ascribe the prayer found in frgs. 4 i+5 to him. See Wise et al., *Dead Sea Scrolls*, 234; Pollak, ibid.; A. P. Jassen, "Literary and Historical Studies in the Samuel Apocryphon (4Q160)," *JJS* 59 (2008): 30, 32; A. D. Gross, "The Vision of Samuel," *Outside the Bible*, 2:1517. However, such an attribution lacks textual support in the prayer itself.
173 If correct, the composition found in 4Q160 and 4Q382 belongs with a few literary works preserved at Qumran both on leather and papyrus. See a list of these in Tov, *Scribal Practices*, 48.

Title

Since 4Q160 1 deals with 1 Sam 3, Allegro entitled it 4QVision of Samuel. To better account for the contents of its other fragments, such titles as ParSam, Apocryphon of Samuel, and An Account of the Story of Samuel were proposed.[174] Yet, if 4Q160 and 4Q382 are indeed copies of the same literary work recasting Samuel-Kings, both scrolls need to be renamed.

Previous Editions

Following the publication of Allegro's *editio princeps*, Strugnell offered several significant improvements to his edition.[175] A new edition of 4Q160 has been recently published by Qimron.[176]

Present Edition

This edition of 4Q160 features several new readings based on the digitalized images of the scroll, both recent and old. Moreover, a previously unnoticed textual overlap between 4Q382 and 4Q160 led to a new suggestion regarding the arrangement, reading, and reconstruction of frgs. 2, 6, and 10.[177]

---

174 E. Tov, S. Pfann, DJD 39:49; Vermes in Schürer, *History*, 3.1:335; Vermes, *Complete Dead Sea Scrolls*, 587; Wise et al., *Dead Sea Scrolls*, 235.

175 Strugnell, "Notes en marge," 179–183.

176 Qimron, *Hebrew Writings*, 3:26–27. Prof. Qimron kindly shared with me a draft of his edition prior to its publication. His contributions are gratefully acknowledged below. Alex Jassen is preparing a new edition of 4Q160 to be included in the revised DJD 5 edited by G. J. Brooke and M. J. Bernstein. Meanwhile, see A. P. Jassen, "Intertextual Readings of the Psalms in the Dead Sea Scrolls: *4Q160* (Samuel Apocryphon) and Psalm 40," *RevQ* 22 (2006): 403–430; idem., "Literary and Historical Studies," 21–38.

177 I have discussed it in A. Feldman, "An Unknown Prayer from 4Q160 and 4Q382," *Meghillot* 11 (2014), forthcoming.

Text and Commentary

Frg. 1[178]

כ]יא נשבע]תי ל[בית]	1
וי]שמע שמוא]ל א]ת דב]ר]∘[	2
ו]שמואל שׁוֹכב לפני עלי ויקום ויפתח את ד]לתות	3
ו]לֹ]א [הֹגיד את המשא לעלי ויען עלי וֹ]יאמר	4
הו]דיעני את מראה האלוהים אלֹנֹ]א	5
אם תכחד ממני ד]בר	6
שמואל ∘]∘	7

Reconstruction with 1 Sam 3:14–17 (MT)

] כ]יא נשבע]תי ל[בית [עלי אם יתכפר עון בית עלי בזבח]	1
[ובמ]נֹ]חה עד עולם וי]שמע שמוא]ל א]ת דב]ר יהוה	2
[ו]שמואל שׁוֹכב לפני עלי ויקום ויפתח את ד]לתות בית יהוה ושמואל]	3
[ירא ו]לֹ]א [הֹגיד את המשא לעלי ויען עלי וֹ]יאמר שמואל בני ויאמר הנני]	4
[ויאמר הו]דיעני את מראה האלוהים אלֹנֹ]א תכחד ממני כה יעשה לכה אלוהים]	5
[וכה יוסיף [אם תכחד ממני ד]בר מכל הדבר אשר דבר אליכה	6
[ ] שמואל[∘]∘	7

Notes on Readings

The DJD edition places a small fragment (designated as frg. 2 on the photograph B-298173) to the right of frg. 1, lines 2–3. Though the shapes of the edges of the two fragments do not match, the resulting text seems to support this placement.

1 נשבעֹ]תי. This is Strugnell's reading confirmed by the photographs (e.g., B-295518). Allegro read נשב]עתי.

2 ובמ]נֹ]חה. A trace of a base stroke appears on frg. 2. Strugnell plausibly read it as a base of a medial *nun*. The DJD edition offers no reading here. Qimron prefers a *bet*, ו.]בֹ]מנחה.

3 שׁוֹכב. This is Strugnell's reading, improving on Allegro's שכב.

---

178 Lengths of the reconstructed lines 3–5 are 59, 61, and 63 letter-spaces respectively.

4 לֹ[א]לְֹ[ו. The DJD edition reads להגיד, yet, as Qimron correctly observes, the *lamed* appears at some distance from the *he*, precluding the reading להגיד.

ויאמר]וֹ. This is the reading of the DJD edition. Strugnell, followed now by Qimron, suggested that the first letter is a *bet*. On the photographs (e.g., B-295518) a vertical stroke curving left at the bottom is visible. The hook-shaped top seems to suit better a *waw* (some of the *waw* letters in this scroll tend to curve to the left), than a *bet*.

5 אלֹֹ[א. This is Strugnell's reading supported by the photographs (B-295518). Allegro offers no reading here.

Translation

1. ["f]or I have swor[n to] the house of [Eli that the iniquity of Eli's house shall not be expiated by sacrifice]
2. [or of]f[erring forever." And] Samue[l] heard the wo[rd of YHWH   ]
3. [and]Samuel was lying before Eli. And he arose and opened the do[ors of the house of YHWH. And Samuel]
4. [was afraid and did]n[ot] tell the oracle to Eli. And Eli answered and[said, "Samuel, my son." And he said, "Here I am."]
5. [And he said, "Let]me know the vision of God. Plea[se], do not[withhold (it) from me. May God do thusly to you]
6. [and may he add,]if you withhold from me a w[ord of what he told you."   ]
7. [   ]Samuel.[   ]

Comments

1–2 כ]יֹא נשבעֹֹ]תי ל[בית [עלי אם יתכפר עון בית עלי בזבח] / [ובמ]נֹ]חה עד עולם. This line follows 1 Sam 3:14. While the MT reads ולכן, the fragment has כיא. This suggests that the scroll paraphrases 1 Sam 3:13.[179]

2 ויֹ[שמע שמוא]ל א[ת דב]ר יהוה. This clause, missing from the MT and the ancient translations, seems to conclude the scroll's account of the divine revelation to

---

179 Strugnell, "Notes en marge," 180, suggested that the scroll might have read ולא כן כ]יֹא נשבעֹֹ]תי, arguing that this is the reading underlying the LXX rendering of vv. 13–14: καὶ οὐδ' οὕτως ὤμοσα (reading ולכן as ולא כן and relegating it to v. 13). Yet this is far from certain, as the conjunction כי/כיא is absent from the LXX's rendition of v. 14, whereas it is consistently represented elsewhere in the Septuagintal version of this chapter (see vv. 6, 8, 9, 10, 13, 20, 21).

Samuel.[180] The reconstruction דב]ר יהוה relies on 1 Sam 3:21, yet דב]ר (ה)אלוהים is equally possible, for it remains unknown whether the scroll used the Tetragrammaton.

ו]שמואל שׁוֹכב לפני עלי ויקום ויפתח את ד]לתות בית יהוה 3. This line depends on 1 Sam 3:15: וישכב שמואל עד הבקר ויפתח את דלתות בית יהוה ("And Samuel lay there until morning; and then he opened the doors of the House of the Lord"). The wording of the fragment diverges from the MT in several respects. First, it replaces וישכב שמואל with שמואל שׁוֹכב[ו], a construction found in 1 Sam 3:3. Second, it clarifies the location of Samuel's night rest, לפני עלי (for this phrase cf. 1 Sam 3:1). Frg. 7 4 also refers to Samuel's lying down/sleeping (the verb שכב may stand for sleeping as well) in front of his master's bed, לפני יצוﬠ[יו]. Third, the scroll omits the temporal עד הבקר. Fourth, it adds the verb ויקום.[181] In a similar fashion the LXX reads καὶ κοιμᾶται Σαμουηλ ἕως πρωὶ καὶ ὤρθρισεν τὸ πρωί (which can be retroverted into Hebrew as וישכב שמואל עד הבקר וישכם בבקר; cf. 1 Sam 15:12–13, another night revelation to Samuel: ויזעק אל יהוה כל הלילה וישכם שמואל לקראת שאול בבקר). The rewritten version of 1 Sam 3 in LAB 53:12 also reads "Samuel arose in the morning."[182] See Discussion.

שמואל שׁוֹכב[ו]. Strugnell suggested that the LXX's καὶ κοιμᾶται Σαμουηλ reflects a Hebrew *Vorlage* identical to that of the scroll. However, it more likely that the Greek renders וישכב שמואל.

ושמואל / ירא ו[ל]א [ה]גיד את המשא לעלי 3–4. Paraphrasing 1 Sam 3:15, the scroll reads ו[ל]א [ה]גיד, while the MT has מהגיד. The scroll also refers to the divine message that Samuel was afraid to disclose as המשא, "pronouncement,"[183] instead of the MT's המראה, "vision." See Discussion.

לעלי. The MT reads אל עלי. The אל/על interchange is frequently attested in the Dead Sea Scrolls.[184]

---

180 Cf. Pseudo-Philo's version of the story adding "when Samuel heard these words" (LAB 53:11). See Jacobson, *Commentary*, 180.

181 On the possibility that this addition reflects phraseology common to dream accounts (e.g., Dan 8:27), see F. Flannery-Dailey, *Dreamers, Scribes, and Priests: Jewish Dreams in the Hellenistic and Roman Eras* (JSJSup 90; Leiden, Boston: Brill, 2004), 134.

182 On this passage see D. J. Harrington, "The Biblical Text of Pseudo-Philo's Liber Antiquitatum Biblicarum," *CBQ* 33 (1971): 14.

183 HALOT, 639–640.

184 See, for instance, E. Y. Kutscher, *The Language and Linguistic Background of The Isaiah Scroll (1QIsaᵃ)* (Leiden: Brill, 1974), 408.

ויקרא עלי את שמואל) **ויען עלי וֹ[יאמר שמואל בני ויאמר הנני 4**. Dependent on 1 Sam 3:16
(MT]) ויאמר הנני, this line utilizes a frequently attested construction, ויען... ויאמר.
instead of the rare ויקרא... ויאמר.

הו[דיעני את מראה האלוהים אלֹנֹ]א תכחד ממני 5. This line reworks 1 Sam 3:17. Unlike
the MT, reading מה הדבר אשר דבר אליך, the fragment has הו[דיעני את מראה האלוהים.
For the phrase מראה האלוהים cf. מראות אלהים of Ezek 1:1; 8:3; 40:2. Hence the translation "the vision of God," though "God's vision" is equally possible. See Discussion.

    אלֹנֹ]א. The scribe wrote these two words as one (for other instances of attach-
ing נא/נה to the preceding word see 4Q364 4b-e ii 4; 4Q382 9 6).

כה יעשה לכה אלוהים] / [וכה יוסיף]אֹם תכחד ממני דֹ]בר מכל הדבר אשר דבר אליכה 5–6.
The fragment follows 1 Sam 3:17 MT.

7 שמואל[ ]○. Perhaps, restore with v. 18: ויגד לו]שמואל[. Still, the MT's wording of
vv. 17–18 is too short for the lacunae in lines 6 and 7. Apparently, the scroll extends
the scriptural account.

Frgs. 2+6+10
The wording of frgs. 2, 6, and 10 bears a close resemblance to 4Q382 104 ii 1–4.
Before offering a combined text of the three fragments, each of them will be pre-
sented separately.

Frg. 2
This fragment seems to preserve the top and the right margins.

Top margin

אותם ולהבר כפים ל[

Frg. 6

Top margin

[לכה ואתה תהיה להמה ות○]	1
כ]יא אתה למרישונה בעֹ[	2
]לֹ[	3

Notes on Readings

2]בֿעֿ. Allegro offers no reading for the second letter. The traces of the tops of two vertical strokes suit well an *ayin*.

3 The trace of a *lamed* is visible on B-295525.

Frg. 10

[הֿייתה לֿהֿ]

Notes on Readings

This fragment is absent from the DJD edition (see Manuscript).

Frgs. 2+6+10: Combined Text Reconstructed with 4Q382 104 ii 1–4

Reconstruction A:

Top margin

1   אותם ולהבר כפים ל]מען יהיו [לכה ואתה תהיה להמה ותצֿ]דק[

2   [בדבריכה ותזכה בשפטכה   כ]יא אתה למרישונה בעֿ]לתם[

3   [ו]הֿייתה לֿהֿ]ם לאב ולאלוהים ולוא עזבתם בידי מ]לֿ]כים ולוא[

According to this placement of frgs. 2, 6, and 10, the reconstructed lines 1 and 3 are 50 letter-spaces long. Since the reconstructed frgs. 1 and 4 i+5 have longer lines (averaging 61 and 59 letter-spaces respectively), the following arrangement of the fragments appears to be preferable, as it results in longer lines (58 letter-spaces in line 1).

Reconstruction B:

Top margin

1 אותם ולהבר כפים ל]מען יהיו [לכה ואתה תהיה להמה ותצֿ]דק בדבריכה[

2 [ותזכה בשפטכה   כ]יא אתה למרישונה בעֿ]לתם ו]הֿייתה לֿהֿ]ם[

3 [לאב ולאלוהים ולוא עזבתם בידי מלֿכים ולוא המש]לֿ]תה בעמך   [

Translation

1.   them and to cleanse hands s[o that they will be]to you and you will be to them. And you will be found ri[ghteous [in your words]

2. [and just in your judging.   F]or you became [their] ow[ner] from the beginning, [and]you were for them

3. [as a father and as God. And you have not abandoned them in the hands of k]i[ngs, and you have not made ma]s[ter over your people   ]

Comments

See Comments to 4Q382 104 ii in Chapter 3.

Frg. 3 i

רֹאה[   ] 4

Notes on Readings

A single word survives in frg. 3 i. It appears opposite to frg. 3 ii 4.

Translation

4. [   ](he) saw

Comments

רֹאה[. רֹאה is a 3rd masc. sg. Qal *qatal* of ראה, "to see." Allegro restored it as מ[רֹאה, "a vision," suggesting a link between this line and the reworking of 1 Sam 3 in frg. 1.

Frg. 3 ii

[מים הואהֹ   ] 1
[ו]בֹּארצות ובימיֹם[   ] 2
אתה בראתה[   ] 3
וה○[   ] 4

Notes on Readings

The blank space at the top of the fragment is slightly larger than an average interlinear space in this fragment. Perhaps these are the remains of an upper margin.

1 מים‎[. A trace of ink is visible in the beginning of the line. Allegro read it as a *shin*, ה[שׁמים, while Strugnell (followed now by Qimron) preferred לא[ומים. However, both readings are highly uncertain.

Translation
1. [ ].... he[
2. [and]in the lands and in the seas[
3. you have created[
4. ...[

Comments

2 [ו]בֿארצות ובימיׂם]. Perhaps this line can be restored with 4Q302 3 ii 9–10: [ו]בֿארצות ובימיׂם] ממשלתך.

3 אתה בראתה. Allegro and Strugnell suggested that this fragment belongs with the prayer in frg. 4 i and offered a combined text of frgs. 3 ii and 4 i (Allegro) or frgs. 3 ii, 4 i, and 5 (Strugnell). However, frgs. 3 ii and 4 i lack thematic and lexical links (thus also Qimron), whereas an attempt to join frgs. 3 ii, 4 i, and 5 produces significantly longer lines.

Frgs. 4 i+5
Since both frgs. 4 i and 5 allude to Ps 40:3, Strugnell placed the two side by side. While this proposal is supported by the wording of the fragments, far less convincing is his attempt (following Allegro) to introduce here also the text of frg. 3 ii (see Comments ad loc.). Before offering a combined text of frgs. 4 i and 5, each fragment will be presented separately.

Frg. 4 i

Top margin

עֿבֿדֿכה לוא עצרתי כוח עד זואת כיא	]	1
יֿ[קֿוו אלוהי לעמכה ועזרתה היה לו והעלהו	]	2
לֿ[ ]וֿ[הֿ]העמד להמה סלע למרואש כיא תהלתכה	]	3
מק[ד]ישֿוֿ ובזעם שונאי עמכה תגביר תפארת	]	4
[וממלכה וידעו כול עמי ארצותיכהֿ]	]	5
יֿ[בינו רבים כיא עמכה הואֿ]	]	6
קדו[שֿיכה אשר הקדשתֿ]ה	]	7

Notes on Readings

3]לֹֿ[. As Strugnell observes, a trace of an upper vertical stroke of a *lamed* is visible on PAM 43.434.

Frg. 5

[מטיט יון]	1
מ[עֹוז עמכה ומ]חסהו	2
[יראתכה על בֹֿ]וֹ[לֹֿל	3
]∘∘[	4

Notes on Readings

3]בֹֿ[וֹ]לֹֿל. Allegro offers no reading for the first two letters. Strugnell reads]בֹֿל. Yet the photographs reveal no trace of a second letter.

4 Traces of two illegible letters are visible in this line on the photographs (e.g., PAM 43.348; 43.434). Qimron tentatively suggests את[הֹֿ יֹ]הוה.

Frgs. 4 i+5: Combined Text[185]

Top margin

[עֹבֹדֹכה לוא עצרתי כוח עד זואת כיא	]	1
י[קֹוו אלוהי לעמכה ועזרתה היה לו והעלהו	]	2
[מבור שאון ו]מטיט יון[הצי]לֹ[ם ו]הֹעמד להמה סלע למרואש כיא תהלתכה	]	3
[היא מ]עֹוז עמכה ומ]חסהו ואתה מק]דֹֿשֹׁוֹ ובזעם שונאי עמכה תגביר תפארת	]	4
[ותתן]יראתכה על בֹֿ]וֹ[לֹֿל] עם וגוי]וממלכה וידעו כול עמי ארצותיכהֹֿ] כיא[	]	5
[	וֹ[בֹינו רבים כיא עמכה הוא]	]∘∘[	]	6
[	קדו]שֹׁיכה אשר הקדשתֹֿ]ה		]	7

Translation

1. [   ]your servant. I retained no strength until this, for

2. [   ](they) shall put (their) hope, O my God, in your people. And be of a help to him. And lift him up

3. [from a miry pit and]from slimy clay[re]s[cue them. And] establish for them a rock as beforehand. For your praise

---

185 The reconstructed lines 3–5 have 56, 60, and 62 letter-spaces respectively.

4. [is the s]tronghold of your people and [his] r[efuge. And you are the one sanc]tifying him. And in the fury of those who hate your people you shall make (your) glory prevail.

5. [And you shall put]your fear on ev[e]ry[people, nation,]and kingdom. And all the nations of your lands shall know[for]

6. [   ]..[and]many [will]understand that this is your people[   ]

7. [   ]your [san]ctified ones whom you sanctifie[d   ]

Comments

1 עד זאת כיא. עְֿבֿדכה לֹוֿא עצרתי כוח עד זאת כיא[. The anonymous speaker refers to himself as God's servant, עְֿבֿדכה. Qimron restores ואני[עְֿבֿדכה. A reconstruction כיא אני עְֿבֿדכה[(with Ps 116:16) is equally possible. Jassen (*apud* Wise) prefers שמע נא אלוהי לְ[עְֿבֿדכה.

לֹוֿא עצרתי כוח. Attested to in Dan 10:8, 16, this phrase depicts the speaker's inability to maintain his/her strength (Allegro; Jassen).[186] Such translations as "I have never yet held back,"[187] "I did not control my strength,"[188] or "I have not restrained my strength until this [moment]"[189] seem to fail to express the feeling of exhaustion implied here.

עד זאת. The phrase is synonymous to עד הנה and עד כה frequent in biblical Hebrew.

2 קֿוֿו אלוהי לעמכה[יֿ. Allegro read and restored the first word as a 3rd pl. Piel jussive of קוה, "to hope," יֿ]קֿוֿו. According to this reading, the speaker prays that others, e.g., רבים of line 6, will put their hopes in God's people. The wording of Ps 40:2: קוה קויתי יהוה (v. 3 of this psalm is paraphrased further on in this line) supports the reading of קֿוֿו[as a form of קוה, "to hope," yet also suggests a possibility of קֿוֿו[being a phonetic spelling of קֿוֿה, a Piel infinitive absolute utilized as an imperative (Qimron).[190] Given the graphic resemblance between *waw* and *yod* in this scroll, a reading קֿוֿֿי אלוהי[, "](those) who trust in my God," ought also to be considered. Strugnell (followed by Vermes, García Martínez and Tigchelaar, Wise, and Jassen) parsed יֿ]קֿוֿו as a 3rd pl. Nifal jussive of קוה, "to assemble." According to this reading, this line is a plea for others to join God's people (cf. Jer 3:17). Jassen

186 HALOT, 870.

187 Wise et al., *Dead Sea Scrolls*, 235.

188 García Martínez, Tigchelaar, *Study Edition*, 313.

189 Vermes, *Complete Dead Sea Scrolls*, 587.

190 Private correspondence. Cf. Joüon-Muraoka, *Grammar*, 398–399.

goes on to suggest that this is a sectarian prayer expressing a hope that other Jews will join the ranks of the speaker's community.

לו היה ועזרתה. היה should be read as an imperative (Strugnell), rather than as a *qatal* (Allegro). For the phrase עזרה/תה היה see Ps 63:8.[191] The antecedent of the 3rd masc. sg. pronoun in לו is, apparently, עמכה.

2–3 הצי[ל]ל[ם] / [מבור שאון ו]מטיט יון והעלהו. The scroll depends here on Ps 40:3a: ויעלני מבור שאון מטיט היון ("He lifted me out of the miry pit, the slimy clay;" Strugnell). Unlike the MT's היון, the scroll reads יון. It seems that both והעלהו and הצי[ל]ל[ם] refer to עמכה mentioned earlier on.

והעלהו. This is another imperative, and not a *qatal*, as Allegro suggested.

הצי[ל]ל[ם]. Strugnell restores הצל רג[ל]ל[ם], yet the available space calls for a shorter reconstruction.

3 והֿ[עמד להמה סלע למרואש. The request to establish a rock (as opposed to "slimy clay") for the people paraphrases Ps 40:3b: ויקם על סלע רגלי ("and set my feet on a rock"). The replacement of the biblical ויקם with the imperative והֿ[עמד reflects the widely attested preference for עמד in the late biblical Hebrew (Jassen).[192] The construction למרואש, absent from the Hebrew Bible (cf. למרישונה in frgs. 2+6+10 2), should be understood adverbially: "as beforehand" (thus Jassen; Strugnell, followed by others, rendered it as "establish for them a rock from of old").[193]

3–4 כיא תהלתכה / [היא מ]עוז עמכה ומ[חסהו ואתה מק]דֿשֿוֿ. Given the use of Ps 40:3 in the preceding lines, the noun תהלתכה may point to v. 4 of this psalm: ויתן בפי שיר חדש תהלה לאלהינו ("He put a new song into my mouth, a hymn to our God"). The reconstruction מ]עוז עמכה ומ[חסהו follows Joel 4:16. Qimron prefers מ[עוז עמכה ומ[בטחו with Ps 40:5: אשרי הגבר אשר שם יהוה מבטחו ("Happy is the man who makes the Lord his trust"). While the letters דֿשֿוֿ[suggest a form of קדש, the restoration ואתה מקֿ[דֿשֿוֿ (with Exod 31:13: כי אני יהוה מקדשכם), i.e., a masc. sg. Piel participle of קדש, is tentative.

191 On the form עזרתה (cf. Ps 44:27) see Gesenius-Kautsch, *Grammar*, § 90g, p. 251.

192 See A. Hurvitz, "The Linguistic Status of Ben Sira as a Link between the Biblical and the Mishnaic Hebrew: Lexicographical Aspects," in *The Hebrew of the Dead Sea Scrolls and Ben Sira* (ed. T. Muraoka, J. F. Elwolde; STDJ 26; Leiden: Brill, 1997), 78–85; H. Dihi, "The Morphological and Lexical Innovations in the Book of Ben Sira" (PhD diss., Ben-Gurion University of the Negev, 2004), 514–516 (Hebrew).

193 HALOT, 1169.

4 ‏ובזעם שונאי עמכה תגביר תפארת. The construction ‏שונאי עמכה is absent from biblical and Qumran Hebrew (cf. ‏לשנא עמו [Ps 105:25]). Similarly unattested is the construction ‏תגביר תפארת, with ‏תגביר being a 3rd masc. sg. Hifil jussive, rather than a
yiqtol, of ‏גבר, "to prevail, be mighty, strengthen."[194] It is tempting to suggest that
this plea to God to make his glory prevail amidst the fury of his people's enemies
reflects one of the many conflicts between the Jewish population of the Land of
Israel and the Gentile powers in late Second Temple times.

5 ‏כיא[‏וֹיראתכה על בֹּ[ו]לֹ[עם וגוי ‏וֹממלכה וידעו כול עמי ארצותיכה[‏וֹתתן]. This formulation seems to expand on Ps 40:4c: ‏יראו רבים וייראו ויבטחו ביהוה ("May many see
it and stand in awe, and trust in the Lord"). The reconstructions ‏וֹיראתכה[‏וֹתתן]
(Qimron) and ‏על בֹּ[ו]לֹ[עם וגוי ‏וֹממכלה], elaborating on ‏רבים of this verse, follow
the biblical idiom (e.g., Ezek 30:13; 1 Kgs 18:10; 2 Chr 32:15). Although the text is
broken, the next line suggests that the knowledge implied by the phrase ‏כול וידעו
‏עמי ארצותיכה (for the language cf. Josh 4:24; 1 Kgs 8:43[=2 Chr 6:33]) has to do with
the covenantal relationships between God and his people.

6 ‏וֹ[בינו רבים כיא עמכה הוא]. ‏וֹ. "Many," ‏רבים, alludes to Ps 40:4c: ‏יראו רבים. Both ‏וידעו
of the preceding line and ‏וֹ[בינו of this line seem to elaborate on ‏יראו.

7 ‏קדו[שיכה אשר הקדשתֹה. This is the second reference to the divine sanctification
of the chosen people in this prayer (cf. line 4; see also the expression ‏לקדשך אותם
in frgs. 2+6+10 and 4Q382 104 ii 1). Perhaps restore ‏עם קדו[שיכה (with Dan 8:24).

Frg. 4 ii

Top margin

1   ‏מחלה את ‏ו°[

2   ‏שמֹ[ו]

Notes on Readings
1 °[. A trace of a letter is visible on B-295520.

---

194 D. J.A. Clines (ed.), *The Concise Dictionary of Classical Hebrew* (Sheffield: Sheffield Academic Press, 2009), 61.

Translation

1. appeasing(?) the .[
2. his name[

Comments

1 מחלה את. The *nota accusativi* suggests that מחלה is a participle, either a Hifil participle of חלה, "to make sick," or, assuming that the line read מחלה את פֹּ[נִי/ה/ו/הם, a Piel participle (unattested in biblical Hebrew) of חלה, "to appease" (see Comment to frg. 7 3).[195]

2]שׁמׄוׄ. One may read the extant letters as a noun שֵׁם, "name," with a 3rd masc. sg. possessive suffix, or as a 3rd masc. pl. Qal *qatal* of שׂים, "to put."

Frg. 5
See above frgs. 4 i+5.

Frg. 6
See above frgs. 2+6+10

Frg. 7

[ׄנׄׄ֯י ויקו ע]ׄל	1
לו	
[וׄגרתי עמו מועֵדי ונלויתי מ[נעורי	2
לוא]יׄחלתי פניה רכוש והון ומחיר] לוא לקחתי	3
[אׄדוני ובחרתי לשכוב לפני יצועֵ]יו	4
Bottom margin	

Notes on Readings

1 ׄנׄׄ֯[. Allegro read the first letter as a medial *pe*, yet the extant trace of ink can belong to several letters. Given the uncertainty, no reading is proposed here.

ויקו. This reading is supported by PAM 40.618. Allegro read יהי.

---

195 HALOT, 317.

2 וְגֹרתי[. The DJD edition offers no reading for the first letter. Strugnell (followed now by Qimron) read it as a *he*. The traces of ink, as are seen on B-295523, are consistent with a *waw/yod*.

מ[נעורי. Allegro read a trace of a letter next to the *mem*. This is not supported by the photographs.

4 אֲ[דוני[. Allegro offered no reading for the first letter. Strugnell correctly reads an *alef* (cf. B-295527).

Translation

1.]... and (he) hoped f[or
2.]and I dwelt with him my whole life and I joined myself to him from[my youth
3.]I have [not]sought her/its favor. Property, and wealth, and money[I have not taken
4.]my master and I chose to lie before [his] bed[

Comments

1 ‹י› ויקו על[ל. Since line 3 seems to paraphrase 1 Sam 12:3, it may well be that this fragment contains a reworking of Samuel's farewell address. Appropriately, most of the verbs in this fragment are in the 1st person. The only exception is ויקו, a 3rd masc. sg. Piel *wayiqtol* of קוה, "to hope," perhaps, referring to Ei, who is spoken of in the 3rd person in lines 2–3. In biblical Hebrew Piel forms of קוה, "to hope," usually take prepositions ל- and אל (e.g., Hosea 12:7; cf. frgs. 4 i+5 2). The construction ויקו על[ל reflects the אל/על interchange frequent in the Dead Sea Scrolls (see Comment to line 2).[196]

2 וְגֹרתי עמו מועדי ונלויתי ‹ל› מן[נעורי[. Although מועדי can be read as the noun מוֹעֵד with a 1st masc. sg. possessive suffix, i.e., "my appointed time," it is more likely that this is a phonetic spelling of מֵעוֹדִי, "since I am, my life long" (Qimron).[197] The reconstruction ונלויתי ‹ל› מן[נעורי, standing in poetic parallelism with the preceding clause, follows 1 Sam 12:2: ואני התהלכתי לפניכם מנערי עד היום הזה ("and I have been your leader from my youth to this day"). Since the next line seems to rework 1 Sam 12:3, it is likely that this entire formulation is an expansion of v. 2. Yet, while in the scriptural passage Samuel speaks of his service to the people, here

196 See Kutscher, *Language and Linguistic Background of The Isaiah Scroll*, 408.
197 HALOT, 796.

he reflects upon the years spent with Eli, referred to in the 3rd person, עמו, לו. Perhaps this elaboration was prompted by the reference to Samuel's "youth" in the scriptural verse.

ונלויתי לו. In biblical Hebrew Nifal forms of לוה, "to join oneself," appear with prepositions אל, על, and עם, while here -ל is utilized. Apparently this is another instance of the interchange of prepositions in this fragment (see Comment to line 1).[198]

3 לוא [יחלתי פניה. The verb יחלתי can be parsed as a 1st masc. sg. Piel *qatal* of יחל, "wait for, hope for" (cf. כי לדברך יחלתי, Ps 119:74).[199] However, in biblical Hebrew Piel forms of יחל do not take a direct object. Furthermore, the construction יחל פניו is not attested in the ancient sources. Qimron suggests that this verb should be understood as a form of חלה, "to appease, entreat a favor of" (García Martínez and Tigchelaar also translate it this way).[200] The expression חלה פניו occurs frequently in the Hebrew Bible (cf. Pr 19:6: רבים יחלו פני נדיב; note also the possible usage of this expression in frg. 4 ii 1). The antecedent of the 3rd fem. sg. suffix in פניה is lost. Yet, in light of the following list of material goods that Samuel seems to have rejected, it is likely that the negative לוא preceded the verb יחלתי.

רכוש והון ומחיר] לוא לקחתי. This list, opening a new clause, may paraphrase 1 Sam 12:3: את שור מי לקחתי וחמור מי לקחתי ... ומיד מי לקחתי כופר ("Whose ox have I taken, or whose ass have I taken? ... From whom have I taken a bribe?"). The noun מחיר ("equivalent value, purchase price, money"), paraphrasing the biblical כופר, is used in poetic parallelism with שחד, "bribe," in Micah 3:11.[201] Hence the rendering "bribery" in several translations of this fragment (Wise; Gross).

4 [א]דוני ובחרתי לשכוב לפני יצוע]יו. The appellation אדוני refers to Eli (cf. Hannah's address to Eli: לא אדני in 1 Sam 1:15, and Elisha's reference to Elijah in 4Q481a 3 4: א]ב ואדון [see Chapter 4]). Samuel presents his service to Eli, epitomized by the phrase "to lie before [his] bed" (cf. frg. 1 3), as his own choice, ובחרתי, rather than as a decision made for him by his mother/parents (1 Sam 1:22–23). This choice might have been contrasted here with the opportunities to accumulate רכוש והון ומחיר, which Samuel refused to pursue.

198 BDB, 530–531.
199 Ibid., 103–104.
200 HALOT, 317.
201 Ibid., 569.

לשכוב. While in biblical Hebrew, as well as in the DSS, the form לשכב is dominant, לשכוב is attested also in 4Q223–224 V, 3 (cf. 1QS VII, 10: ישכוב).[202]

Frg. 11

Three minute scraps of leather, designated as frg. 11, appear on B-294984 (see Manuscript). There are no legible traces of letters on these scraps.

Discussion

Scriptural Exegesis in 4Q160

The comparison between frg. 1 and the Masoretic Text of 1 Sam 3:14–18 reveals the following similarities and differences (the latter are set in bold type):

4Q160 1	**1 Sam 3:14–18 MT**
כ[יא נשבע]תי ל[בית [עלי אם יתכפר עון בית עלי בזבח	וְלָכֵן נִשְׁבַּעְתִּי לְבֵית עֵלִי אִם־יִתְכַּפֵּר עֲוֹן בֵּית־עֵלִי בְּזֶבַח
ובמ[נ]חה עד עולם ו[י]**שמע שמוא**[ל א]**ת דב**[ר יהוה	וּבְמִנְחָה עַד־עוֹלָם:
ו[שמואל **שוכב לפני עלי ויקום** ויפתח את ד[לתות בית יהוה	**וַיִּשְׁכַּב** שְׁמוּאֵל **עַד־הַבֹּקֶר** וַיִּפְתַּח אֶת־דַּלְתוֹת בֵּית־יְהֹוָה
ושמואל ירא ו[ל]**א** [ה]גיד את **המשא לעלי וי**ען עלי ו[י]אמר	וּשְׁמוּאֵל יָרֵא מֵהַגִּיד אֶת־הַמַּרְאָה אֶל־עֵלִי: **וַיִּקְרָא** עֵלִי
שמואל בני ויאמר הנני ויאמר הו]**דיעני את מראה האלהים**	**אֶת־שְׁמוּאֵל** וַיֹּאמֶר שְׁמוּאֵל בְּנִי וַיֹּאמֶר הִנֵּנִי: וַיֹּאמֶר **מָה הַדָּבָר**
אל[נ]א תכחד ממני כה יעשה לכה אלוהים וכה יוסיף [אם תכחד	**אֲשֶׁר דִּבֶּר אֵלֶיךָ** אַל־נָא תְכַחֵד מִמֶּנִּי כֹּה יַעֲשֶׂה־לְךָ אֱלֹהִים וְכֹה
ממני ד]בר מכל הדבר אשר דבר אליכה	יוֹסִיף אִם־תְּכַחֵד מִמֶּנִּי דָּבָר מִכָּל־הַדָּבָר אֲשֶׁר־דִּבֶּר אֵלֶיךָ:
[שמואל °[	וַיַּגֶּד־לוֹ שְׁמוּאֵל

The majority of scholars consider the differences between these two texts to be significant enough to classify frg. 1 as a rewriting of 1 Sam 3:14–18.[203] As is frequently the case with rewritten Scripture,[204] it is difficult (and in many cases

---

202 See Qimron, *Hebrew of the Dead Sea Scrolls*, 50.

203 Jassen, "Studies," 24–25, believes that frg. 1 contains a form of a biblical text, rather than a rewriting thereof. His main argument seems to be that the wording of the fragment lacks exegetically driven alterations characteristic of a rewriting. The following remarks demonstrate that the fragment indeed attempts to resolve some of the difficulties embedded in the scriptural account.

204 See, for instance, E. Tov, "The Temple Scroll and Old Testament Textual Criticism," *Eretz-Israel* 16 (1982): 100–111 (Hebrew); G. J. Brooke, "Some Remarks on 4Q252 and the Text of Genesis," *Textus* 19 (1998): 1–25; J. C. VanderKam, "The Wording of Biblical Citations in Some Rewritten Scriptural Works," in *The Bible as Book: The Hebrew Bible and the Judaean Desert Discoveries* (ed. E. D. Herbert, E. Tov; London: British Library; New Castle, DE: Oak Knoll Press, 2002), 41–56; Feldman, *Rewritten Joshua Scrolls, passim*.

impossible) to distinguish between the scroll's scriptural *Vorlage* and modifications introduced through the process of rewriting.[205] It is tempting to suggest that a variation in the use of prepositions (לעלי), a minor syntactical change (הֹגִיד]א ל[ֹ ו ירא[), a slight expansion (ויקום ויפתח), and a preference for a more common expression (ויען עלי וֹ[יאמר) belong to the scroll's *Vorlage*, while the readings presented below as exegetically driven reflect 4Q160's tampering with the scriptural text. Yet, one must also allow for the possibility that any of these could have been already present in the scroll's *Vorlage*.[206] Be this as it may, two aspects of the scroll's rewriting of 1 Sam 3:14–18 deserve further consideration.

First, while 1 Sam 3:15 concludes the description of the divine revelation to Samuel by saying that he "lay there until morning" (וישכב שמואל עד הבקר), frg. 1 3 reads "[and]Samuel was lying before Eli" (שמואל[ו] שוֹכב לפני עלי). The construction ושמואל שוכב occurs in 1 Sam 3:3 (MT):

ויהי ביום ההוא ועלי שכב במקמו ... ונר אלהים טרם יכבה **ושמואל שֹכַב** בהיכל יהוה אשר שם ארון אלהים

One day, Eli was asleep in his usual place ... the lamp of God had not yet gone out, and Samuel was sleeping in the temple of the Lord where the Ark of God was.

According to the consonantal Masoretic Text, Samuel slept that night in the sanctuary, בהיכל יהוה. The notion of someone (even a Levite or a priest[207]) sleeping in the sanctuary, perhaps even in the Holy of Holies, as the phrase "where the Ark of God was" may imply, was bound to be found disturbing, at least by some readers.[208] Indeed, ancient sources exhibit a variety of attempts to do away with this difficulty. Thus, considerations of space suggest that the scroll 4QSam[a] (III, 43) omitted the phrase יהוה אשר שם ארון אלהים.[209] The Aramaic

---

205 See the cautious remarks of A. D. Gross, "The Vision of Samuel," *Outside the Bible*, 2:1518.

206 Strugnell, "Notes en marge," 180, argues that 4Q160 follows an LXX type of text, but many of his suggestions are doubtful (see Comments to frg. 1).

207 While according to the scriptural record Samuel was a Levite (1 Chr 6:13; cf. *Ant.* 5.353), several ancient sources depict him as a priest (Sir 46:13 [Heb; "officiating as a priest," מכהן]; LAB 51:6; *Apos. Con.* 8.5.1–4 [D. A. Fiensy, D. R. Darnell, OTP 2:687–88]). In the scriptural account Samuel assists Eli at the Tent of Meeting and offers sacrifices (1 Sam 7:9–10, 9:12–13, 16:5). Cf. also Ps 99:6.

208 Compare the omission of Exod 33:11b, mentioning Joshua's constant presence in the Tent, from 4Q368 1 4, which may reflect similar concerns. See further A. Feldman, L. Goldman, *Scripture and Interpretation*, 166.

209 F. M. Cross, D. W. Parry, R. J. Saley, DJD 17:40, 46. See also A. Rofé, "Midrashic Traits," 83. LAB 53:2 seems to omit this part of the verse as well, reading: "Samuel was sleeping in the

Targum locates Samuel in the Court of the Levites: ושמואל שכיב בעזרת ליואי וקלא אשתמע מהיכלא דיי דתמן ארונא דיי ("and Samuel was sleeping in the court-yard of the Levites. And a voice was heard from the Temple of the Lord where the ark of the Lord was"). The Masoretic punctuation places an *athnaḥ* under ושְׁמוּאֵל שֹׁכֵב: שכב.[210]

It seems that 4Q160 1 reflects a similar concern with the location of Samuel's sleep. Borrowing the phrase [ו]שמואל שׁוֹכֵב from v. 3, it situates Samuel "before Eli," of whom the scriptural account says in v. 2 that he was lying down "in his place," במקמו, a far more neutral designation than that of Samuel's location in v. 3. Such an interpretation might have been suggested by the wording of v. 9, where Samuel, upon his third and last return from from Eli, is reported to lie down, במקומו, "in his place".[211]

Samuel's sleeping before Eli is mentioned once again in frg. 7, which reworks Samuel's farewell address (1 Sam 12). Elaborating on his time spent with Eli in his youth, Samuel states that he "chose to lie before [his] bed" (line 4). This choice seems to be contrasted with the opportunity to amass "property, wealth, and money," mentioned in the previous line. It appears that here the imagery of Samuel's sleeping by his master's (אֹדוני) bed is evoked as a quintessential expression of Samuel's service to Eli. While this particular imagery is absent from the scriptural account, it may echo the description of the young Samuel in 1 Sam 3:1: והנער שמואל משרת את יהוה לפני עלי ("the young Samuel was in the service of the Lord under [literally, "in front of"] Eli"). Another passage describing Samuel's service is 1 Sam 2:11, which states that once brought to Eli, the "boy entered the service of the Lord under the priest Eli" (והנער היה משרת את יהוה את פני עלי הכהן). For a reader familiar with the Pentateuchal regulations setting the minimal age for Levites entering the service at the sanctuary at 25 (Num 8:24),[212] the notion of a "boy" officiating in some capacity at the Tent of Meeting could be unsett-

---

temple of the Lord." On LAB's treatment of 1 Sam 3, see H. Jacobson, "Samuel's Vision in Pseudo-Philo's Liber Antiquitatum Biblicarum," *JBL* 112 (1993): 310–311; idem, *Commentary*, 1116–1130. Josephus's version of the story completely ignores Samuel's whereabouts (*Ant.* 5.348).

210 The late Midrash Shemuel 9:5 envisions Samuel sleeping outside the Sanctuary: נעל הכהן מבפנים ובן לוי ישן מבחוץ ("the priest locked [the door] from inside and the son of Levi slept out-side"). Cf. also Rashi and Kimḥi to 1 Sam 3:3. See further M. Z. Segal, *The Books of Samuel* (Jeru-salem: Kiryat Sepher, 1956), 33 (Hebrew).

211 As a result, the extant wording of the scroll may suggest that the revelation to Samuel oc-curred while he was lying down by Eli.

212 Num 4:3, 23, 30 specify the age of 30, while 1 Chr 23:24 and Ezra 3:8 refer to the age of 20.

ling.[213] At the same time, since both 1 Sam 2:11 and 3:1 mention Samuel's service in relation to Eli, it is not difficult to imagine how Samuel's service might have been interpreted as a service to *Eli himself*.[214] Perhaps, it is such a (nomistic?) reading of the scriptural story that underlies the scroll's description of Samuel's youth in frg. 7 2, 4.[215]

The other aspect of 4Q160's version of 1 Sam 3 worth looking into is its description of Samuel's night experience. The scriptural account uses several terms to describe the revelation to Samuel. The opening verse (v. 1) notes that the "word of the Lord" (דבר יהוה) and the "vision" (חזון) were rare in those days. As the story unfolds, God is said to "call" (ויקרא) Samuel (vv. 4, 6, 8, 10) and to "speak" (ויאמר) to him (v. 11). Eli speaks of "the word" (הדבר אשר דבר אליך) and Samuel reports to him "all the words" (כל הדברים; v. 17). While all these suggest an auditory experience, the biblical story also mentions God's "coming and standing there" (v. 10) and Samuel's "vision" (מראה, v. 15), indicating that the revelation might have also had a visual aspect.[216] Of the ancient sources dealing with 1 Sam 3, both LAB 53 and *Ant.* 5.348 present the revelation to Samuel as auditory.[217] LAB even introduces a divine soliloquy explaining why it would be advisable for the deity to avoid any visual manifestation.[218] However, 4Q160 allows for an experience that is both visual and auditory. When it refers to the divine message of doom pertaining to Eli's house, it fittingly uses the nouns דבר ("word"; line 2 [cf. also line 6]) and משא ("pronouncement"; line 4 [replacing the MT's מראה; see Comment ad loc.]),[219] yet as it paraphrases Eli's request to Samuel to disclose what happened

---

213 LAB states that Samuel was 8 years old at the time of the divine revelation, whereas Josephus says that he was 12 (*Ant.* 5.348).

214 Compare Elisha's ministering to Elijah (וישרתהו) in 1 Kgs 19:21 (cf. 4Q382 9 3 and Comment ad loc. in Chapter 3). See also Rashi to 1 Sam 2:11.

215 It is quite likely that the scroll's depiction of Samuel's sleep near his master's bed is influenced by the scriptural sources alone. Still, note the (limited) evidence regarding the Roman practice of having slaves sleep in their master's chamber: see M. George, "*Servus* and *Domus*: The Slave in the Roman House," in *Domestic Space in the Roman World: Pompeii and Beyond* (ed. R. Laurence, A. Wallace-Hadrill; Michigan: Portsmouth, RI, 1997), 22.

216 See discussion in R. Fidler, '*Dreams Speak Falsely*'? *Dream Theophanies in the Bible: Their Place in Ancient Israel Faith and Tradition* (Jerusalem: Magnes Press, 2005), 279–285 (Hebrew; and the pertinent bibliography cited there).

217 On Josephus see further R. K. Gnuse, *Dreams and Dream Reports in the Writings of Josephus: A Traditio-Historical Analysis* (AGJU 36; Leiden; Brill, 1996), 170.

218 Jacobson, *Commentary*, 179.

219 V. A. Hurowitz, "Eli's Adjuration of Samuel (1 Samuel III 17–18) in the Light of a 'Diviner's Protocol' from Mari (AEM I/1, 1)," *VT* 44 (1994): 488 note 20, suggests that the use of משא fits א[ ]ל[ו] הֿגיד better than מראה.

during the night, it describes it as מראה האלוהים ("the vision of God;" line 5), a phrase reminiscent of Ezekiel's visions, rather than the MT's הדבר אשר דבר אליך ("it that he told you").[220]

---

220 While the MT speaks of מַרְאָה, the scroll uses a masculine מַרְאֶה. In the MT both forms denote "sight, appearance, vision," yet the feminine מַרְאָה occurs more frequently, predominantly with reference to prophetic visions. See HALOT, 630; A. Brenner, "מַרְאֶה and מַרְאָה," *Beth-Mikra* 25 (1980): 374 (Hebrew). Fidler, *Dreams Speak Falsely*, 283, deducing from Num 12:6, 8 that the masculine מַרְאֶה denotes a higher level of divine communication, suggests that 4Q160 brings Samuel closer to the status granted to Moses in Num 12:8. Yet it is also possible that the scroll's wording reflects the synonymy of these two nouns (see Ezek 43:3; Dan 10:1, 7, 8). A similar interchange, this time מַרְאָה→מַרְאֶה, is attested in 1Q34[bis] 3 ii 6, rewriting ומראה כבוד (Exod 24:17) as במראת כב[ו]ד, and in 4Q422 III, 4, rephrasing הַמַּרְאֶה הגדול הזה (Exod 3:3a) as [במראת.

Chapter 3: 4Q382

The Manuscript

The scroll 4Q382 is a papyrus inscribed in a semiformal Hasmonean hand.[221] It survives in 152 fragments.[222] Three additional fragments, edited in the DJD edition as frgs. 93, 98, and 103, may belong to another manuscript (see Appendix).[223] The vast majority of the fragments are small. Some of them preserve upper (frgs. 14?, 25?, 27?, 38, 49?, 71?, 77?, 88?, 95?, 104, 107), bottom (frgs. 8, 16, 60, 61?, 91?, 98?), and intercolumnar margins (frgs. 15, 16?, 41, 56, 57, 93?, 95?, 104, 105, 137?). The shapes of the extant fragments, frequently broken along the fibers, offer little material evidence to help reconstruct their sequence in the original scroll. One possible exception is frg. 10, which contains the remains of two sheets of papyrus glued together. The remains of the right sheet reveal no traces of ink. This blank space is considerably wider than the intercolumnar margins preserved elsewhere in the scroll. Perhaps frg. 10 preserves remains of an uninscribed handling sheet, a *page de garde* (note also the two holes that might have been used to attach a string fastening the scroll), and the first column of the scroll.[224] Also, in the case of frgs. 1 and 3, their shape and contents suggest that they can be joined together. Finally, frgs. 9 and 11 rework the same scriptural pericope and must have appeared in close proximity to each other in the scroll.

Contents

Several fragments of 4Q382 deal with biblical episodes involving Elijah, Ahab, Jezebel, Obadiah, and Elisha (frgs. 1+3, 2, 4, 5, 6?, 9, 11, 30, 47). Yet the vast majority of its extant fragments feature speeches (frgs. 12, 13, 15 1–4, 23, 44, 131) and prayers (7, 16, 25, 37, 40, 47, 49, 50, 104 ii, 111, 114, 115, 127). The settings of these rhetorical and liturgical passages are mostly unclear. The two exceptions are frg. 15, containing a prayer with a superscription akin to those found in the book

---

221 S. Olyan, DJD 13:363, notes a similarity between the script of 4Q382 and that of 1QS, dated by F. M. Cross (*Scrolls from Qumrân Cave 1* [Jerusalem: The Albright Institute of Archaelogical Research and the Shrine of the Book, 1972], 4) to 100–75 BCE. Davis, "Elijah," 9, dates 4Q382 to the late Hasmonean or the early Herodian periods.
222 On the Qumran papyri see Tov, *Scribal Practices*, 44–55.
223 Davis, "Elijah," 83, observes that the preliminary edition of 4Q382 by Wacholder and Abegg (*Preliminary Edition*, 3:201) includes a fragment (#38) missing from its photographs and from the DJD edition. The fragment reads ‫כפר ל]עֹ‬[.
224 If correct, this would be the only extant specimen of the beginning of a literary papyrus from Qumran. On the absence of the beginnings and endings from Qumran literary papyri, see Tov, *Scribal Practices*, 44. For the use of a *page de garde* in the Qumran manuscripts, and on this method of fastening leather scrolls from Qumran, see Tov, ibid., 41, 114–115.

of Psalms (frg. 15 5–9), and frg. 46 4–5, preserving a prayer ascribed to King Hezekiah. One of the fragments seems to mention someone's fall "into the hands of Chaldeans," perhaps, a reference to the Babylonians' conquest of Judah (frg. 39 7). Finally, there is a fragment that appears to describe eschatological events (frg. 31).[225]

The Textual Overlap between 4Q160 and 4Q382

4Q382 104 ii and 4Q160 2+6+10 overlap. This may imply that the two scrolls are copies of the same literary work (see Chapter 6). Since some of the extant fragments of 4Q160 rework 1 Sam 3 and 12, this putative composition rewrote both Samuel and Kings.

Title

Initially entitled by Strugnell as "papTehilot Ha-'Avot," the scroll 4Q382 was finally edited by Olyan as "4Qpap para-Kings et. al."[226] The latter title reflects Olyan's conclusion that the remains of 4Q382 contain more than one composition (see Discussion). Others refer to this scroll as "An Apocryphon of Elijah" and "Paraphrase of Kings."[227] If 4Q382 and 4Q160 are indeed copies of the same composition, there is a need for a title that accounts for their treatment of both Samuel and Kings.

Previous Editions

The editorial work on 4Q382 was at first entrusted to Strugnell. His transcription of the scroll is embedded in the Preliminary Concordance. The readings recorded in this concordance were utilized by Wacholder and Abegg in their edition of 4Q382.[228] The final edition of the scroll for the DJD series was prepared by

---

225 Davis, "Elijah," 15, suggests a sectarian provenance for this scroll, adducing the terms יחד (frg. 20 2), פשרו (frg. 46 1), קץ (frgs. 31 2; 62), and המחקק (frg. 9 2, which he reads and understands in light of CD VI, 7–11, as "the Interpreter of the Law"). The former two examples are doubtful readings, while the latter two can be interpreted differently (see Comments ad loc.). All in all, the extant fragments of 4Q382 contain no vocabulary or worldview characteristic of Qumran sectarian literature. On the criteria for distinguishing between sectarian and non-sectarian texts from Qumran, see recently D. Dimant, "The Vocabulary of the Qumran Sectarian Texts," in idem, *History, Ideology and Bible Interpretation in the Dead Sea Scrolls* (FAT 90; Tübingen: Mohr Siebeck, 2014), 57–100.

226 On the initial title see E. Tov, S. Pfann, DJD 39:63.

227 Wise et al., *Dead Sea Scrolls*, p. 437; Vermes, *Complete Dead Sea Scrolls*, 589.

228 Wacholder, Abegg, *Preliminary Edition*, 3:190–220. Their edition excludes multiple small fragments of the scroll. With only limited access to the Preliminary Concordance, I was able to

Olyan.[229] It appears that he had no access to Strugnell's preliminary transcription.[230] Some corrections to Olyan's readings were offered by García Martínez and Tigchelaar in their selective edition of 4Q382 (six fragments only), and by Bernstein in his review of DJD 13.[231] An extensive revision of Olyan's text in light of Strugnell's readings and early photographs was undertaken by Davis.[232] A new edition of selected fragments of 4Q382 (seventeen in total) has been recently published by Qimron.[233]

Present Edition
This edition of 4Q382, while relying on the work of previous scholars, is based on a fresh examination of the fragments and their photographs, both old and new. As a result, it features numerous new readings and reconstructions. To facilitate its use, most of the minute fragments of 4Q382 are grouped together and presented last.

Text and Commentary

Frgs. 1+3

] ○○○ ○ ○○ ○ [	1
ויקח עבדיה מאה נביאי[ם̊ ויחביאים חמשים חמ̊[ש]י̊ם במ̊]ערה	2
ועבד[י̊ה̊ ירא מאיזבל ומאחאב מ̊ל̊ך ישׂ̊ר̊אל̊]	3
וילך ע[ב̊ד̊י̊ה̊ בא̊]רץ [ישׂ̊ר̊אל̊ ל̊]בדו	4

---

verify only some of Strugnell's preliminary readings. In most cases I had to rely on Wacholder and Abegg's reconstruction of the text based on the *Preliminary Concordance*.

229 Olyan, DJD 13:363–416.

230 Olyan's numbering of the fragments differs from that of Strugnell (and hence of Wacholder and Abegg). As Davis, "4Q382," 7, notes, Olyan numbered the fragments according to their placement on the most recent PAM images of the scroll (43.365, 43.366, 43.367). He goes on to observe that these images seem to be the primary source of the readings in the DJD edition of 4Q382, neglecting the important evidence available on earlier PAM photographs.

231 García Martínez, Tigchelaar, *Study Edition*, 763–765; M. Bernstein, "Review of Qumran Cave 4, VIII: Parabiblical Texts, Part 1, by H. Attridge, et al. Discoveries in the Judean Desert 13; Oxford: Clarendon Press, 1994," *DSD* 4 (1997): 102–112.

232 Davis, "Elijah." Dr. Davis graciously sent me a copy of his thesis, for which I am grateful.

233 Qimron, *Hebrew Writings*, 3:144–150. I am grateful to Prof. Qimron for sharing with me a draft of his new edition. His new readings and reconstructions are acknowledged below.

Notes on Readings

The DJD edition presents frgs. 1 and 3 separately. Frg. 3 reads:

1   [אֹים בֹמ]

2   מ[לֹךְ יִשְׂרָאֵל]

It seems highly plausible that lines 1 and 2 of frg. 3 are a continuation of lines 2 and 3 of frg. 1.

2   נביא[יֹם. While the editor offers no reading for the trace of a letter in the beginning of the line, on PAM 41.991 a right vertical stroke is visible. Although there is no trace of a base stroke (perhaps due to the damage to the surface), the shape of the letter seems to be consistent with a final *mem*.

     במ]ערה. The DJD edition reads ב[○. On PAM 43.464 the base and oblique strokes of a medial *mem* are clearly visible (Strugnell).[234]

3   ועבד[יֹה. The DJD edition has]○○. García Martínez and Tigchelaar and Davis correctly read correctly יה[. Qimron prefers כֹ[.

     מֹלֹךְ. The first letter is found on frg. 1. While Olyan had difficulty in identifying it, Davis reads it as a medial *mem* (cf. PAM 41.991; 43.288; 43.464). The traces of a second letter, *lamed*, unnoted in Olyan's transcription of frg. 3, are visible on PAM 43.464 (Davis).

Translation

2.   and Obadiah took a hundred prophet]s and hid them, fi[f]ty to a c[ave

3.   and Obad]iah feared Jezebel and Ahab the King of Israel[

4.   and O]badiah [went] through the l[and] of Israel a[lone

Comments

2   במ]ערה חמֹ[ש]יֹם חמשים ויחביאֹם מאה נביא[יֹם ויקח עבדיה. This line follows 1 Kgs 18:4. Unlike the MT's ויחביאם חמשים איש, the scroll reads, apparently with v. 13, ויחביאֹם חמשים חמֹ[ש]יֹם. This resolves the somewhat difficult wording of v. 4, reporting that Obadiah took a hundred prophets and hid (only?) fifty of them in a cave (cf. S: חמשין חמשין גברין; Tg: חמשין חמשין גברא; a similar understanding of v. 4 is reflected in LXX: κατὰ πεντήκοντα and V: et abscondit eos quinquagenos).[235] For the plene orthography נביא[יֹם (vs. נבאים, MT) see frg. 31 5.

---

234 *Preliminary Concordance*, 2:724.

235 Like our fragment, LXX and V lack an equivalent of איש. It remains unclear whether it is

ויחביאֹם. While the MT reads ויחביאם, the scroll introduces a *yod* as a *mater lectionis* for ṣere.[236] Qimron prefers ויחביאוֹם.

3 וֹעבד[יֹה ירא מאיזבל ומאחאב מֹלֹך יֹשׂראֹל]. It is unclear whether this line speaks of Elijah (cf. 1 Kgs 19:3: וַיַּרְא [according to MT and Tg; yet read as וַיִּרָא in LXX, V, and S]) or of Obadiah (1 Kgs 18:9, 14). Since the preceding and the following lines are concerned with the latter, perhaps one may restore here וֹעבד[יֹה. The scriptural account refers to Obadiah's fear of Ahab, yet the fragment also mentions Jezebel, introducing her name before that of the king (for the title מלך ישראל see 1 Kgs 20:2, 13). See Discussion.

4 וילך ע[בֹדֹיֹה בֹאֹ]רץ [יֹשׂרֹאֹל לֹ]בדו. The reconstructions follow 1 Kgs 18:6 (Qimron prefers לֹ]עבור בה). For the short form ע[בֹדֹיֹה (vs. עבדיהו), see Obad 1:1; Ezra 8:9. While the verse speaks of הארץ, the scroll prefers a more explicit בֹאֹ]רץ [יֹשׂרֹאֹל.

Frg. 2

```
]○  ○[        1
]אֹחאב הֹ[      2
]אֹ[ת אֹלֹיה    3
]לֹ[ ]○יֹה וֹלֹהֹ[  4
```

Notes on Readings

4]לֹ[ ]○יֹה. The DJD edition has עֹוֹב[דֹיה. A trace of a vertical stroke of a *lamed* is visible at the right edge of the fragment (PAM 43.288). The letter before *yod* is illegible.

וֹלֹהֹ[. Olyan reads ○לֹ○[. On PAM 43.464 the hook-shaped top of a vertical stroke is visible. This is most likely a *waw*. The last letter is a *he*. Its upper horizontal stroke appears on the fragment and its photographs.

——————

omitted as superfluous (as seems to be the case in this fragment) or because of the conventions of the target languages. Commenting on frgs. 1+3, 9, 11, Olyan, DJD 13:364, suggests that the scroll's *Vorlage* was close to that of the Septuagint. Yet given the paucity of the evidence, one can only observe the harmonistic tendency reflected in both frgs. 1+3 and 9.

236 Qimron, *Hebrew of the Dead Sea Scrolls*, 19–20.

Translation

2.]Ahab .[
3.]. Elijah[

Comments

2 הֹ אחאב[. Olyan restores ה]מלך הֹ[אחאב (cf. דויד המלך [1 Chr 26:26, 32]). However, in the Hebrew Bible Ahab is usually referred to as מלך ישראל (e.g., 1 Kgs 20:2, 13; see also frgs. 1+3 3) or מלך שמרון (1 Kgs 21:1).

3 ת[א. אלִ֯יה. For the short form אליה (vs. אליהו) see 2 Kgs 1:3, 4, 8, 12; Mal 3:23 (the photograph PAM 43.464 makes it clear that no *waw* followed). Perhaps this line depends on 1 Kgs 18:17: ויהי כראות אחאב את אליהו ("When Ahab caught sight of Elijah"). Qimron places frg. 2 beneath frgs. 1+3.

Frg. 3
See frgs. 1+3.

Frg. 4

[עֹבדיהֹ[ ]	1
ויח[דל אחֹאֹ[ב	2

Notes on Readings

1] עֹבֹדיֹה[. The DJD edition reads עו]בֹדִי[ה. On PAM 43.464 traces of an *ayin* are visible. The meager remains of the last letter suit well a *he*. Next to it a letter-size blank space is visible.

2 ויח[דל. Olyan reads ישר]אֹל. Davis suggests וי]חל. However, the photograph PAM 43.464 seems to favor a *dalet*.
אחֹאֹ[ב. The DJD edition has א[. Davis proposes אֹח]אב. There appear to be traces of two letters next to the *alef*, tentatively read here as a *ḥet* and an *alef*.

Translation
1.   ]Obadiah [
2.   and]Aha[b ce]ased[

Comments
The fragment apparently belongs to the recasting of 1 Kgs 18:1–16, where both Obadiah and Ahab are mentioned.

Frg. 5

ויאומר [אֹלֹיה אֹל אחאֹ]ב	1
] *vacat* [	2
[שריה בֹן מֹ]	3
]∘א בן לֹ∘∘[	4

Notes on Readings
1 אֹלֹיה[. This is Strugnell's reading (PAM 43.290).[237] The DJD edition has א]ליה.

3]מֹ. Olyan offers no reading. On PAM 43.290; 43.464 a short vertical stroke with an upper bar and a base stroke, as in a medial *mem*, are visible.

4 לֹ∘∘[. The DJD edition reads אֹל[. The first letter (or two letters) is illegible.]א∘. Olyan suggests that the vertical stroke at the end of the line is a *yod*.

Translation
1.   and]Elijah [said] to Aha[b
2.   ]   [
3.   ]Seraiah son of .[
4.   ].. son of ..[

237 *Preliminary Concordance*, 1:155.

Comments

1 ב[אחא אל אׄל[יה [**ויאמר**. The fragment seems to deal with an encounter between Elijah and Ahab (cf. 1 Kgs 17:1, 18:18–19, 41). Assuming that the space in line 2 indicates a change in the train of thought, perhaps it reworks the concluding exchange between the prophet and the king in 1 Kgs 18:41.

3 [מׄ בֿן שׂריה[. The name שְׂרָיָה is borne by several biblical figures (e.g., 2 Sam 8:17; 2 Kgs 25:18, 23; Jer 40:28, 51:59, 61). None of these has a patronymic beginning with a *mem*, or occurs in a context related to Elijah.

4 [לׄ∘ בן א∘[. This is, apparently, another name.

Frg. 6

[עׄינׄי בׄי לי [	1
[בׄי ישבח וׄ[	2
[רוחנֹוׄ ישׄ[י	3
ים[לׄשׄחקׄ לה[ע	4

Notes on Readings

2 [בׄי ישבח וׄ[. The DJD edition reads] ׄשׁ וׄמֹשׁׄבֹה [. The first letter, a *waw*(?), belongs to the preceding word. The *yod* and the *bet* of ישבח are visible on PAM 43.290. As to the last two letters, Davis correctly reads [כׄי.

3 [ישׁׄיׄ. The DJD edition has [יׄב. On PAM 43.290 the left stroke of a *shin* is visible. On the same photograph a tiny scrap of papyrus is placed to the right of line 3. It is unclear whether it belongs here.

Translation

1.   ] to me, because my eyes[
2.   ]. (he) will praise, for[
3.   (he) will]let (us) regain our strength[
4.   (he) we]nt up to the cloud[s

Comments

1 [עׄינׄי בׄי לי. This is a first person address. The identity of the speaker is unknown, but see Comment to line 4.

2]בֹ֗ל תשבח. The fragment appears to employ a *yiqtol* or a jussive of שבח, "to sing praises."[238]

3]שֹ֗יב רוחנו[י. Given the use of a 3rd masc. sg. *yiqtol*/jussive in the preceding line, the first word can be restored as שֹ֗יב[י (cf. מֹ֗שֹ֗יב רוחו in frg. 46 2). In Judg 15:19 and 1 Sam 30:12 the phrase שבה רוח stands for regaining one's strength or vigor.[239] Davis prefers "our spirit (he) will ret[urn."

4 עֹ[לה לשֹחקֹ]ים. Since several fragments of this scroll deal with Elijah, this line may refer to Elijah's ascent (2 Kgs 2:1, 11). If this is correct, the first person discourse found in this fragment ought to be compared to Elisha's lament following Elijah's disappearance in 4Q481a 3 3–5 (see Chapter 4).

Frg. 7

]אֹ֗ל֗ תֹ[	1
]קֹ לבדכה[	2
מ[וֹצא פיכהֹ]	3
[כֹּול חֹטאותֹ]	4

Notes on Readings

1]תֹ֗ אֹ֗ל֗[. This is Qimron's reading. Olyan reads]אֹ֗ל֗תֹ֗[.

2 קֹ[. The DJD edition has]ה. Davis reads a *qof* (cf. PAM 41.991; 43.290; 43.464).

3 מ[וֹצא. Olyan reads מ[וצא. On PAM 41.991 a vertical stroke of a *waw* is visible.

Translation

2.   ]. you alone[

3.   what c]omes forth from your mouth[

4.   ]all the sins of[

238 HALOT, 1387.
239 BDB, 925; HALOT, 1198, 1433.

Comments

1]תֹ לֹאֹ[. לֹאֹ can be read as the negative אַל or the preposition אֶל. Olyan prefers to take these letters as one word, i.e., a construct of אָלָה, "a curse."[240]

3]מ[וֹצֹא פיכהֹ. The wording of lines 2–4 indicates that this is a 2nd person address, perhaps a prayer. While in biblical Hebrew the constructions יצא מפה and מוצא שפתים are found, the Dead Sea Scrolls attest to what appears to be a combination of both, מוצא פה (4Q414 2 ii, 3, 4 7; 4Q416 2 iv 9).

Frg. 8

]אֹתֹ [ ]לֹ[	1
ה[קשיֹבֹוֹ]	2
]עֹל פֹֹ[ ]○[	3
Bot]tom marg[in?	

Notes on Readings

The uninscribed space below line 3 may be either a *vacat* in line 4 or a bottom margin.

1]לֹ[. According to PAM 41.991; 43.464, in the beginning of the line a vertical stroke, projecting below the imaginary bottom line, is visible. Perhaps this is a diagonal stroke of a *lamed*. The last letter seems to be a *taw* (PAM 43.464), rather than a *ḥet* (DJD).

3 עֹל[ ]○[. Olyan reads עֹל[. Davis notes a trace of ink before the *ayin*.

]פֹֹ. The DJD edition has]○°. According to PAM 41.991, the first letter is consistent with a medial *pe*. The second letter is represented by a vertical stroke, perhaps a *yod*.

Translation

2.   li]sten [
3.   ].[ ]according to[

---

240 HALOT, 51.

Comments

2]הֹקשׁיֹבֹו[. This is either a 2nd masc. pl. imperative or a 3rd pl. *qatal* Hifil of קשב, "to listen."

Frg. 9

[	הֹקֹ oֹהֹ[]o[	] 1
[	עֹתֹה וֹמֹיֹמֹן הֹמֹחֹקֹק לֹ[]	] 2
[	וֹחֹבֹב וֹמתניֹה המשֹרֹתיֹם]	] 3
[	משתחוֹ[ים ועובדים לצֹבֹא השמיֹם]	] 4
[ויאומרו אליו היד[עֹתה בֹי היום //// לוקח אֹ]ת אדניכה מעל ראושכה ויאומר גם אני ידעתי[		] 5
[החשו ויאומר אלי]הֹ אֹל אלישע שיבנה בנֹ]י פה כי //// שלחני יריחו ויאומר אלישע[		] 6
[חי ////] וֹחי נפש]כה אמ אעזֹוֹבֹכֹה]		] 7	ויבאו יריחו ויגשו[
[בני הנביאים אֹ]שֹׁרֹ בירֹיֹחו] oo		] 8
[	ק לשוֹנֹבֹם וֹאֹ oֹלֹ[]o	] 9
[	הֹ כול הירֹדֹ דוֹ]מֹה	] 10
[	]o[	] 11

Notes on Readings

1]o[הֹ oֹהֹקֹ. DJD has]הֹ רֹ[א. According to the photographs (esp. 42.500), the first letter is represented by a vertical stroke and an upper bar curving downwards at its left extremity as in *he* (cf. *he* in עֹתֹה[[line 2]). The second letter is clearly a *qof*. It is followed by a vertical stroke. Next to it, at some distance (perhaps an interval between two words) two vertical strokes, probably a *he* or a *ḥet*, are visible. After a letter-size lacuna, traces of both vertical and base strokes, as in a medial *kaf*, *mem* or *nun*, appear.

2 עֹתֹה[. Olyan reads]תֹהֹo[. On PAM 42.500 both left and right strokes of an *ayin* are visible in the beginning of the line (cf. *ayin* in היד[עֹתה [line 5]). As to the last letter, the editor mistakenly joined here the traces belonging to the folowing word, reading them as a final *mem*. However, there is letter-size blank space after the *he* of עֹתֹה[.

וֹמֹיֹמֹן. The DJD edition has ץoo. According to PAM 42.500, the first letter is a *waw*. It is followed by a medial *mem* and a *yod*, shaped like an inverted "v." A medial *mem* and a final *nun* follow.

3 וֹחֹבֹ[. Olyan reads ○בֹ○[. The first letter appears to be a *waw* or a *yod*. The second letter is either a *he* or a *ḥet* (cf. *ḥet* in בִּירִיחוֹ [line 8]). The fourth letter is most likely a *bet* (Wacholder and Abegg). A faint trace of its base stroke is visible on PAM 42.500.

המשֹׁרתיֹם. The DJD edition has המש[ר]תים. The *resh* is visible on PAM 42.500 (Davis).

6 אלֹ[יֹהֹ. This is Strugnell's reading (cf. PAM 42.500).[241] Olyan reads אלֹ[.

שיבנה. Wacholder and Abegg read שובנֹה. Qimron notes that שובנה suits better the Qumran Hebrew (see Comment ad loc.).

בֹנֹ[י. This is Wacholder and Abegg's reading. The DJD edition has פֹהֹ[.

7 אמ. Olyan reads אם. The last letter is clearly a medial *mem*.

9 קֹ○[. The DJD edition has קֹחֹ[. The penultimate letter is difficult to read. On some of the photographs (PAM 41.991; 42.500) traces of an upper bar, a vertical stroke, and a base as in *bet* seem to be visible. Hence, one possible reading would be תד[בֹק.

ואֹ○לֹ○[. Olyan reads ואלֹ[, yet there appear to be traces of two illegible letters, one before and one after the *lamed*.

10 דֹז[מה. The DJD edition has חֹ[י. The traces of the first letter are consistent with a *dalet*, while the second letter may be either a *yod* or a *waw*.

Translation

2. [   ]now and trustworthy is what has been decreed for/by[ ]
3. [   ]and Hobab and Mattaniah serving[   ]
4. [prostrat]ing and worshiping the host of heaven[   ]
5. [and said to him, "Do you k]now that //// will take [your master from your head today?" He replied, "I know it too;]
6. [be silent." And Eli]jah[said] to Elisha, "Stay [here], my son,[for //// has sent me on to Jericho." And Elisha said,]
7. ["As //// lives and as]you[live,] I will not leave you."[And they went on to Jericho. And came to him]

---

8. [the sons of the prophets w]ho were at Jericho ..[   ]
9. [   ].. your tongue and ....[   ]
10. [   ]. anyone who goes down into sil[ence   ]

Comments

2]לֹ הַמֹחֹקק וֹמֹ֫מֹן וֹעֹתה[. The first word may be vocalized as an adverb עֹתה, "now," or restored as a 2nd masc. sg. *qatal* verb, e.g., ד[עֹתה יד (אשר) or שמ[עֹתה (אשר). In the latter case, this line contains direct speech.

וֹמֹ֫מן. This appears to be a phonetic spelling of the Aramaic passive Afel participle of אמן, מהימן (cf. 1Q20 V, 8), "trustworthy," akin to the Hebrew נֶאֱמן (for other instances of phonetic spellings in this scroll see line 6 and frgs. 1+3 2).

]לֹ הַמֹחֹקק. This is a masc. sg. Pual participle of חקק, הַמְחֻקָק, "what is decreed" (Pr 31:5; 4Q417 1 i 15).[242] An alternative reading would be a Piel participle of the same root, הַמְחֹקֵק, denoting either a "commander" or a "ruler's staff," yet it does not seem to fit the context. In the Dead Sea Scrolls forms of חקק, including the construction ל- חקק, are used to denote a deterministic view of history, as in 4Q417 1 i 15: כי חרות מחקק לאל ("For engraved is that which is ordained by God").[243] In light of the following quotation from 2 Kgs 2:3–5, this line may present the events related to Elijah's ascent as a part of the divine plan.

3] הַמְשֹׁרתים וֹמתניה וֹחֹבב[. Though borne by several individuals mentioned in the Hebrew Bible,[244] the names חֹבב and מתניה are absent from the Elijah-Elisha cycle.[245] The *waw* in וחבב indicates that another name(s) might have preceded it. Of both Hobab and Mattaniah the scroll says that they are הַמֹשֹׁרתים, a masc. pl. Piel participle of שרת, "to serve." In the Hebrew Bible שרת frequently occurs with reference to the duties of priests and Levites (1 Sam 2:11, 3:1; Jer 33:21, 22; Ezek 44:11). What remains unclear is whether חֹבב and מתניה are the names of the sons of the prophets at Bethel, whose question to Elisha is cited in line 5 (cf. 1 Kgs 19:21 describing Elisha as serving Elijah, וישרתהו), or whether they are the ones to whom the wording of the next line, "prostrat]ing and worshipping the host of heaven," applies.

---

242 HALOT, 347.
243 Clines, *The Concise Dictionary of Classical Hebrew*, 130.
244 E.g., Hobab, Moses' father-in-law (Num 10:29), and several Levites named מתניה/ו (1Chr 25:4, 16; 2 Chr 29:13).
245 While Olyan renders ומתניה as "and the loins of," Bernstein, "Review," 110, correctly points out that this is a proper noun, Mattaniah.

4 [מ‏שתחו]ים ועובדים לצבא השמ‏ים. While the phrase מ‏שתחו]ים ועובדים may refer to the men whose names are listed in the preceding line, it is also possible that it describes the inhabitants of Bethel in general (on Bethel as a center of the idolatrous worship, see 1 Kgs 12:29–33; Hos 10:15). The reconstruction follows Deut 4:19 and 2 Kgs 21:3. While biblical Hebrew prefers the construction עבד את, the fragment employs the preposition ל- as a marker of the direct object. On the worship of "the host of heaven" in the Northern Kingdom, see 2 Kgs 17:16. The notion that in Elijah's time people worshiped the host of heaven (not made explicit in the biblical account) could have been derived from the wording of 2 Kgs 21:3–4, comparing the days of Manasseh to those of Ahab.

5–6 החשו ... את אדניכה / לוקח א]ת //// עתה כי היום / היד]. The scroll quotes 2 Kgs 2:3. The scribe represented the Tetragrammaton with four diagonal vertical strokes, a scribal technique attested in 4Q306 3 5; XHev/Se 6 2 7; 4Q248 5.[246] Cf. also frg. 78 where a similar technique seems to be used.

6 יריחו ... פה י]בנה בו]ל אלישע שובה אל ה[אלי אליו ויאומר. This line depends on 2 Kgs 2:4. Unlike the MT's אליהו אל לו ויאמר, the fragment reads אלישע אל ה[אלי ויאומר, assimilating the wording of v. 4 with v. 2, as, apparently, in LXX (καὶ εἶπεν Ηλιου πρὸς Ελισαιε), S (לאלישע אליא ואמר), and V ("dixit autem Helias ad Heliseum").

פה י]בנה שיבנה. The reading שיבנה assumes the use of a *yod* as a *mater lectionis* for *ṣere*. Qimron prefers שובנה, suggesting that שוב is either a phonetic alternative of שֵב or an imperative of שוב. The *alef* in נא has been replaced by a *he*. For the writing of נה/נא without an interval, cf. אמנא in 4Q364 4b-e ii 4. Elijah's addressing Elisha as בו]י should be viewed in light of the biblical passages describing the relationship between a prophet and his apprentice with father/son language (see 1 Sam 3:6 and, particularly, 2 Kgs 2:12, where Elisha addresses Elijah as אבי אבי; cf. also 4Q481a 3 4).

6–7 יריחו ויבאו אם אעזובכ]ה נפש]כה וחי / חי //// / אלישע ויאומר. The scroll quotes 2 Kgs 2:4b. While the MT reads אֶעֶזְבֶךָ, the scroll employs a non-pausal form, אעזובכה.[247] The reconstruction אלישע ויאומר, instead of the MT ויאמר, follows v. 2, as the available space allows for a longer wording.

---

246 On this scribal technique, along with the so-called *Tetrapuncta*, see Tov, *Scribal Practices*, 218–221.
247 Qimron, *Hebrew of the Dead Sea Scrolls*, 50–52.

7–8 בֿיריחו א[שֿׁר הנביאים] / [ויגשו. The fragment follows here 2 Kgs 2:5, but, apparently, expands it, given the available space.

9 ק[לשׁוֹנֿכֿם ואֿ̊ס̊ל̊̊ס[. Possibly, this line paraphrases Elisha's plea to the sons of the prophets in Jericho, החשו. One is tempted to read and restore here תד[בֿק לשׁוֹנֿכֿם (cf. תדבק לשוני לחכי [Ps 137:6]).

10]ה כל הירד̇ דו]מה. The scroll seems to borrow here from Ps 115:17: לא המתים יהללו יה ולא כל ירדי דומה ("The dead cannot praise the Lord, nor any who go down into silence"). See Discussion.

Frg. 10

]ooo[ ]	1
]o וֿברֿצ̊ו̊ן	2
]oo בֿו̇	3
]oבֿ̇	4
לֿהֿ̊יוֿ]ת	5
]	6
]	7
]ooo	8
]oֿהֿ̊לֿ	9
לֿשׁ̇ו̊]	10

Notes on Readings

This fragment preserves the remains of two sheets of papyrus glued together. The remaining part of the right sheet is blank. Since this blank space is wider than the intercolumnar margins in this scroll, the right sheet could have served as a *page de garde*. The two circular holes visible in what remains of the right sheet might have been used to insert a string used to fasten the scroll (see Manuscript).

2]o וֿברֿצ̊ו̊ן. This is Strugnell's reading (cf. PAM 42.500).[248] The DJD edition reads]oo בֿ̇ר̇o.

3]ooבֿ̇. Olyan suggests]oלo. According to the photographs (PAM 42.500; 43.290; 43.464), there are no traces of a *lamed* in this line. There are remnants of three or

248 *Preliminary Concordance*, 4:1780.

four letters. The first one is represented by an upper vertical stroke with a short serif at its left extremity and a base as in a *bet*. The second letter is a vertical stroke, perhaps a *waw* or a *yod*.

4 רבֿ]◦. This is Davis's reading. The editor offers no reading here.

5 לֹהֹוֹ[ת. This is a reading by Davis. The DJD edition has ל̊ל̊א ◦].

9 לֹהֹ◦]. The editor suggests no reading. The traces of the first letter (PAM 42.500) are consistent with a *lamed*, while the second is a *he*.

10 לֹשֹ[. Olyan reads ל̊ל̊א̊[ש. According to the photographs, the second letter is a *shin*; all of its three strokes are visible.

Translation
2. in the will of .[
5. to b[e

Frg. 11

כי א[לֹוֹהיﬦ שלחני עד] בית אל

Notes on Readings
אֿ]לֹוֹהיﬦ. This is Strugnell's reading corroborated by the photographs (PAM 41.988; 43.289; 43.464).[249] The DJD edition has יֹהוֹה [.

Translation
for G]od has sent me on to[Bethel

Comments
This seems to be a quotation from 2 Kgs 2:2: כי יהוה שלחני עד בית אל ("for the Lord has sent me on to Bethel"). If the scroll follows the scriptural order of events, it should be placed above frg. 9 1. Olyan suggests that this fragment cites 2 Kgs 2:4:

---

249 *Preliminary Concordance*, 4:1856.

כי יהוה שלחני יריחו. He assumes that the scroll's *Vorlage* diverges from the MT and is similar to that of the LXX, reading εἰς Ιεριχω (cf. εἰς Βαιθηλ in v. 2). If correct, the fragment belongs with frg. 9, line 6 (thus also Qimron). Unlike the MT, which employs the Tetragrammaton in both verses, the scroll reads א[לוהים.

Frg. 12

] ○ [	1
אר[צֹות רבות וגדֹולֹות פֿ○ן]	2
החר[שֹתי בלבבֿי פֿ○ן אֿ]	3
להשי[בֿ לאיש כֿפֿ]עֿלו	4
○[ ]○[עֿ[שֹו ואין לאמֿ]ץ כוח	5
○[נֿאצו והגדו לי אֿלֿ]	6

Notes on Readings

2 אר[צֹות. Olyan reads אֿת[. According to the photographs (PAM 41.991; 42.500; 43.289; 43.464), there are traces of two letters before the *taw*, probably a medial *ṣade* and a *waw*.

פֿ○]. In the DJD edition וגדֹולֹות is the last word surviving in this line. Traces of three additional letters, פֿ○], are visible on PAM 41.991 (on other photographs this part of the fragment is lost). Davis reads ○ן○[.

3 החר[שֹתי. Olyan suggests חֹי[. The second letter is a *taw* (Strugnell).[250] As to the first letter, a vertical stroke resembling that of a *shin* is visible on PAM 41.991.

אֿ] פֿ. This is Strugnell's reading.[251] The DJD edition offers no reading here.

4 להשי[בֿ. While the editor reads ○[, the photographs suggest that this is a *bet*.
כֿפֿ]עֿלו. This is Qimron's reading. The DJD edition has כֿי].

5 There is an illegible trace of a letter in the beginning of the line (see PAM 42.500).
לאמֿ]ץ. This is Qimron's reading. The editor reads לאבֿ].

---

250 *Preliminary Concordance*, 3:1194.
251 Ibid.

Translation

2.   lan]ds many and great so that .[
3.   ]I[kept sil]ent in my heart so that I may[
4.   to repa]y everyone according to[his]d[eed
5.   ].[(they) d]id and there is no exer[ting strength
6.   ]. they despised. And they told me, "Do not[

Comments

2 אר[צׄוׄת רבות וגדׄוׄלׄוׄת פׄן. For the language cf. Jer 28:8.

3 החר[שׁתי בלבבי. The extant wording indicates that this is a 1st person speech, perhaps a prayer. The reconstruction is tentative, as the expression is not attested in the Hebrew Bible or the Dead Sea Scrolls.

4 להשי[בׄ לאיש כפ]ועלו. The reconstruction is that of Qimron (cf. Pr 24:12, 29).

5 ואין לאמׄ]ץ כוח. This is Qimron's restoration. For the phrase אמץ כח see Amos 2:14; Nah 2:2.[252]

6]ׄ○[. Perhaps read and restore את שמכ[ׄה נאצו וׄ]נאצו והגדו לי אׄלׄ[(with Ps 74:10, 18). For other instances of the use of נאץ in this scroll, see frgs. 47 4 and 122 2. For a possible context compare frg. 30 reworking 1 Kgs 19. Qimron suggests that the blank space between והגדו and לי is a scribal oversight and reads והגדילו (cf. Zeph 2:8, 10). However, such an emendation appears to be unnecessary.

Frg. 13

רעׄ[תנו וׄחטאׄ]תנו   1

]ׄהׄ הׄבׄׄׄרׄנו[○○ׄהׄ   2

Notes on Readings

2]ׄהׄ הׄבׄׄׄרׄנו[○○ׄהׄ. The DJD edition reads]נו ○ כ ○○[. On PAM 43.464 traces of a *he*, concluding the first extant word, as well as the traces of a *he* and a *resh* of the second word, are visible.

---

252 HALOT, 65.

Translation

1.]our[wicked]ness and [our] si[n
2.　　　　]... we acknowledged[

Comments

2 רע[תנו וחטא]תנו. This fragment contains a first person address, apparently a confession of sins. The reconstruction follows 1 Sam 2:19.

2]הٔכֲּרֲנו. This Hifil form of נכר, "to recognize, acknowledge," may also be rendered as "(he) recognized us."[253]

Frg. 14

Top margin?

לה[שֵׁכיל למת]　　　1

[מד בֹּאָ]　　　2

Translation

1. to in]struct ...[

Comments

1]לה[שׂכיל למת. For a Hifil of שכל in the sense of instructing see Neh 9:20.[254] It is tempting to restore the line with the term מתנדבים, "volunteers," frequently used in the Qumran sectarian texts.[255]

---

253 HALOT, 699–700.
254 Ibid., 1328–1329.
255 On this term see D. Dimant, "The Volunteers in the Rule of the Community: A Biblical Notion in Sectarian Garb," *RevQ* 23 (2007): 233–245.

Frg. 15

This fragment preserves the right intercolumnar margin.

למען]	שמו] אֹו[הֹ֗בֹ֗וֹ חושבי	1
[	תֹבינו בכול נפֹ֗]לאות	2
[	[ ]∘∘ וֹהֹנה מ[ ]	3
[	[ ]∘ה למעולמֹ֗י֗ן] עולמים	4
[	*vacat* למנצח בֹ֗]	5
[	אלוהים בשנתֹ]	6
[	תורת אלוהים ∘∘[ ]	7
[	קֹדֹוש ישראל וֹאֹל֗]	8
[	[ ] ∘∘∘[ ]	9

Notes on Readings

1 אֹו[הֹ֗בֹ֗וֹ]. This is Qimron's reading. The editor suggests ∘ב[.

חושבי. The DJD edition has והשמן. Qimron reads correctly חושבי.

2 נפֹ֗]לאות. Olyan reads נו[. Strugnell suggests that the second letter is a medial *pe* (cf. PAM 40.600; 43.288).[256]

3 וֹהֹנה. The editor suggests ∘∘נה[. According to PAM 43.288, the first two letters are a *waw* and a *he*. There are traces of two more letters in the beginning of the line. The second one has a hook-shaped top, characteristic of a *waw* or a *yod* (see esp. PAM 43.288).

4 למעולמֹ֗י֗ה∘[. The DJD edition reads כֹול מעולם[. According to the photographs (esp. PAM 43.288), the trace of the first illegible letter is followed by two vertical strokes consistent with a *he*. The *lamed* belongs with the second word.

בֹ֗]. Olyan reads י[. On PAM 40.600 traces of a *bet* are visible (Qimron).

8 וֹאֹל֗]. The DJD edition offers no reading for the last two letters in this line. Davis reads correctly וֹאֹל֗] (cf. PAM 43.288).

Translation

1. [those lov]ing him and thinking [of his name   so that]
2. you may understand all the won[ders
3. [ ].. and behold ..[
4. [ ].. forever[and ever
5.   To the director on[
6. God in the year of[
7. God's law ..[
8. the Holy One of Israel and ..[

Comments

1 שמו [וֹאֻ]הֻבֻו חושבי]. In light of the plural חושבי, [וֹאֻ]הֻבֻו ought also to be read as a plural, אוהבי(ו).[257] The reconstruction (Qimron) follows Mal 3:16: ויכתב ספר זכרון לפניו ליראי יהוה ולחשבי שמו ("and a scroll of remembrance has been written at his behest concerning those who revere the Lord and esteem his name"). If this is correct, the fragment replaces יראי יהוה, "(those) fearing YHWH," with [וֹאֻ]הֻבֻו, "those who love him, his friends."

2 תביגו בכול נפֻ]לאות / [למען. The wording of this line suggests that lines 1–4 contain a 2nd person address. For the language compare Job 37:14; 1QS XI, 19.

4 עולמים [למעולמֻי. While the expression עולמי עולמים occurs in several texts from Qumran (4Q405 6 4; 4Q491 26 1), this is its only occurrence with the prepositions ל- and מ-. Compare למן עולם ועד עולם (Jer 7:7, 25:5; note also [ל{מ}עולם [4Q377 2 ii 12]).

5 ל]מנצח בֻ. This is a superscription preceding what appears to be a non-Masoretic psalm. Perhaps restore למנצח ב]נגינות (e.g., Ps 4:1). Among the many non-Masoretic psalms found among the Dead Sea Scrolls, this seems to be the only instance of a superscription employing this term.

6 אלוהים בשנת]. The construct noun בשנת] may clarify the occasion at which the ensuing psalm was composed, or that which it commemorates.

7 תורת אלוהים. The phrase תורת יהוה frequently occurs in the Hebrew Bible (e.g., Exod 13:19). As in frg. 11, the scroll seems to prefer here אלוהים for the Tetragrammaton.

---

257 See Qimron, *Hebrew of the Dead Sea Scrolls*, 33–34.

8 ‫קְדוֹשׁ יִשְׂרָאֵל וֹאֵל[‬. For the appellation ‫קדוש ישראל‬ see, e.g., 2 Kgs 19:22; Isa 1:4. The letters ‫וֹאֵל[‬ may also belong to a divine title (cf. the use of ‫אל‬ in frg. 38 6). The preposition ‫אֶל‬ (Qimron: ‫וֹאֵל] תורתו‬) or the negation ‫אַל‬ are equally possible.

Frg. 16

In addition to the bottom margin, this fragment may also preserve the right inter-columnar margin.

1	‫[∘קֹֿבֿ∘ רְצֹוֹנכה תֿ∘]‬
2	‫[∘כֿ∘בֿ∘ה הֿיֿוֿתֿ]לֿ[‬
3	‫[עֲמֿכה ותֿ∘∘ ∘∘]‬
4	‫[בֿרֿיתכה יֿ∘∘ לֿהֿ]‬
	Bottom margin

Notes on Readings

1 ‫∘קֹֿבֿ∘[‬. According to the photographs (esp. PAM 43.289; 43.464), the second and the third letters seem to be a *qof* and a *bet*.

‫רְצֹוֹנכה‬. Olyan reads ‫∘∘∘כֿתֿ‬. Wacholder and Abegg suggest ‫רנינכה‬. According to PAM 42.500, the second letter is a medial *ṣade*. The third letter may be read either as a *waw* or as a *yod*.

2 ‫לֿ[הֿיֿוֿתֿ]ה∘בֿ∘‬. The DJD edition has ‫מ[∘שׁׄיֿחֿ יֿשֿׂרֿ[א]לֿ∘∘]‬. Next to an illegible letter in the beginning of the line there are a medial *kaf*, another illegible letter, and a *he* (not a *ḥet*; see PAM 43.289). After an interval, traces of a *he*, a *waw*, a *yod*, and a *taw* are visible. Next to a hole in the leather, a vertical stroke of a *lamed* appears. There are no traces of ink after the *lamed*.

3 ‫עֲמֿכה ותֿ∘∘ ∘∘]‬. This is a reading by Wacholder and Abegg. Olyan reads ‫[∘ כֹחֿוֹ ∘∘∘ ∘]‬.

4 ‫בֿרֿיתכה‬. This reading follows that of Wacholder and Abegg (cf. PAM 43.289). The DJD edition has ‫[∘בֿנֿהֿ‬.

‫יֿ∘∘∘לֿהֿ]‬. Olyan suggests ‫הֿ[∘∘∘∘]‬. The first letter is consistent with a *waw/yod*. Traces of a *lamed* and a *he* in the end of the line are visible on PAM 43.464.

Translation
1.].... your will ..[
2.].... to be[ ].[
3.] your people and .. ..[
4.] your covenant .....[

Comments
The phrases רצוֹנכה, עֻמֹכה, and בְּרִיֹתכה indicate that this is a prayer.

Frg. 17

אמ[תֹ וצדק]	1
]∘בֹ נֻוֹ∘[	2
]∘זֹ הֹזֹ∘[	3
]∘∘[	4

Notes on Readings
1 תֹ[אמ. The editor sees no traces of ink here. Davis reads a *taw* (cf. PAM 43.289; 43.464).

וצדק. The DJD edition reads the first letter as a *yod*.

2]∘בֹ נֻוֹ∘[. Olyan suggests]∘ עֻזוֹ[. The trace of the first letter is illegible. Next to it a medial *nun* and a *waw/yod* are visible. After an interval, a *bet* appears (PAM 43.289).

Translation
1. tru]th and righteousness [

Comments
1 תֹ[אמ וצדק. Perhaps, restore תֹ[אמ וצדק, a collocation frequently found in the Dead Sea Scrolls (1QS IV, 2; 1Q36 15 2; 4Q404 5 6; 4Q444 1–4 i+5 3). It occurs also in frg. 34 2.

Frgs. 18–20: See Minute Fragments

Frg. 21

] ∘∘∘ ∘∘ ∘∘∘[ ]∘∘[	1
]∘ [פז ו]תועב[ת̇ נדה	2
]א̇ו̇ בתיהם̇[ ]א∘[	3
]י[שיב דבר כי אשר ל̇	4
]ות לו[	5

Notes on Readings

1 The DJD edition reads a *dalet* at the end of the line. The shape of the letter lends itself to different interpretations.

2 פז∘[. The editor suggests ם∘[. The first letter is illegible, but the second and the third ones are clearly a medial *pe* and a *zayin* (cf. PAM 43.464).

תועב]ת̇ו. Qimron correctly reads a *taw*, whereas Olyan suggests a *bet*.

נדה. This is Wacholder and Abegg's reading. The DJD edition has נדה.

3]בתיהם̇. This is Strugnell's reading.[258] Olyan reads בתיה]ם.

4 שיב[י. The editor sees a trace of another letter next to the *bet*, but it is absent from the photographs.

ל̇. As Davis notes, there is a trace of a vertical stroke at the end of the line, slightly above it (PAM 43.289; 43.464). This is undoubtedly a *lamed* (missing from DJD's transcription).

5]לו. Olyan offers no reading for the second letter, yet according to PAM 43.289 it is either a *waw* or a *yod*.

Translation

2.	]... and[an abomination of] defilement.[
3.	]..[ ].. their houses[
4.	he will]answer; for that .[
5.	].. to him[

---

258 *Preliminary Concordance*, 1:487.

Comments

2 תועב]ת נדה[ו. This is Qimron's reconstruction (with 1QHª XIX, 14).

4 שיב דבר כי אשר[י. Davis and Qimron restore ואין מ[שיב דבר.

Frg. 22: See Minute Fragments

Frg. 23

אחזׄיׄקׄה ואתׄועׄדדה [ ]∘[	1
ואעשה צ[ד]קׄה ומׄשׁפׄט כי]א[ ]חׄמׄלתׄהׄ[עלי	2
נׄשׄא מׄ ∘∘[	3

Notes on Readings

1 אׄחׄזׄיׄקׄה[. The DJD edition has]∘[ ]אׄהׄ[ ]ה[. The reading proposed here is that of Qimron.

2 צׄ[דׄקׄה. This is the reading by Wacholder and Abegg. The editor reads]נׄדׄׄתׄ.

[א]כׄיׄ[. The DJD edition has כׄוׄל. Qimron suggests a more cautious כ[. A trace of a *yod* is visible on PAM 43.290 (Davis).

חׄמׄלתׄהׄ[. Olyan reads]לת∘∘. Wacholder and Abegg suggest המלוׄנׄ ∘[. The traces of the first letter may be read either as a *he* or a *ḥet*. The letter next to the *lamed* is a *taw* (Davis). A vertical stroke, perhaps a *he* (Qimron), seems to follow.

3 נׄשׄא[. This is Wacholder and Abegg's reading. Olyan reads בא[.

Translation

1.   ].[ ]I shall stand firm and I shall rejoice [
2.   and I will do rig]hteousness and justice fo[r] you showed compassion[to me
3.   ](he/it was?) carried ....[

Comments

1 אׄחׄזׄיׄקׄה ואתׄועׄדדה[. Line 2 suggests that this 1st person discourse is a prayer. It is unclear whether the verb אׄחׄזׄיׄקׄה was preceded by an indirect object (compare בצדקתי החזקתי [Job 27:6] and ועם ידעי אלהיו יחזקו ועשו [Dan 11:32]). Compare the first person speech in frg. 41. Qimron notes that the two verbs found here occur together in 1QHª XII, 37.

ואתׄועׄדדה. The orthography ואתׄועׄדדה reflects a weakening of the gutturals.

2 ‏וֹאעשה צְ[דְקָה וֹמֹשֹפֹטֹ‎. The reconstruction is that of Qimron. For the word pair ‏צדקה ומשפט‎ see, e.g., Gen 18:19; 2 Sam 8:15.

‏כֹ[א]יֹ הֹמֹלֹתֹהֹ] עֹלֹי‎. Qimron suggests that this is a prayer by Hezekiah after he recovered from his sickness (cf. Isa 38). If this is correct, this fragment may belong with frg. 46.

3 ‏נֹשֹׁא[‎. A Qal or Nifal form of ‏נשא‎, "to carry, lift up."[259]

Frg. 24

1	‏לֹה[רים]‎
2	‏] לֹ [‎

Translation

1   to r]aise up[

Comment

Cf. frg. 37.

Frg. 25

Top margin?

1	‏[עֹנֹו מֹלֹב גוֹי]ם‎
2	‏[ים ולֹבֹי הֹנֹדֹ]כה‎
3	‏[הֹ ידֹיֹכֹהֹ]‎
4	‏[בֹחרט זהב מנובבֹ]‎
5	‏[וֹיֹשוֹבֹוֹ כדי לֹ]‎
6	‏[מֹוֹאֹדה פ‎ooooo]‎
7	‏[ooo]‎

Notes on Readings

1 ‏עֹנֹו[‎. The DJD edition has ‏]הֹשֹׁאֹ[‎. Qimron reads ‏]oעֹנֹו‎. His reading is followed here with one exception: it is unclear whether there is a trace of ink before the *ayin*.

‏מֹלֹב‎. Wacholder and Abegg read ‏מֹלֹב‎. Olyan suggests ‏[לֹב]‎.

---

259 HALOT, 724.

גוי[ם. The editor reads]גי, yet there is another *waw/yod* at the end of the line (Davis).

2 ולבי. The DJD edition has א[ה]וֹ[י. On PAM 41.988 traces of a *waw* (not *alef*) and a *bet* (mistaken for a *waw*) are visible.

הנד]כה. The editor reads חנו[ת. The first letter is clearly a *he*. As to the third letter, a vertical stroke, which may well belong to a *dalet*, is visible on the photographs.

3 ידיכֹהֹ[הֹ. The DJD has]ירי *vacat* [. The proposed reading is supported by PAM 41.988; 43.290.

5 וֹיֹשֹובֹוֹ[. Olyan reads וֹיֹשֹימֹוֹ[. The traces of the penultimate letter are more consistent with a *bet*. The preceding letter can be either a *waw* or a *yod*.

כדי לֹ[. The DJD edition disregards the *yod*, reading]כדל.

6 מֹוֹאֹדה[. Wacholder and Abegg read correctly מֹוֹאֹדה[, while Olyan suggests בֹוֹגדה[.

Translation
1.   ]willfully oppressed? nation[s
2.   ].. and my cru[shed] heart[
3.   ]. your hands[
4.]a hammered gold with a stylus[
5.]and they will return in order to[
6.   ]very .....[

Comments
1 עָנָו מלֹב גוי[ם. The extant phrase is difficult. Perhaps עָנָו is to be read as a 3ʳᵈ masc. sg. Piel *qatal* of ענה, "to oppress," as in כי לא ענה מלבו (Lam 3:33).[260]

2 ולבי הנד]כה. This is a first person address, perhaps a prayer, as suggested by the phrase]ידיכֹהֹ in line 3. For the language compare לב נשבר ונדכה (Ps 51:19).

3]ידיכֹהֹ. The addressee is probably God.

---

260 HALOT, 853.

4 ‪בֹּחרט זהב מנובֹב‬]. The first word can be read either as חֶרְ(י)ט, "a bag, purse," or, more likely, as חֶרֶט, "a stylus".[261] Qimron observes that a masc. sg. participle מנובֹב may denote "glittering" (deriving it from נוב, "to make to flourish, prosper"),[262] yet in the recent edition of 4Q382 he interprets it as "hammered" (cf. ‪ניב/נוב זהב‬ in Sir 35:5 referring to a piece of jewelry).[263] Qimron suggests that this might be a reference to the golden calves made by Jeroboam and restores: ‪ויצור‬ ‪בֹּחרט זהב מנובֹב‬].

Frg. 26

‪ת ויאומֹ]ר‬   1
‪יש[‬∘‪ימו שו‬]   2
‪[‬∘∘‪ה ‬∘]   3
‪וי[תפלל ‬∘∘]   4

Notes on Readings

1 ‪ויאומֹ]ר‬. The DJD edition has ‪וי‬∘]. On the photographs (PAM 41.991; 43.290; 43.464) a vertical stroke is visible next to the *alef*. Its hook-shaped top suggests that this is a *waw* or *yod*. Next to it the right extremity of a base stroke appears. Perhaps it belongs to a medial *mem*.

2 ‪יש[לימו‬. The editor reads ‪לימי‬[, but the last letter can also be read as a *waw*.

3 ‪ה‬∘∘[. Olyan sees traces of one letter before *he*. However, the photographs (esp. PAM 43.464) indicate that there are traces of two letters.

4 The DJD edition has ‪ת פ‬∘]. Wacholder and Abegg correctly read ‪וי[תפלל‬.

261 HALOT, 352–353.

262 Private correspondence. Cf. BDB, 626; HALOT, 677. Dr. Noam Mizrahi (private correspondence) notes that an affinity between the semantic field of growth and flourishing and that of light is reflected in several Hebrew roots, e.g., נצץ. See further S. Morag, "'Light is Sown' (Psalms 97:11)," *Tarbiz* 33 (1964): 140–148 (Hebrew); idem, "'Well-Rooted Like a Robust Native Tree' (Psalms 37:35)," *Tarbiz* 41 (1971–72): 4 (Hebrew).

263 It is rendered into Greek as κόσμος, "an ornament, a decoration." See Dihi, "The Morphological and Lexical Innovations in the Book of Ben Sira," 419–420.

Translation
1.   ].. and (he) sai[d
2.   they will ful]fill ...[
3.   ]....[
4.   and he p]rayed ..[

Frg. 27

To]p mar[gin?

א[לֿיֿנוֿ]   1

] נח ◦[2

Notes on Readings

What Olyan considers to be a *vacat* in the first line, is most likely an upper margin.

1 א[לֿיֿנוֿ. On PAM 43.464 there seems to be a trace of a *lamed* before the *yod* (unnoticed by the editor).

Translation
1.   to]us [
2.   ] (he/it) rested .[

Frg. 28: See Minute Fragments

Frg. 29

]◦ [1

]שֿמֿעֿ[2

] ◦ [3

Translation
2.   ](he) heard[

Frg. 30

]○שמ[ ]בֿ[	1
א[ת אשמוֹ]ת	2
כי אין לע[מֹוד לפניכ]ה על זאת	3
אלי[שע בן שֹ]פט	4
]○ תֿ[	5

Notes on Readings

1]בֿ[. This is Davis's reading supported by PAM 43.288.

]○שמ. On PAM 43.288 a trace of a vertical stroke appears after the medial *mem*. Davis and Qimron restore ים]שמ[ב, yet the available space appears to be too short to accommodate an interval between two adjacent words and a *bet*.

2 ת]אשמוֹ. Olyan reads]שמן[ ]○. Wacholder and Abegg suggest אשמוֹת. The *taw* is not extant on the fragment.

3 דֹ[מֹוֹ. This is the reading of Wacholder and Abegg. Olyan reads the traces of the first letter as an *ayin*.

5]○ תֿ[. The editor offers no reading for the first letter, yet on PAM 41.991; 43.288; 43.465 traces of a *taw* are visible.

Translation

2.   th]e guil[t of
3.   for one cannot s]tand before yo[u on this account
4.   Eli]sha son of Sha[phat

Comments

2 ת]אשמוֹ. For the language compare ואשמותי ממך לא נכחדו (Ps 69:6; cf. also 2 Chr 28:10).

3 כי אין לע[מֹוד לפניכ]ה על זאת. The reconstruction follows Ezra 9:15. For another allusion to Ezra 9, see frg. 104 8.

4 אלי[שע בן שֹ]פט. The mention of the name of Elisha, including the patronymic, may point to God's revelation to Elijah at Horeb in 1 Kgs 19, at the end of which the latter is commanded to anoint Elisha as a prophet (v. 16).[264] In 1 Kgs 19:10, 14 Elijah refers to Israel's sins, as does line 2. Cf. frg. 47.

Frg. 31

]○○[	1
֙	
ג[ֿדֿולה לתתֿם ביד כול גוי]ֿ הארץ	2
[לקץ יעמֿוד איש הפֿל]א	3
○[כֿ לכֿוֿל רוחות יישבֿ]ו	4
הג[ֿבֿיאים]○	5

Notes on Readings

1 ֿדֿולה[ג. The DJD edition has ֿיל[. Here Strugnell's reading and reconstruction are adopted (a trace of an upper bar of a *dalet* is visible on PAM 43.465).[265]

גוי]ֿ. This is Qimron's reading. Olyan suggests]○○ג.

2 הפֿל]א. Strugnell reads correctly הפֿל[(cf. PAM 43.288).[266] The DJD edition has חיל[.

4 יישבֿ]ו. Olyan reads]ויש○. The trace of a letter next to the *shin* may belong to a *bet*. The first letter can be read as either a *waw* or a *yod*.

Translation

2. g]reat, to deliver them into the hand of all the nations[of the earth
3.]at the end the man of wond[er] will arise[
4.]. for at all sides (of the world) they will dwe[ll
5. the pr]ophets .[

264 Thus also G. J. Brooke, "Parabiblical Prophetic Narratives," in *The Dead Sea Scrolls after Fifty Years* (ed. P. W. Flint, J. C. VanderKam; Leiden: Brill, 1998), 1:276–277.
265 *Preliminary Concordance*, 2:550
266 Ibid., 1:82.

Comments

2 הארץ [גו]ל כול ביד לתתֹם דֹולה[ג. The first word is, apparently, the adjective גדולה. Perhaps it can be restored as מכה גדולה (Josh 10:10; Judg 11:33) or מהומה גדולה (Deut 7:23; 1 Sam 5:9; 1QM I, 6). The reading גדֻלה is less likely in this context. The reconstruction כול גו[י] הארץ follows a frequently attested biblical idiom.

3 הפל]א איש יעמֹד לקץ[. The noun קץ here probably denotes an "end" (cf. Hab 2:3; Dan 12:13), rather than a "period of time" (cf. also frg. 62).[267] For a similar formulation cf. הגדול השר מיכאל יעמד ההיא ובעת (Dan 12:1).

איש הפל]א. While in biblical Hebrew the noun פלא is only rarely used in construct (one exception is קץ הפלאות in Dan 12:6), in the Dead Sea Scrolls such phrases as רזי פלאו (CD III, 18), גבורות פלאו (CD III, 8), מעשי פלאכה (1QHᵃ XV, 35), סוד פלאכה (1QHᵃ XII, 29), and אלוהי פלא (4Q511 10 7) are attested. Still, the expression איש הפלא (הפל]אות; Qimron) is unique to this scroll. Since several fragments of 4Q382 deal with Elijah, some identify איש הפל]א with the eschatological Elijah (see Discussion).

4 יש̇בֹ]ו רוחות לכֹ̇ול כֹ̇י. The plural רוחות may stand here for the points of the compass (see Jer 49:36; Zech 2:10; cf. also Sir 5:9). The subject of יש̇בֹ]ו (for the double *yod* cf. יישבו in 4Q158 14 8) is unknown. Perhaps it refers to Israel, envisioned as dispersed all over the inhabited world. On the possibility that this fragment evokes a hope for an ingathering of the dispersed Israel (cf. Deut 30:3–4; Isa 54:7; 1 En 90:33; 2 Macc 2:7), see Discussion.

5 הנ]בֹיאים. For possible reconstructions cf. כאשר דבר ביד כל עבדיו הנביאים (2 Kgs 17:23) and כדבר יהוה אשר דבר ביד עבדיו הנביאים (2 Kgs 24:2)

Frgs. 32–33: See Minute Fragments

Frg. 34

1   כול]ת̇[א
2   צדק]ו̇ מֹ̇[א

---

267 Clines, *The Concise Dictionary of Classical Hebrew*, 399.

Notes on Readings

1 תֿ[א. The DJD edition disregards the trace of a letter in the beginning of the line. Davis correctly identifies it as a *taw* (see PAM 43.465).

2 וֿ מֿֿת[א]צדק. Olyan suggests]◦ תֿ◦[. Wacholder and Abegg correctly read וֿ מֿֿת[א].

Translation

1.]all [t]he[
2. t]ruth and[justice

Comments

2 וֿ מֿֿת[א]צדק. The reconstruction follows frg. 17 1 (see Comments ad loc.).

Frg. 35

]לכול[	1
]ל [	2

Translation

1.]to all[

Frg. 36

]שֿלֿמֿה[

Comment

This may be a reference to King Solomon (for a similar orthography cf. 4Q385a 1a–b ii 5). Yet, other vocalizations, e.g., שַׂלְמָה, "a garment," are likewise possible.

Frg. 37

]◦◦[	1
]◦ לה[רים	2

Translation

2   to r]aise up .[

Comment

Cf. frg. 24.

Frg. 38

Top margin?

ה[ו̇ד̇ה וישׂר̇אל ויש̇ oo]יה   1

יׄמ̇ oooo[בׄח̇נתני כ̇י   2

לה[ש̇בׄיׄל ב]ד[בׄר̇כה ולעשות [משפט וצדקה   3

 o]ה oooo[דב̇ר̇ צ̇ד̇ק   4

על̇[ולוא oo]   5

[ה כי ישׂר̇ אׄל̇]   6

ת[צׄ כי עזב א̇]ȯ   7

ה[מ̇שׂילו בׄכלם]   8

[ולׄ̇הׄביׄא oo]   9

[ ] i̇o o oo[10

Notes on Readings

1 וישראל. The reading is that of Wacholder and Abegg. The DJD edition has ו[ש]ר̇אל.
ויש̇oo[. Olyan reads וישׂ̇רׄאׄל̇. The traces of ink next to the *shin* are illegible.

2]oooמ̇י. Olyan proposes no reading for the second letter, but Davis correctly identifies it as a medial *mem*. Its traces are quite visible on PAM 43.288.

3 ש̇בׄיׄל[לה. The DJD edition has שׁלׄם o[. The proposed reading follows that of Wacholder and Abegg, בׄול̇ ש[, yet assumes that these are the remains of a single word. *Waw* and *yod* are frequently indistinguishable in this scroll.
בׄר̇כה[ד]ב. The editor reads פ̇יׄכה. The tentative reading proposed here is another attempt to decipher the almost illegible traces of writing.

4 ה̇ooo[. Olyan incorrectly attaches the *he* to the next word.

5 על̇[. The editor proposes no reading for the second letter. The traces of a *lamed* are visible on PAM 43.288 (Wacholder and Abegg).

6] יֹשֶׁר אֵל. The DJD edition reads יֹשֶׁר ∘∘∘[. Wacholder and Abegg note correctly that the traces of the two letters next to the *resh* are consistent with an *alef* and a *lamed* (יֹשראֵ֗ל). There is a small interval between the *resh* and the *alef*.

7 According to PAM 43.288; 43.465 there is a trace of a letter before *ṣade*, unnoticed by Olyan. The last letter in this line resembles an *alef* (DJD provides no reading).

8 מֹשׁילו[ה. The editor suggests שׁילו[. The trace of a letter preceding *shin* (PAM 43.465) can be construed as a medial *mem* (Wacholder and Abegg).

בֹּכֹּלֹם. This is Wacholder and Abegg's reading. Olyan reads לם∘∘.

10] ֹיֹ ∘∘ ∘∘. The DJD edition has וחֹגֹר. Aside from the last letter, which is consistent with a *waw/yod*, the rest of the letters are illegible.

Translation

1.   J]udah and Israel and ....[
2.   ]you have tested me for .....[
3.   to u]nderstand your [w]ord and to do[justice and righteousness
4.   ].... word of righteousness .[
5.   ]... and not on[
6.   ]. for God is upright [
7.   ].. for he forsook [
8.   ](he) made him a ruler over everyone[
9.   ] and to bring ..[

Comments

2 בֹּחֹנתני ֹכֹּ. The wording of lines 2–3 suggests that this is a prayer (cf. Jer 12:3; Ps 26:2). One may also read בֹּחֹנתנו (as in Ps 66:10).

3 לה[ה שֹׁכֹּיל ב[ד]בֹּרֹכֹה ולעשות [משפט וצדקה. For the language cf. להשכיל אל דברי התורה (Neh 8:13). The reconstruction ולעשות [משפט וצדקה follows Jer 23:5. Cf. frg. 23 2.

4 דבֹּרֹ צֹֹדֹק. One may construe the first word as a noun, דְּבַר צדק (cf. Ps 45:5; 4Q372 1 28; 4Q403 1 i 18), or as a Piel verbal form of דבר (cf. דִּבֶּר צדק [Isa 45:19]).

6 כי יֹשֶׁר אֵֹל. Unlike lines 2–3, lines 6 and 8 refer to God in the 3rd person. For the wording cf. כי ישר יהוה צורי (Ps 92:16). The scroll seems to prefer אֵ֗ל to the Tetragrammaton.

8 ‏בْלם[ה.‏מْשׁילו בבْלם]. In the Hebrew Bible and, more frequently, in the Dead Sea Scrolls, a Hifil of ‏משל‏ is used with reference to human dominion over creation (cf. Ps 8:7; 4Q301 3a-b 6; 4Q422 1 9). For another instance of the use of ‏המשיל‏ in this scroll, see frg. 104 4.

Frg. 39

]∘[	1
אמת ו[צْדْקה]	2
איש לרْעْה]ו	3
תْו את יה]	4
ואין]מْרפא עْד]	5
דו]רْותיהْםْ]	6
בْיْד כשׁדْיْםْ]	7
]∘∘[	8

Notes on Readings

1 The DJD edition reads here ‏כ‏, but the trace of ink is illegible.

3 ‏לרْעْה[ו‏. The editor reads]∘∘‏ל‏. On the photographs traces of the tops of three letters are visible. The first two are horizontal strokes, perhaps a *resh* and a *he*. The third one is a vertical stroke, a *waw/yod*.

4 ‏תْו את יה]‏. A similar reading has been proposed by Wacholder and Abegg (]‏תْואתיה‏). Olyan suggests]‏יה‏∘∘‏[.

5 ‏עْד]‏. This is Davis's reading. The DJD edition has]∘ ‏מْרפא]‏.

6 ‏דו]רْותיהْםْ]‏. Olyan reads]‏ריהם‏∘∘‏[. In the beginning of the line the upper bar of a *resh* is visible. Next to it comes a vertical stroke of a *waw* or a *yod*. The third letter is clearly a *taw*.

7 ‏בْיْד כשׁדْיْםْ]‏. The DJD edition has]‏תْחדْשׁ‏[. Davis suggests]‏מْוْד כשׁדْיْ‏[. The letters ‏בْיْד‏ and the final *mem* in ‏כשׁדْיْםْ‏ are visible on PAM 42.500.

Translation

2.　　　　　truth and]righteousness [
3.　　　　　] man to [his] fellow[
4.　　　　　]......[
5.　and there is no]healing until[
6.　　　　　]their [ge]nerations[
7.　　　　　]into the hand of Chaldeans[

Comments

2 אמת ו[צְּדֹקה. The reconstruction follows a biblical idiom (cf. frgs. 17 and 34). Other restorations, e.g., משפט ו[צְּדֹקה (as in frg. 38 3), are equally possible.

4 את יה]. The last two letters are likely to belong to a proper noun, perhaps a theophoric name. In light of line 7, one might consider את יה]ודה.

5 מׁרפא]אין ל. For the language cf. Pr 6:15. The same expression may occur in frg. 112 1.

7 בׁיׁד כׁשׁדׁיׁם]. The phrase ביד כשדים with the verb נתן appears several times in the book of Jeremiah (e.g., 22:5, 32:24, 25). It is likely that the fragment refers to the desolation of Judah by the Babylonians. What remains unclear is whether it is presented as a past, present, or future event.

Frg. 40

1　　　　　[בׁן אדׁם וׁקׁם אׁקׁ]וׁם
2　　　　　[ל אלהׁיׁם] [יׁשמרנׁי הׁ]

Notes on Readings

1 אדׁם. The reading is that of Davis (cf. PAM 41.991; 43.289). Olyan suggests אד]ם[.

אׁקׁ]וׁם. The DJD edition has אׁ[o]. Wacholder and Abegg read the last letter as a *qof*, which is clearly visible on PAM 43.289; 43.465.

2 לׁo[. Olyan reads אׁל[. The traces of one or more letters preceding the *lamed* are illegible.

אלהׁיׁם]. The editor reads אלי]ה/שע. The proposed reading follows that of Wacholder and Abegg.

]ה֯ י֯שמרני֯[. This is Wacholder and Abegg's reading. The DJD edition has]○ ד֯ה֯○○○[.

On PAM 41.991 a scrap of papyrus is attached to the left extremity of this fragment. It is unclear whether it belonged there originally. This scrap is absent from the other PAM images and the plate (XXXIX) in the DJD edition. If it indeed belonged here, the fragment would read:

1]בׄן אדׄם ו֯קׄם אׄקׄ]ום]אופ[

2]○כ֯ל אל֯ה֯י֯ם֯[ ]י֯שמרני֯ ה֯○[ ]○מו[ ]

Translation

1.]man and I will cer[tainly] rise[
2.].. God will guard me ..[

Comments

2 אל֯ה֯י֯ם֯[ ]י֯שמרני֯. This is another fragment containing 1st person speech.

Frg. 41: See Minute Fragments

Frg. 42

1]ה֯ אלוהי[ם

2]○ עם ○[

Note on Readings

1 ה֯[. This is a reading by Wacholder and Abegg. Olyan offers no reading for the first letter.

Translation

1.]. Go[d
2.]. people .[

Comments

1 אֱלוֹהִֿ]ם ‬הֿ[. While the phrase יהוה אלוהים lends itself easily as a possible reconstruction, other fragments of this scroll indicate that it refrains from using the Tetragrammaton.

2 עם. This word can also be read and rendered as "with."

Frg. 43

פ[לִֿיֿטֿה לבֿית יעֿ]קוב	1
עֿ[טֿרת תפארתֿ]	2
[בִֿישראל כי יֿ]ֿ	3

Notes on Readings

1 פ[לִֿיֿטֿה. This is Wacholder and Abegg's reading. Olyan suggests ב[טֿח. Qimron prefers מ[בֿטֿהֿ. The last letter is clearly a *he*, as its upper bar curving downwards indicates.

יעֿ]קוב. Wacholder and Abegg correctly identify the second letter as an *ayin* (PAM 41.991). The DJD edition has יֿשֿ[ראל.

Translation

1.	sur]vivors to the house of Ja[cob
2.	a cr]own of glory[
3.	]in Israel, for .[

Comments

1 פ[לִֿיֿטֿה לבֿית יעֿ]קוב. For the language cf. Isa 10:20 (ופליטת בית יעקב; the construction פליטה ל- occurs in Judg 21:17; 1 Chr 4:43). Frg. 45 3 also refers to פליטה.

2 עֿ[טֿרת תפארתֿ]. This phrase occurs in several scriptural passages, e.g., Isa 62:3.

Frg. 44

$$
\begin{array}{rr}
]\circ\circ[& 1 \\
\text{יש}[\text{מורכֿה}] & 2 \\
\text{נֿ}[\text{יות}] & 3 \\
\text{כֿה ת}[& 4 \\
]\text{לֿ} \circ [\text{לֿוֿאֿ}] & 5
\end{array}
$$

Notes on Readings

2]יש[מורכֿה. This a reading by Wacholder and Abegg. The DJD edition has]ירכֿתֿ◌[.

4 כֿה[. Olyan offers no reading for the first letter. However, its traces, as visible on PAM 43.465, resemble those of a medial *kaf* or a *bet*.

Translation

2.　　he will g]uard you[

5.　　　　]. no[

Comments

2]יש[מורכֿה. This fragment contains 2nd person address (note also the suffix כֿה[in line 4).

Frg. 45

$$
\begin{array}{rr}
]\circ \text{פֿ} \text{עֿלֿ} [& 1 \\
]\text{מ}[\text{נֿוֿחֿת} & 2 \\
\text{שאר}[\text{יֿת ופלֿ}]\text{יטה} & 3 \\
]\text{לֿוֿא יֿשֿ}[& 4
\end{array}
$$

Notes on Readings

1]◌פֿ עֿלֿ. This is a reading by Wacholder and Abegg. The DJD edition has]קֿ◌◌[.

3 שאר[יֿת ופלֿ]יטה. Olyan offers no reading for the first and last letters. On PAM 43.288 traces of a *yod* and a *lamed* are visible.

Translation

1   ] on ..[
2.   the r]est of [
3.   a remna]nt and a sur[vivor
4.   ]not ..[

Comments

3 שאר]ֿוֿת ופלֿ]יטה. For the language see, e.g., 2 Kgs 19:31; Ezra 9:14. It is unclear whether the fragment envisions that a remnant will remain, or that the destruction will be complete (cf. Ezra 9:14). The reference to the "rest" in line 2 lends some support to the former interpretation. פליטה is mentioned also in frg. 43 1.

Frg. 46

]ooo̊פ הֿרֿבֿא oo[	1
]משיב רוחי כֿi[	2
] *vac* מעמכה o[	3
דבֿרי תפלה ותחנ]ֿונים [	4
]ֿיֿחֿזֿקֿיֿהֿ מלֿךֿ] יהודה	5

Notes on Readings

1 הֿרֿבֿא. The DJD edition has א̊ooה oo[. Davis and Qimron read הֿובֿא. The second letter as visible on PAM 43.288 may also be read as a *resh*.

]ooo̊פ. The traces of the two or three letters at the end of the line are difficult to decipher. Wacholder and Abegg read]ה̊ מ̊. Olyan suggests]פֿשֿע̊, whereas Davis reads]פֿשֿרֿוֿ.

3 מעמכה. This is a reading of Wacholder and Abegg. Olyan suggests מעמדכה.

4 ותחנ]ֿונים. The reading follows that of Wacholder and Abegg. The DJD edition has]o̊חתנ.

5]מלֿךֿ יֿחֿזֿקֿיֿהֿ̊. Thus read Wacholder and Abegg, Davis, and Qimron. Olyan suggests]לֿוֿא̊. On PAM 41.991 a scrap of papyrus containing the proposed reading is visible. It is missing from the other photographs and the DJD plate (XXXIX).

Translation

1.].. many ....[
2.]allowing (me) to regain my strength, for[
3.]. from your people [
4.] words of a prayer and a suppli[cation
5.]Hezekiah king of[Judah

Comments

1 הרבא. This is either a *qatal* or an infinitive absolute of רבה in the Hifil, "to multiply." Here the latter reading, הַרְבֵּה, "many," is assumed (cf. frg. 114 1). In either case, the scribe wrote an *alef* instead of a *he*, another attestation to the weakening of the gutturals.

2 [מְשִׁיב רוחי כֹי]. This is a 1ˢᵗ person address, perhaps a prayer. The construction השיב רוח occurs in frg. 6 3 (see Comment ad loc.).

3 מעמכה. The extant word may be vocalized as מֵעַמְכה, "from your people," or מֵעִמְכה, "from you." A blank space after מעמכה seems to indicate the end of a literary unit, as is also suggested as by the contents of line 4.

4 דבֹרי תפלה ותחנֹ[ונים. Lines 4 and 5 contain a superscription preceding a now lost prayer. For the phrase תפלה ותחנונים cf. Dan 9:3, but the wording of the scroll here is unique. Qimron adds והודות לאלוהים.

5 [יֹחֹזֹקֹיֹֹה מלֹֹך] יהודה. This line continues the superscription found in the preceding line. The reconstruction follows an appellation occurring several times in the Hebrew Bible (cf. particularly 1 Chr 4:41: יחזקיהו מלך יהודה). Qimron restores יֹחֹזֹקֹיֹֹה[אשר התפלל. It is possible that one of the prayers attributed to Hezekiah in the Hebrew Bible followed (see 2 Kgs 20:2–3 [=Isa 38:2–3]; Isa 38:9–20; 2 Chr 30:18, 19). However, given the unique wording of the superscription, it seems more likely that this is a non-scriptural prayer ascribed to Hezekiah. This may elaborate on one of his prayers recorded in the Hebrew Bible, or it may be an expansion of a biblical account, such as 2 Chr 32:20 (Sennacherib's siege of Jerusalem), which depicts Hezekiah praying without providing the actual wording of the prayer.

[יֹחֹזֹקֹיֹֹה. For the spelling יֹחֹזֹקֹיֹֹה[(vs. the recurring חזקיהו/יחזקיהו), see Hosea 1:1; Micah 1:1.

Frg. 47

א[ל אליהֿ]	1
ל[	2
[בים דבֿ]ֿר	3
שמכ[ה לנאצֿ]ו	4
הר[שיעו ע]מכה	5
[אֿה לאורֿד] ימים	6
[הֿמֿהֿ]	7

Notes on Readings

1 ל[א אליהֿ]. This is Wacholder and Abegg's reading. The DJD edition has ל[אֿ∘∘].

4 לנאצֿ[ו]. The editor reads a final *ṣade*, yet the photographs suggest a medial *ṣade* (esp. PAM 41.991; 43.288).

6 [אֿה. The DJD edition leaves the first letter undeciphered. According to PAM 43.465, the trace of ink is consistent with the left stroke of an *alef*.

לאורֿד[. Olyan reads לאורֿ ∘[. The vertical stroke of the final *kaf* is readily visible on all the photographs.

7 [הֿמֿהֿ. The editor offers no reading here. On PAM 43.288 traces of a *he*, a medial *mem*, and another *he* are visible.

Translation

1.	t]o Elijah[
2.	].[
3.	]... wor[d
4.	you]r[name] to treat [it] disrespectfully[
5.	your]p[eople ac]ted wickedly[
6.	].. for many[years
7.	]they[

Comments

1 ל[א אליהֿ]. If, as suggested below, lines 4–5 contain an address to God, perhaps this line quotes the latter's speech to Elijah, e.g., ויאומר //// א[ל אליהֿ].

4 שׂמכ[ה לנאצּו]. The reconstruction (cf. Ps. 74:10, 18) assumes that this line, along with line 5, is an address to God. The occasion is unclear, yet Elijah's address to God at Mt. Horeb in 1 Kgs 19:10–18 should be considered (cf. frg. 30). A form of נאץ occurs also in frg. 12 6.

5 הר[שׁיעו ע]מכה. Another possible reconstruction is הר[שׁיעו ע]בדיכה.

6 אֹה לאורֹך] ימים. The restoration follows the recurring biblical expression (e.g., Ps 93:5).

Frg. 48

]∘∘ ∘∘[	1
]∘∘ ∘[	2
וי[עֲֹנו כי כֹ]	3
דב[רי פי]ו	4
כ]ל ישׂראֹ]ל	5
[הֹרבֹו]	6

Notes on Readings

3 וי[עֲֹנו. This is Davis's reading. Olyan suggests ∘י[.

5 ל[. This letter is not represented in the DJD transcription, yet the vertical stroke of a *lamed* is easily visible on all the photographs (Davis).

6 [הֹרבֹו]. The editor suggests]ידבֹר[. Wacholder and Abegg read ם]הֹרבֹּי[. The last letter, either a *waw* or a *yod*, is followed by a blank space.

Translation

3.   and they an]swered, because.[
4.   wo]rds of [his] mouth[
5.   al]l of Israe[l
6.   ](they) increased [

Comments

3 וי[עֲֹנו כי כֹ]. Lines 4–6 may contain a response implied by this verb.

Frg. 49

Top margin?

]oooo[	1
]○ מ ○[	2
וֹימיׄ] ○[	3
והישר [הׄטוֹבׄ] לעשות [לֻעׄוֹלֹםׄ ○[	4
על שכל עבדכה [לוֹא אׄיש בׄיׄנׄה וב]	5
ואין [לׄעׄוֹלׄׄהׄ להופיע אתכׄ]ה	6
בהשפטכׄ]ה ○[ ]○ [○ [	7
בבו]שׄת פנים ובכלמה]	8
חטאיׄ והבׄ] ○[	9
לוא א[עזבכה ולוׄ]א	10

Notes on Readings

2 וֹימיׄ]. The DJD edition has]○ בֹדׄזׄ. According to PAM 42.500, the first two letters are consistent with *waw/yod*. The third letter is a medial *mem*. The fourth letter could be a *yod*.

4 לֻעׄוֹלֹםׄ] ○[. There is a trace of ink in the beginning of the line unnoticed by Olyan (see PAM 41.988). The last letter may also be read as a medial *mem* (Davis; Qimron).

5 וב]על. This is Qimron's reading. The editor reads the second letter as a medial *mem*.

6 לׄעׄוֹלׄׄהׄ[. This is the reading of Strugnell.[268] Olyan, Davis, and Qimron suggest לׄעׄוֹלׄםׄ[. On the photographs, particularly on PAM 42.500, the traces of a *he* are clearly visible.

אתכׄ]ה. The DJD edition has]○יׄא. Wacholder and Abegg read אתהׄ[. The vertical stroke of the third letter can also belong to a medial *kaf* (see PAM 41.988).

7]○ [ ]○. Olyan reads הׄ[צ]דׄק[. Wacholder and Abegg suggest תׄצׄדׄק. Qimron reads וׄהׄצׄדׄק. The curving vertical stroke of the last letter seems to belong to a final *nun*, rather than to a *qof*, for the typical upper stroke of a *qof* is missing from the photographs. The preceding letters are illegible.

---

268 *Preliminary Concordance* 4:1471.

9 חטאיו‎ °[. The editor reads °° [ת]חטא. The two vertical strokes with hook-shaped tops, most likely a *yod* and a *waw*, visible on the fragment are at some distance from the *alef* of חטא. Perhaps this is due to the sloppy placement of the scrap containing the letters חטא. In fact, it is unclear whether this scrap (including the entire text of line 10) belongs here.

Translation

3.   ]. and days of[
4.   ]. forever[to do]what is good[and right
5.   your servant is]not a man of understanding, nor one possessing in[sight
6.   and no] injustice will appear with y[ou
7.   ].[ ].. when yo[u] enter a judgment[
8.   in sh]ame and dishonor [
9.   ]. his sins [
10.   I will not]forsake you and (will) no[t

Comments

4 והישר [הטוֹב֗] לעשות [לעוֹלם֗]. The reconstruction follows Deut 12:28.

5 [לוֹא אִ֗יש בִּינה וב֗]על שכל עבדכה. For the phrases איש בינה and בעל שכל (Qimron), not found in biblical Hebrew, see 4Q426 10 2 and 4Q423 5 7 respectively. The reconstruction עבדכה assumes with lines 6 and 7 that this is a prayer.

6 [לְעוֹלֹה להופיע אתב֗]ה ואין. The first word can be vocalized as עַוְלָה, "injustice, malice."[269] The infinitive להופיע is understood here as "to come forth, appear," as is common in rabbinic Hebrew.[270]

7 בהשפטכ]ה. This is a Nifal infinitive of שפט, "to enter a judgment" (cf. Ezek 20:35, 36).[271]

8 בבו]שֹׁ֗ת פנים ובכלמה. For the language cf. Ps 35:26.

10 [עזבכה לוא א]לוֹא א[עֹזבכה ולו]א. Qimron restores ועבדכה לוא א[עזבכה ולו]א.

---

269 HALOT, 798.
270 Jastrow, *Dictionary*, 586.
271 HALOT, 1626.

Frg. 50

T]op mar[gin

]דֹּבֵּר[	1
תו[כֹּתתכהֹ]	2
[בֹּאֹור הֹבֹּ]וקר	3
[לֹכֹבֹוֹדֹ]	4
ה[חֹלֹוֹ הֹ]	5

Notes on Readings

1 דֹּבֵּר[. This is the plausible suggestion of Wacholder and Abegg. The DJD edition has] ס⸱ר ⸱ס[.

2]כֹּתתכהֹ[תו. This is Wacholder and Abegg's reading.[272] The editor suggests] ⸱כ את⸱[.

3 בֹּאֹור[. The DJD edition has ⸱ר⸱ס⸱[. Wacholder and Abegg correctly read או⸱ר[. On PAM 42.500 an upper bar and a base of a *bet* are visible.

 הֹבֹּ]וקר. All previous editions offer no reading for these two letters. According to PAM 42.500, the first letter is represented by two vertical strokes and an upper bar. It may be a *he*. Of the next letter a vertical stroke, a short upper bar and a base stroke consistent with a *bet* are visible (PAM 42.500).

5 ה[חֹלֹוֹ הֹ. Olyan reads]אלֹֹהֹֹיֹם[. The letter he reads as an *alef* is more consistent with a *ḥet*. The last letter, *he*, opens a new word. There are no traces of ink next to it.

Translation

1.   ]speaking [
2.   ]your [re]buke[
3.   ]in the light of mor[ning
4.   ]for an honor[
5.   (they) b]egan .[

---

272 *Preliminary Concordance* 4:1929.

Comments

2 ‏תו[כֹֿחתכֹה]‏. This is a 2nd person address, perhaps a prayer.

3 ‏[בְּאוֹר הֹבֹּ]וקר‏. For the language cf. Micah 2:1.

Frgs. 51–52: See Minute Fragments

Frg. 53

]ooo‏ו‏ ‏תֿ‏ooo[	1
‏בֹּק ושׂעְ‏רֹ‏וֹ‏רִ‏]‏ה‏	2
]ooo‏לֿ‏ o‏אֹֿ‏לֿ‏ o[	3

Notes on Readings

1]ooo‏ו‏ ‏תֿ‏ooo[. The DJD edition has ‏ה]יֹ‏הֹ‏ו‏ ‏תֿ‏ooo[. With the exceptions of a *taw* and a *waw/yod*, the letters seem to be illegible.

2 ‏בֹּק ושׂעְרֹורִ]ה‏. Olyan reads ‏א]וֹנֹשׂישׂעְרֹורִ]ה‏. Wacholder and Abegg read]‏קo ושׂעְרֹורֹ[יה‏. As to the first letter, on PAM 43.465 faint traces of a *bet* are visible. At the end of the line, a vertical stroke, perhaps a *yod*, can be seen (PAM 41.988).

Translation

2.   ].. and something horr[ible

Frg. 54

‏ים לעד אל]‏[	1
]‏לֿ‏[	2

Notes on Readings

1 ‏לעד‏. This reading follows that of Wacholder and Abegg. Olyan reads ‏לעץ‏.

Translation

1.   ].. forever God[

Frg. 55

] ▭°°° °° [1

[עֿה והפלא עדֿלֿמֿ]ואדה   2

] ° ליום הואֿהֿ [3

[   ]   4

] °°°°°הֿ[ולה   5

Notes on Readings

The stretch of the papyrus containing line 4 is missing.

1 A final *mem* is legible at the end of the line.

2 עה[. Olyan offers no reading for the first letter. On the photographs the left and base strokes of an *ayin* (or *bet*) are clearly visible.

    עדֿלֿמֿ[אדה. This is Qimron's reading (PAM 43.289). The DJD edition has ע°לל°[.

Translation

2.].. and he acted e[xceedingly] wondrously[

3.]. to day he [

Comments

2 והפלא עדֿלֿמֿ[ואדה. The verb והפלא apparently has God as a subject (cf. 1QHᵃ VII, 20). For the construction עדֿלֿמֿ[ואדה, written without an interval, cf. Isa 64:8. For the spelling מואדה see frg. 25 6.

Frgs. 56–58: See Minute Fragments

Frg. 59

] אלפֿ[י   1

[והוֿאֿ[לֿ   2

Notes on Readings

1 לֿ]והוֿאֿ[. The DJD edition has]ותיֿ°[. On PAM 43.466 a vertical stroke of a *lamed* is visible in the beginning of the line. After a short blank space, perhaps an interval between adjacent words, a *waw*, a *he*, and another *waw* are visible. The remains of the last letter resemble an *alef*.

Translation
1.] thousand[s of
2.]. and he[.

Frgs. 60–61: See Minute Fragments

Frg. 62

] ‏לֹקׄצׄ‎[	1
]ooo[	2

Note on Readings
1] ‏לׄקׄצ‎[. This is Wacholder and Abegg's reading. The DJD edition reads]‏שצ‎[.

Translation
1.]to the end [

Comment
For another instance of the use of the noun ‏קץ‎ in this scroll, see frg. 31 3.

Frg. 63: See Minute Fragments

Frg. 64

]o[	1
]oooo[	2
]‏ריׄאל‎ o[	3
]o[	4

Notes on Readings
2 Olyan reads]∘ה̊ו̊[, but the traces are illegible.

Translation
3.   ]. without[

Frgs. 65–69: See Minute Fragments

Frg. 70

]ה̊ו̊א̊[	1
]∘ל̊[	2

Notes on Readings
2]∘ל̊[. Olyan reads here]ה̊[. In the beginning of the line a vertical trace of a *lamed* is visible (Davis). The rest of the traces are illegible.

Translation
1.   ]no[

Frgs. 71–74: See Minute Fragments

Frg. 75

]ל̊ ד∘[	1
]ב̊ה[	2
]הזכי̊ר	3

Notes on Readings
2]ב̊ה[. Olyan reads]כ̊ה[, yet the size and the shape of the first letter suggest that this is a *bet* (Davis).

Translation
3.](he) caused to remembe[r

Frgs. 76–77: See Minute Fragments

Frg. 78

]בְּנֵי[	1
//]// ר[	2

Translation
1.]sons of[

Comment
2 The two extant dots (or, rather, strokes, for the second one is longer than the first one and appears to be a stroke) most likely represent the Tetragrammaton, as in frg. 9.

Frg. 79

]ת ∘[	1
]ולוא[	2
]∘ מים[י	3
]ו נח[	4

Notes on Readings
1]ת. Olyan reads a medial *kaf*, yet the photographs (PAM 43.289; 43.466) exhibit two vertical strokes and an upper bar as in a *taw* (Davis).

3]∘ מ[. The DJD edition offers no reading for the first letter. On the photographs in the beginning of the line traces of a medial *mem* are clearly visible.

4]ו. Olyan considers the first letter to be illegible. The vertical stroke curving downwards at the top is most likely a *waw* or a *yod*.

Translation

2.]and not[
3. d]ays .[
4.]. (he) rested[

Frgs. 80–81: See Minute Fragments

Frg. 82

1]לְבֹבָם[
2] נָשָׂא ֯ ○[

Notes on Readings

2 As Davis observes, there is a trace of ink in the beginning of the line (unnoted in the DJD edition; cf. PAM 43.466).

Translation

1.]their heart[
2.]. (he) carried[

Comments

For לבבם and נשא cf. frgs. 104 1 and 23 3 respectively.

Frgs. 83–92, 94–95: See Minute Fragments. For **frg. 93:** see Appendix.

Frg. 96

וֹמֹמֹלֹכוֹ]ת ○[

Notes on Readings

Davis notes that there is a trace of ink in the beginning of the line (absent from the DJD edition). The word may also be read as וֹמֹמֹלֹהֹת[.

Translation

]. and kingdom[s

Frgs. 97, 99–100: See Minute Fragments. For **frg. 98:** See Appendix

Frg. 101

[ذ]

Translation

]son[

Frg. 102: See Minute Fragments

Frg. 103: See Appendix

Frg. 104 i

[ ]ל[2 [

Notes on Readings

While the DJD edition reads the *lamed* as a part of frg. 104 ii 2, it is more likely that this letter belongs with the preceding column. Such a reading is supported by the fact that lines 1–4 open with completely preserved words.

Frg. 104 ii
Parallel text: <u>4Q160 2+6+10 1–4</u>

Top margin

מדבריך ולתמוך בבריתכֹה ֹלהיות לבֹבֹם [ל]ֹך לקדשֹךֹ] <u>אותם ולהבר</u>[1

<u>כפים למעֹן יהיו לכה ואתֹה להם ותצדק</u> בֹ[ד]בֹרֹיֹבֹה] <u>ותזכה בשפטכה</u>[2

<u>כי אתה</u>   <u>למֹירֹישֹוֹנֹֹה בֹעלתם</u> והייתה להם לאב ולֹאֹ[לוהים ולא[3

עזבתם בידי מלכיֹם] ולא [הֹמֹשלתה בֹעמֹךֹ ○○ לֹי[ ]○ ○[ ]○[4   [

]○○○○○○○○ לֹוֹא ○○ ○○[5   [

]   6   [

וסֹ[וֹרֹ מֹמֹצֹוֹוֹתֹיֹכה הנתתה להם ביד מושֹה] עבדכה   7   [

מֹ]שֹפֹטֹכֹה ועוֹן עמכה מעלה לרוֹ]ש   8   [

○○ וֹבֹאֹוֹרֹךֹ אפיכה ורובֹסֹלֹיֹחֹוֹתֹיֹ]כה   9   [

Notes on Readings

1 לֹבֹבֹם [ל]ֹךֹ לקדשֹךֹ]. Olyan reads לֹבֹבֹם ○[ ]ו[לקדשׁוֹ]. The reading proposed here follows that of Qimron (in the final publication he prefers מֹקדשׁךֹ). Yet while he reconstructs the entire word לֹךֹ, on the photographs there is a trace of ink visible right after לֹבֹבֹם. It may well belong to a final *kaf*.

2 בֹ[ד]בֹרֹיֹבֹה. Olyan reads ○[ ]○○יֹכֹה. On PAM 42.500 the traces of two letters, a *bet* and a *resh*, are visible.

3 לֹמֹירֹישֹוֹנֹֹה. Olyan reads לֹמוֹרֹישׁ ○○. The proposed reading suits the traces of ink and is supported by a parallel text from 4Q160.

4 בֹידֹי. The editor reads בֹיד. On PAM 42.500 a *yod* after the *dalet* is visible.

מלכֹיֹם. Olyan suggests מלביהֹ[ם]. The extant traces of the last letter are consistent with either a medial *kaf* (Strugnell: מלבֹיֹכֹ[ה]²⁷³) or a final *mem* (Qimron: מלכֹיֹם).

הֹמֹֹשׁלתה[. The DJD edition has וֹ[הֹבֹשׁלתה]. Strugnell's reading הֹמֹשׁלתה is equally possible and contextually preferable.²⁷⁴

בֹעמֹךֹ. The DJD edition has בעמ○. Qimron's reading adopted here better suits the traces of the letters. He also suggests reading the remaining traces of ink as יֹד לֹאֹוֹמֹ]ים.

273 *Preliminary Concordance*, 3:1357.
274 Ibid., 3:1357.

5 Qimron reads כִּֿ לֹוֹאֿ.

7 וֹ[סו. This is Davis's reading. Olyan reads יֹ[.

מֹמִצְוֹוֹֹתֿיכה. The editor reads ב∘∘∘ חיכה. Davis's reads correctly מִמִּצְוֹֹוֹתיכה.

9 וֹבֹאֹוֹרֿךֿ ∘∘[. The DJD edition has אֹרֿךֿ ∘∘∘[. Traces of the two letters preceding the *alef* may be read as a *waw* and a *bet*. On the photographs a hook-shaped trace of a *waw* after the *alef* is visible.

וֹרוֹבסֿלֿיֿחֿוֹתֿ]יכה. Olyan reads ∘∘∘ [כול ורוב. Wacholder and Abegg suggest ורוב סֿלֿיֿחֿה. Here Qimron's reading is adopted.

Translation
1. from your words, and to hold on to your covenant. And that their hearts may be t[o] you, so that you may sanctify[them. And to cleanse]
2. hands, so that they may be to you and you to them. And you will be found righteous in your words [and just in your judging.]
3. For you became their owner from the beginning and you were for them as a father and as God. And you have not
4. abandoned them in the hands of kings [and] you have [not]made master over your people .. .. [ ]..[ ]
5. [ ].... and not .... [ ]
6. [ ]
7. [and str]aying from your commandments which you have given them by the hand of Moses[your servant.]
8. [ ]your judgment and the iniquity of your people is higher than the hea[d]
9. [ ].. and in your indulgence and the abundance of merc[ies]

Comments
1–2 מדבריך ולתמוך בבריתכה ולהיות לבבם [ל]ךֿ לֿקדשׁךֿ [ל]היות לבבם / אותם ולהבר] / כפים. The beginning of this prayer is lost. Its extant text opens with the speaker elaborating on what is required of the subject of his prayer, apparently, the nation of Israel, in order to maintain relationship with God, "so that they may be for you and you for them" (line 2). These are presented utilizing infinitives, ולהיות, ולתמוך, and ולהבר.

מדבריך. The phrase מדבריך can be reconstructed as מדבריך / [ליראה] (cf. 1 Sam 28:20; Ezek 2:6) or מדבריך / לוא לסור] (cf. Deut 17:11; Qimron). Throughout this column a longer form of a 2nd masc. possessive suffix is dominant, with a short suffix being attested also in line 4, בֿעמֿךֿ.

ולתמוך בבריתכֿהֿ. The construction תמך בברית, expressing the idea of "holding on to the covenant,"[275] does not occur in the Hebrew Bible, but appears in 1QH^a X, 23–24; XII, 2(=4Q432 7 4); XXII, 14–15.

ולהיות לבבֿםֿ [לֿ]ךֿ לֿקדשֿךֿ [אותם]. The speaker pleads that the heart of his people may belong to God so that he may sanctify them. While the wording is peculiar to the scroll, the notion itself is well at home in the Hebrew Bible (cf. והטו את לבבכם אל יהוה [Josh 24:23]; והכינו לבבכם אל יהוה [1 Sam 7:3]). The construction ולהיות לבֿבֿםֿ [לֿ]ךֿ is reminiscent of Deut 5:29: מי יתן והיה לבבם זה להם ליראה אתי ("Oh, that they had such a mind [literally, "heart"] as this always, to fear me," RSV). The reconstruction לֿקדשֿךֿ [אותם] is based on the parallel text from 4Q160 2+6+10 1 (see Chapter 2). For God's sanctifying His people see, e.g., Exod 31:13; Lev 20:8. This motif appears also in a prayer found in 4Q160 4 i+5 4, 7 (see Chapter 2).

ולהבר] / כפים. The reconstruction follows 1QH^a VIII, 28. The juxtaposition of לבֿבֿםֿ and כפים follows the frequent biblical pairing of the pure heart and hands, as, e.g., in Gen 20:5 (בתם לבבי ובנקיק כפי) and Ps 24:4 (נקי כפים ובר לבב).

2 למען יהיו לכה ואתה להם. If Israel acts according to what is said in lines 1–2, they will be God's people and he will be their God. The wording of this line is reminiscent of several biblical passages. Cf., for instance, Jer 11:4: והייתם לי לעם ואנכי אהיה לכם לאלהים ("that you may be my people and I may be your God"). The parallel text in 4Q160 2+6+10 1 is slightly longer: לֿ[מען יהיו לכה ואתה תהיה להמה].

ותצדק בֿ[ד]בֿריֿכֿהֿ [ותזכה בשפטכה]. This proclamation of God's justice, relying on Ps 51:6 (למען תצדק בדברך ותזכה בשפטך), may hearken back to a confession of sins made earlier on (in the now-lost section of this prayer), or point to the one found in line 8. It seems that the wording of 4Q160 here is again somewhat longer.

בֿ[ד]בֿריֿכֿהֿ. Ps 51:6 MT reads בְדָבְרֶךָ, i.e., a Qal infinitive construct of דבר, whereas the scroll has a plural of דָבָר, "a word." A similar reading of this verse seems to be attested in 4Q393 1 ii, 2 2: למען תצדק בדבֿרֿ[י]ֿךֿ / תֿזֿ[ו]כה בשופ[טכֿה and in 4Q379 17 3: בֿדבריו [יצדק. The Greek translation of Ps 51:6 (50:6 LXX) also reads: ἐν τοῖς λόγοις σου.

3 כי אתה למֿיֿרֿיֿשֿוֿנֿהֿ בעלתם. The conjunction כי links the affirmation of divine justice in line 2 to the review of God's past dealings with Israel in lines 3–4. The prayer first evokes the divine election of Israel as God's own property. The verb בְעלתם, a 2nd masc. sg. Qal qatal of בעל, "to own, be a master," describes the divine ownership of Israel in several biblical passages, such as Jer 31:32.[276] As in Jer 31:32,

---

275 HALOT, 1751.
276 Ibid., 142.

the phrase בְּעָלתם לְמִירִישׁוֹנֹה (the adverb לְמִירִישׁוֹנֹה is otherwise unattested, but cf. למבראשונה in 1 Chr 15:13) seems to refer to the events of Exodus (cf. the expression ברית ראשנים with reference to the Sinai covenant in Lev 26:45).

לְמִירִישׁוֹנֹה. In addition to dropping a quiescent *alef* and introducing a *yod* as a *mater lectionis* for an 'i' sound after the *resh* (cf. הרישון in 4Q219 II, 35), the fragment also places a *yod* as a *mater lectionis* for 'i' after the preposition -מְ. According to the Tiberian vocalization, an 'e' is expected here (cf. מֵרֵאשׁוֹן in Jer 17:12).[277]

והייתה להם לאב ולֹא[ל]וֹהים. This clause explicates the import of the divine ownership of Israel: from now on YHWH is their father and God. While a father-son relationship between God and his people is mentioned in several biblical passages, the scroll may again allude here to Jer 31: בעת ההיא אהיה לאלהים לכל משפחות ישראל ("At that time ... I will be God to all the clans of Israel, and they shall be my people," v. 1) and כי הייתי לישראל לאב ("For I am ever a father to Israel," v. 9). See Discussion.

3–4 בְּעמֵךְ [הֹמֹשׁלתה] ולא [מלכים] עזבתם בידי / [ולֹא. Given the preceding reference to a father-son relationship between God and Israel, it is unlikely that a depiction of the deity forsaking his people could follow; hence is the reconstruction [ולֹא] ... עזבתם / [ולֹא [הֹמֹשׁלתה. According to this reconstruction, God as Israel's father initially ruled over them directly (cf. 1 Sam 8:7; for the phrase עזב ביד see 2 Chr 12:5; the construction המשיל ב- occurs in Ps 8:7; see also frg. 38 8). Alternatively, the scroll may imply that although God appointed kings over Israel, he did not abandon them. Finally, a vocalization מַלְ(א)כִים, i.e., a plural of מַלְאָךְ, "angel," should be considered.[278] Such writings as 1 En 86–90 attest to the belief that God entrusted Israel into the hands of angelic beings.[279] However, Jub 15:30–32 and Sir 17:17 insist, as this fragment may also do, that while God appointed angels over all the nations, he did not do so for Israel, who is his own portion.[280]

---

277 Joüon-Muraoka, *Grammar*, 312.

278 See N. Mizrahi, "'Kings' or 'Messengers' in 1 Sam 11:1? The Linguistic Background of the Masoretic Text," *Textus* 25 (2010): 13–36 (Hebrew); M. Kister, "Ancient Material in Pirqe De-Rabbi Eli'ezer: Basilides, Qumran, The Book of Jubilees," in *"Go Out and Study the Land" (Judges 18:2): Archaeological, Historical and Textual Studies in Honor of Hanan Eshel* (ed. A. M. Maeir et al.; Leiden, Boston 2012), 85–86. My thanks are to Prof. Menahem Kister, who encouraged me to include this interpretation and drew my attention to these studies.

279 See D. Dimant, "Israel's Subjugation to the Gentiles as an Expression of Demonic Power in Qumran Documents and Related Literature," *RevQ* 22 (2006): 373–388.

280 See Kister, "Ancient Material in Pirqe De-Rabbi Eli'ezer," 71–78.

7 [עבדה֗] מושה ביד להם הנתתה מֹצֹוֹֹתֹיכה מֹ֗וֹ[ס].וֹ This line may warn of deviating from God's commandments, as is suggested by Qimron's restoration, וֹ[ס לבלתי מֹצֹוֹֹתֹיכה (cf. Deut 17:20). But, since line 8 depicts Israel's iniquity being "higher than the hea[d," it may well be that the scroll speaks here of the people's forsaking God's commands, as in Dan 9:5: חטאנו ועוינו והרשענו ומרדנו וסור ממצותך וממשפטיך ("We have sinned; we have gone astray; we have acted wickedly; we have been rebellious and have deviated from your commandments and your rules"). Therefore it is proposed to restore here וֹ[ס], an infinitive absolute of סור. Instead of the expected אשר נתתה (cf. Lev 26:46; Neh 10:30) or שנתתה (characteristic of late biblical Hebrew; cf. Ezra 8:20), the scroll reads הנתתה (for a similar usage of -ה, see 1 Chr 29:17).[281] The reconstruction מושה֗ [עבדכה] follows the frequent biblical idiom (e.g., Exod 14:31).

8 [מֹשֹׁפֹּטֹכה ועוון עמכה מעלה לרו]ש. The beginning of the line might have read כי מאסו/וימאסו ב[מֹשֹׁפֹּטֹכה (cf. Lev 26:43; Ezek 5:6, 20:16) or כי סרו/ויסורו מ[מֹשֹׁפֹּטֹכה (cf. Dan 9:5, alluded to in the previous line). The remaining part of the line appears to describe the results of forsaking God's judgment. For the expression עוון עמכה see Num 14:19; Ps 85:3. The reconstruction follows Ezra 9:6: כי עונתינו רבו למעלה ראש ("for our iniquities have risen higher than our heads," RSV; cf. מעלה / ועוונתינו רבו [נ]לראשי [4Q378 6 ii 5]).[282] For the use of ל-מעלה, instead of למעלה, compare 4Q403 1 i 28; 11Q5 XII, 12. The phonetic spelling לרו]ש (or לרו]אש) with a waw as a mater lectionis for 'o' occurs frequently in the scrolls.

9 וֹבֹֹאֹוֹרֹךְ אפיכה ורובסֹלֹיחֹתֹ[יכה. The speaker either pleads for God's forgiveness of Israel or refers to a past event when the divine long-suffering and abundant forgiveness became manifest (cf. Neh 9:17). For the wording compare ארך אפים עמו ורוב סליחות (CD II, 4; cf. רוב סליחה [1QHᵃ XIV, 12]). For writing without leaving a space between adjacent words see frgs. 9 6, 106 4 and more.

---

281 Joüon-Muraoka, *Grammar*, 504.
282 See Feldman, *Rewritten Joshua Scrolls*, 40, 42.

Frg. 105

On PAM 43.467 this fragment appears to consist of two fragments linked by a scrap of papyrus. This is how it is reproduced in the DJD edition (plate XLI). The two fragments appear separately on all other photographs, without the tiny scrap combining them. The right intercolumnar margin has been preserved.

[	]oo[]ooo	1
השיעו עיניהם[	לאֱלֹהִֿיֹםֿ]	2
[	מראות והשמֹנֹ]ו לבבם	3
[	ויבושו עמֹכֹ]ה	4
[	כול הארצ o]	5
[	וֹהֹחֹיֹות הֹ]oֹ	6
	א	
[	וברייה תה]	7
[	[ֹ]ooֹלֹ	8

Notes on Readings

3 והשמֹנֹ]ו. The DJD edition has וֹחֹשֹׁבֹ]o. However, Wacholder and Abegg (השמֹ]ם) correctly identify the first letter as a *he* and the third one as a medial *mem*. The last letter is difficult to decipher, yet the vertical and base strokes visible on PAM 43.467 suggest a medial *nun*.

6 וֹהֹחֹיֹות. Olyan offers no reading for the first letter. Wacholder and Abegg read it as a *waw*.

הֹ]oֹ. The DJD edition provides no reading here. The first two vertical strokes are most likely a *he*. A trace of a vertical stroke next to it is illegible.

Translation

2. to God[they sealed their eyes]
3. from seeing and [they]made [their heart] fat[   ]
4. and yo[ur] people will be ashamed[   ]
5. the entire earth .[   ]
6. the animals ..[   ]
7. and creation ..[   ]

Comments

3 השיעו עיניהם] / מראות והשמנ֗ו לבבם. This line seems to allude to Isa 6:10: השמן לב העם הזה ואזניו הכבד ועיניו השע פן יראה בעיניו ("Make the heart of this people fat, and their ears heavy, and shut their eyes; lest they see with their eyes, and hear with their ears").

והשמנ֗ו. The presence of the medial *nun* precludes reading והשמן here, as in Isa 6:10. The suggested reconstruction assumes a defective orthography of והשמ(י)נו.

4 ויבושו עמכֿ]ה. Apparently this is a 2nd person address. For the language compare Joel 2:26, 27.

7 ובריֿ֞ה תה]. Given the reference to וֿהֿחֿיֿ֞ות in the preceding line, בריֿ֞ה, "creation," might be understood as referring to all living creatures. The line could have read ובריֿ֞ה תה]לל.

Frg. 106

]◦ה ממש◦[	1
]תֿם תמיד ל֗[	2
]◦ל כול הי[מֿ֞ים ל◦[	3
]ה עלעמֿ֞ד]ו	4
]הֿ֞ארץ[	5

Notes on Readings

1]ה◦. There is a trace of ink before the *he* (unnoted by Olyan).

]◦ממש. Under the left stroke of the *shin* (PAM 43.467) there is a tiny trace of ink. Its location suggests that it is not a *lamed* (Olyan). Wacholder and Abegg suggest an *alef*.

2]ל תמיד תֿם[. This is Wacholder and Abegg's reading. The DJD edition has]גֿ֞ם[ ]◦ תמיד.

3]י[מֿ֞ים. This is Davis's reading. Olyan reads the first letter as a *resh*.

4]ו עלעמֿ֞ד. The editor reads]על ◦◦[. As Wacholder and Abegg correctly note, there are traces of a medial *mem* and a *dalet* next to the *ayin*. The two words are written without a separating space.

5 הֿארץ[. Olyan offers no reading for the first letter. On PAM 43.467 there are faint traces of two vertical strokes, perhaps a *he* (Wacholder and Abegg).

Translation
2.].. always .[
3. all the]days ..[
4.]. in [his] place[
5.]the earth[

Comments
3 כול הי[מים. The reconstruction echoes תמיד of the preceding line. Yet מים[, "water," is equally possible.

Frg. 107

]○חת ים[	1
אנו]חטֹ לבֹה ○[	2

Notes on Readings
The fragment may preserve an upper margin.

2 There is a trace of ink before לכה unnoted by the previous editions.

Translation
2.]. to you and [we have] sin[ned

Comments
Perhaps this fragment is a part of a prayer.

Frg. 108

אל[ו̇ה̇י יש̇]ראל

Notes on Readings

Olyan reads the first word as ○○ה̇○[. Here Davis's reading is followed.

Translation

G]od of Is[rael

Frg. 109

[○ב̇ והשאתה]

The editor reads the final letter as a medial *mem*. The vertical stroke projecting below the imaginary base line suits a final *nun* better (Davis).

Translation

]and you have lent .[

Frg. 110

] ○ ○[	1
אברכ]ה̇ בשמכ̇ה̇ ○○○○[	2
[ה̇יו̇ת̇ להם̇ כה○]	3

Notes on Readings

1 Olyan sees no traces of ink in line 1 (see PAM 41.988; 43.467).

2 ה̇[. The editor reads the first letter as a *waw*. The upper horizontal stroke visible on PAM 41.988; 43.467 better suits a *he* (Wacholder and Abegg).

3 להם̇. This is Wacholder and Abegg's reading. Olyan reads ל○○.

Translation

2. I will bles]s in your name ....[
3.   ] your [ ]. to them to be[

Comments

2 אברכ]ה בשמכה. This fragment could be a part of a prayer. The reconstruction (Wacholder and Abegg) follows a biblical idiom (e.g., Deut 10:8).

Frg. 111

] להחרׄיׄבׄ[	1
]ה להכרׄיׄת ׄ◦	2
]הׄרם מכול[	3
]◦ כחסדיכ]ה הטובים	4
]◦ת כי טוׄבׄ]יׄ[ם	5
ע]שה ואני נפל]לבי	6
] לאחרונה]◦[	7

Notes on Readings

1]להחרׄיׄבׄ. The editor reads להחרׄי]ם. Qimron reads a *bet* in the end of the line.

2]הׄ[. Olyan proposes no reading for the first letter. Davis plausibly suggests that this is a *he*.

3]הׄרם[. The DJD edition offers no reading for the first letter. On PAM 43.288 a vertical stroke curving to the left at its top, and a trace of an upper bar reminiscent of a *he* (or a *ḥet*) are visible.

5 טוׄבׄ]יׄ[ם. This is Qimron's reading. Olyan suggests טמא].

6 נפל]. The DJD edition has נפל]תי. However, on the photographs (e.g., PAM 41.988) a blank space follows the *lamed*, indicating that this is the last letter of the word.

Translation

1.   ] to destroy[
2.   ]. to cut off .[
3.   ]raise from all[
4.   according to you]r good[mercies] .[
5.   ].. for good (are)[
6.   (he) d]id. And, as for me, [my heart] failed [
7.   ]. lately[

Comments

1 ‏[להחרׄיֺב‏]. Qimron restores the line as ‏אמר אויב [להחרׄיֺב‏]. He suggests that this fragment contains a prayer by Hezekiah (cf. frg. 46) on the occasion of Sennacherib's invasion (cf. the use of a Hifil of ‏חרב‏ in 2 Kgs 19:17, 24).

3 ‏[הֹרם מכול‏]. Qimron restores ‏הֹרם מכול‏] מלך[. He suggests that this line describes the boastful attitude of Sennacherib (cf. 2 Kgs 19:22–23).

4 ‏כחסדיכ]ה הטובים‏. The adjective ‏הטובים‏ may point to such biblical phrases as ‏דבריך טובים‏ (2 Sam 15:3) or ‏משפטיך טובים‏ (Ps 119:39). The proposed restoration follows 4Q185 1–2 ii 1.

6 ‏ע]שה ואני נפל [לבי‏. The reconstruction ‏נפל [לבי‏ follows 1 Sam 17:32.

Frg. 112

1   לאין מר[פّׄא ולאיֹן]
2   ]‏vacat‏ ‏ובר‏o[
3   החט[אֹה והעוֹנ]ות
4   ]o ‏י[שראל ת‏

Notes on Readings

1 ‏ולאיֹן[‏. The editor reads ‏ולאי]ן‏. On PAM 43.467 there is a trace of ink below the line. Most likely this is a vertical stroke of a final *nun* (Wacholder and Abegg).

2 ‏ובר‏o[. Olyan sees no writing before the *bet*, yet there is a trace of a vertical stroke on PAM 42.500; 43.288.

3 החט[א̇ה. The editor offers no reading for a diagonal stroke visible on the fragment. Most likely this is a left stroke of an *alef*.

והעו̇נ̇]ו̇ת. The last letter is apparently a medial *nun* (Davis). Olyan offers no reading here.

Translation

1.   there is no heal]ing and no[
2.   ]... *vacat* [
3.   the s]in and the iniqui[ties
4.   I]srael ..[

Comments

1 לאין מר[פ̇א ולא̇י̇ן[. The reconstruction follows a biblical idiom (see, e.g., Pr 29:1). This phrase occurs also in frg. 39 5.

3 החט[א̇ה והעו̇נ̇]ו̇ת. Cf. Exod 34:7: נשא עון ופשע וחטאה.

Frg. 113: See Minute Fragments

Frg. 114

```
          ת̇ כיהרב]ה     1
       כאש]ר̇ דברת̇ה̇]    2
            ו̇מ̇י̇ם]      3
```

Notes on Readings

1 ת̇[. There is a trace of a base stroke as in a *taw* (Davis) in the beginning of the line (unnoticed by the editor).

2 כאש]ר̇. This is Wacholder and Abegg's reading. Olyan sees no trace of a letter before דברת̇ה.

דברת̇ה̇[. The DJD edition has דברת[ה. On PAM 43.467 there is a trace of a *yod* (Strugnell) or a *he* in the end of the line.

3 ו̇מ̇י̇ם[. The editor reads מ̇י̇ם[י̇. There is a trace of a hook-shaped top in the beginning of the line (PAM 43.476). Most likely it is a *waw* or a *yod*.

Translation

1.   ]. for many[
2. whe]n you spoke[
3.   ]and water?[

Comments

1 הרב]ה. The scribe left no space between the two words. One may read הרב]ה
as a Hifil *qatal* of רבה, "to multiply" (הרב]ה/ו/ית), or as a Hifil infinitive absolute of
the same root, הַרְבֵּה, "many." Cf. frg. 46 1.

Frg. 115

1   ת[ן כוחכה ל]ֹ

2   ולוא לסו[ר̇ מ̇ן דרך ה̇]חיים

3   [ו̇י̇שׁבֹו כ]ֹ o[

4   ]ooo[

Notes on Readings

1]ֹ. Olyan offered no reading for the trace of ink found in the end of the line, yet
it resembles the bottom part of a *lamed* (Davis).

2 לסו[ר̇. In the beginning of the line a vertical line and an upper bar consistent
with a *resh* appear (Wacholder and Abegg). The DJD edition offers no reading.

ה̇]חיים. The vertical stroke with a trace of an upper bar found in the end of the
line may well be a *he*. Olyan offers no reading.

3 ו̇י̇שׁבֹו. This is Wacholder and Abegg's reading. The editor suggests ה̇o[ ]וֹנֹו.

Translation

1.   giv]e your strength to[
2. and not to stra]y from the way of [life
3.   ]. and (they) will dwell ..[

Comments

1 ת[ן כוחכה ל]ֹ. This fragment is a prayer. The reconstruction follows a biblical
idiom (e.g., Deut 8:18).

2 חיי]ה דרך מן ר[סו לוא ולא. Given the wording of the preceding line, the restoration ולוא לסו]ר seems to be fitting. For the phrase דרך ה[חיים cf. Jer 21:8.

Frg. 116

]לרוב[	1
]ל להרבות[	2
]כה דע°[	3
]° ל[	4

Notes on Readings
1]לרוב[. The DJD edition reads]רוב[. On the photographs (PAM 43.289; 43.467) a bottom diagonal stroke of a *lamed* is visible (see the *lamed* in line 2).

3 ל[. This is Wacholder and Abegg's reading. The editor offers no reading here.

]להרבות. Olyan reads]°להרבי. Vertical and upper strokes in the end of the line can be read as a *taw*.

4]כה[. The DJD edition has]°ה. Wacholder and Abegg read the first letter as a medial *kaf*.

]°דע. The DJD edition offers no reading for the traces of these three letters. The first one is clearly a *dalet* (see PAM 43.289; 43.467). A diagonal vertical stroke next to it resembles an *ayin*.

Translation
1.]abundantly[
2.]. to multiply[

Frg. 117

]אתה[כ°י	1
]ם ואוכל[	2
]°°°[	3

Translation
1. si]nce you[
2.]. and food[

Frg. 118

בֿ בני אֿ]דם [1
הֿארץ לֿ] [2

Notes on Readings

1 There are traces of a *bet* in the beginning of the line (unnoted by the editor).

Translation

1.   ]. me[n
2.   ]the earth/land to[

Frg. 119

מֿן קֿ]∘[1
ועמכה] [2

Notes on Readings

1 Olyan reads]∘קֿ∘[. Before the *qof* there are traces of a medial *mem* and a final *nun*.

2] ועמכה [. The DJD edition has] ועמכה יֿ[. No traces of ink before the word ועמכה are extant on the fragment.

Translation

2.   ] and your people [

Frgs. 120–121: See Minute Fragments

Frg. 122

∘[כה ∘] [1
לנאֿצֿ]ו [2

Translation
1.   ]. thus.[
2.   ]to despise[him

Comments
2 For other occurences of נאץ in this scroll cf. frgs. 12 6; 47 4.

Frg. 123

[בהמות]

Notes on Readings
This is Davis's reading. The DJD edition has]טובות[.

Translation
]animals[

Comments
Alternatively, read בהמות, "hippopotamus" (cf. Job 40:15). Note the reference to "the animals" in frg. 105 6–7.

Frg. 124

[ο כי ο[1
[בּ תמיד]   2

Notes on Readings
1 The DJD edition has]כה ο[. There is a *yod* before the medial *kaf* (Davis). The last letter is illegible.

2]בּ תמיד[. This is the reading by Wacholder and Abegg. Olyan has]ο ביד ο[.

Translation
2.   ]always .[

Frg. 125

$$
\begin{array}{rl}
1 & \ ]\mathring{ה}[\\
2 & \ ]\mathring{דבר}[
\end{array}
$$

Translation

2.   ]spoke/word[

Frg. 126

]תֹוֹכחתכֹה[

Notes on Readings

This is Wacholder and Abegg's reading. The DJD edition has]וֹכחתכֹה[ת.

Translation

]your rebuke[

Comments

Apparently, this is another fragment containing the language of prayer. The same word occurs in frg. 50.

Frg. 127

$$
\begin{array}{rl}
1 & \ ]\circ \ כעם הזה \ \circ[\\
2 & \ ]\mathring{ותיהם} \ ו\mathring{נ}[\\
3 & \ ]ם מבעסים[\\
4 & \ ]\circ\circ[\ ]\mathring{ל}\circ[
\end{array}
$$

Notes on Readings

1 כעם ∘[. Olyan reads]∘כעֹם[. The trace of the first letter is at some distance from the medial *kaf*.

2]וֹתֹיהם. The editor reads]הֹ∘∘הם. The vertical stroke in the beginning of the line could be a *waw*. The trace of the second letter is more consistent with a *taw* than with a medial *nun* (on PAM 42.500 the vertical bar of a *taw* is clearly visible). The third letter is a *waw*/*yod*.

3]נֿוֿ. The DJD edition offers no reading for the second letter. A medial *nun* with its vertical and base strokes is visible on PAM 42.500; 43.288; 43.467 (Wacholder and Abegg).

מבעסים[. This is the reading of Wacholder and Abegg, except for the last letter, which they read as a medial *kaf*, while a final *mem* seems to suit the traces better. Olyan suggests מדע מיכֿ].

Translation
1.   ]. like this people .[
2.   ]their[ ]... and.[
3.   ]. provoking to anger[

Frg. 128

]ׄלֿמרוׄ[1

ם]ׄלֿגוים[2

Notes on Readings
1]ׄלֿמרוׄ[. Olyan reads]ׄגוׄרוׄ[. On the photographs (PAM 43.288; 43.467) a trace of a vertical stroke of a *lamed* is visible. The second letter is clearly a medial *mem*.

2 ם]ׄלֿגוים[. This is Davis's reading. Olyan suggests]גוׄיׄ[.

Translation
2.   ]to the nation[s

Frg. 129: See Minute Fragments

Frg. 130

[להוש]יֹע   1

וֹ[עָֿלֹוּ וּבָֿאֹ]וּ   2

Notes on Readings

1 [להוֹש]יֹע. This is Wacholder and Abegg's reading (cf. PAM 43.467). The DJD edition has [ת]שׁ°°[.

2 [עָֿלֹוּ וּבָֿא]וּ. The editor has [°ל יֹ וב]°[. On PAM 43.288; 43.467 the left and base strokes of an *ayin* are visible (Davis). The trace after the *bet* is difficult to read. The reading proposed here follows a biblical idiom.

Translation

1.   ]to sav[e
2.   and](they) went up and ca[me

Frg. 131

[בֹּשֹׁרֹ וֹ]   1

[אֱלֹ[וֹ]הִיכָֿהֹ]   2

Notes on Readings

1 [בֹּשֹׁרֹ ו]. Olyan reads [אֱשֹׁרֹ ו]. The left extremities of an upper bar and a base stroke are more consistent with a *bet*.

2 [אֱל[וֹ]הִיכָֿהֹ]. This is a reading by Wacholder and Abegg. The DJD edition has [אלו]הִיכָֿהֹ.

Translation

1.   ](he) announced and[
2.   ]your [G]od[

Comment

1 [בֹּשֹׁרֹ. This might be a Hifil *qatal* of בשר, "to announce," or a noun בֶּשָֹׁר, "flesh."

2 [אֱל[וֹ]הִיכָֿהֹ]. This fragment is a part of a 2nd person address.

Frg. 132

[לְעָיֵ֯ף]   1

[א֯תָ֯ ישראֵ֯ל]   2

Notes on Readings

1 לְעָיֵ֯ף[. The editor sees no trace of ink before the *ayin*. The traces are consistent with a *lamed* (PAM 43.288; 43.467).[283] He reads the third letter as a *waw*.

2 תָ֯[א. Olyan offers no reading of the first letter. Davis reads a *taw* (PAM 43.288).

Translation

1.   ]to a tired one [
2.   ]. Israel [

Comment

1 לְעָיֵ֯ף[. Cf. נתן ליעף כח (Isa 40:29).

Frgs. 133–134: See Minute Fragments

Frg. 135

[א֯ο הֹו֯א֯ οο[1

[שֹׁמֹו וימֹ֯ο[2

Notes on Readings

1]οο א֯הֹו֯א֯ ο[. Olyan reads]οοתָ֯ו֯ א֯οο[. The reading proposed here follows that of Davis.

Translation

1.   ].. he ..[
2.   ] his name ....[

---

283 The trace of a vertical stroke of a *lamed* appears on a tiny fragment attached to frg. 132 on the left. This placement is uncertain, for the shapes of the edges of the two fragments do not match.

Frgs. 136–137: See Minute Fragments

Frg. 138

]אֱלׄוׄהׄיׄם[

Translation
]God[

Frg. 139

]לׄהֹם יׄקׄ[

Notes on Readings
]יׄקׄ. Olyan offers no reading for the traces of ink after להם[. Wacholder and Abegg read a *yod* and a *qof*.

Translation
]to them ..[

Frg. 140

]מׄכׄוׄל יושׄבׄיׄ[

Translation
]from all the dwellers of[

Frg. 141

א[בותיהם ○[

Notes on Readings
This is Wacholder and Abegg's reading. Olyan reads ○ותיהם[.

Translation
]their [fa]thers .[

Frg. 142

]∘∘[	1
[אין מקוה]	2
[כול שבת]	3

Translation

2.   ]there is no hope[
3.   ]every Sabbath[

Comments

1]אין מקוה[. For this phrase cf. 1 Chr 29:15.

2]כול שבת[. Since the context is lost, it is unclear whether this line refers to the Sabbath, the fallow year or else.

Frg. 143

[ש ויציל אֹ]ת	1
]∘[ ]יֹ ∘[	2

Notes on Readings

1 אֹ]ת. Olyan reads ויצילוֹ[. The trace of the last letter, which is consistent with an *alef* is at some distance from the *lamed*.

Translation

1.   ]. and (he) will save t[he

Frg. 144

[הֹשֹ ∘[	1
[נפשֹ]	2
[בֹ]	3

Notes on Readings

1]שׁ̇ה. Olyan offers no reading for the last letter in this line. On PAM 43.290; 43.467 traces of two strokes of a *shin* are visible (Davis).

Translation

2.   ]a living being[

Frg. 145

] שׁופט ○[	1
]שׁ א̇ו̇[	2
]א̇○ם̇[	3
]○ת̇י○○ ה[	4

Notes on Readings

1 According to PAM 42.500 there is a trace of a letter before the word שׁופט and a blank space next to it (unnoted by the editor).

2 א̇ו̇[. Olyan offers no reading here. On PAM 42.500 a hook-shaped top of a *waw/yod* and an *alef* are visible.

3]○ת̇י○○ ה[. The DJD edition has]○מ̇י○ ○○[. On the photographs (PAM 42.500; 43.467) an upper part of a *he* is visible in the beginning of the line. Traces of two or three letters follow after an interval. What Olyan reads as a medial *mem* is a *taw* (see PAM 42.500).

Translation

1.   ]. a judge/judging[

Frg. 146

א̇[מתכה יש̇]מרו

Notes on Readings

Olyan offers no reading for the first letter. The horizontal stroke descending from right to left and a base stroke are consistent with a medial *mem*.

Translation

] (they) will ke[ep] your [t]ruth [

Comments

מרו]מֹתכה יש[א. The reconstruction follows Ps 146:6.

Frg. 147

[יכה כול]

Translation

]your[   ] all[

Frgs. 148–149: See Minute Fragments

Frg. 150

ב[הֹשלם בֹּ]ס

Notes on Readings

Olyan reads]ס יֹעֹלֹהֹ ס[. What he reads as a *yod* and an *ayin* is, in fact, a *shin* (Davis). Next to a *lamed* comes a final *mem* (the serif at the left end of its upper bar is visible on PAM 43.467). The first letter of the next word is consistent with a *bet*.

Translation

upon]completion ..[

Comments

ב[הֹשלם. This is apparently a Nifal infinitive of שלם, "to be complete" (cf. 1QS X, 6: בהשלם חוק תכונם).

Frg. 151

שׁק̇ ◦[ ]

Notes on Readings
Olyan offers no reading for the surviving traces of ink. The first two traces resemble a *shin* and a *qof*.

Translation
] a sack .[

Frg. 152: See Minute Fragments

Frg. 153

◦◦◦◦ עָרִים[ ]

Translation
].... cities[

Frg. 154

וְאֶפְרִים הוֹכִיח[ ]

This is Strugnell's reading.[284] Olyan reads]היביא◦◦◦◦◦[.

Translation
]and (he) rebuked Ephraim[

---

284 *Preliminary Concordance* 1:202.

Minute Fragments

Frg. 18

]וא [		1
]יד [		2

Frg. 19

]כֹש[		1
]ג [		2

Frg. 20

] עֹד [		1
]◦ליֹהֹ[		2

Notes on Readings
2]◦ ליֹהֹ[. Olyan reads]הֹיֹדֹ[ה. This fragment appears on PAM 43.464. The shape of the upper horizontal bar of the third letter is more consistent with a *he* than a *ḥet*. The fourth letter may indeed be a *dalet*. Wacholder and Abegg read]◦ ליֹה[א. Yet it is unclear whether the interval between the *he* and the last letter is large enough to be an interval between two consecutive words.

Translation
1   ] until [

Frg. 28

]◦ הם[		1
] ◦ש[		2

Translation
1.   ]they .[

Frg. 32

]◦ עﬥ ם[

Translation

]. on .[

Frg. 33

]◦יֿהֿ[1
]צֿחֿ[2

Translation

2.]shiny?[

Frg. 41

The fragment seems to preserve the left intercolumnar margin.

בֿ[1
בו[2
ו[3
בֿוֿ[4

Notes on Readings

1 בֿ[. The DJD edition offers no reading here. The long base stroke visible on the fragment most likely belongs to a *bet*.

4 בֿוֿ[. The traces of the first letter are consistent with a *bet*. Olyan suggests no reading.

Frg. 51

] טֿ◦[1
]מֿ[2
]ה[3

Frg. 52

]○[	1
]○○[	2
]○○[	3
]○○[	4
]○[	5
]ṁ[	6

Frg. 56

The fragment seems to preserve a right intercolumnar margin.

וממ]	1
צמ]	2
]°○○[	
]	3

Notes on Readings

1]וממ[. Olyan reads]ומט. According to PAM 43.466 the second letter is a medial *mem*, as is suggested by its diagonal stroke.

3 The traces of the letters transcribed by Olyan as line 3 are most likely an interlinear addition. He reads here]י [. There are traces of one or two letters before the *yod*.

Frg. 57

The fragment seems to preserve a trace of a preceding column (unnoticed by the editor) and an intercolumnar margin.

Col. ii		Col. i	
איש]	1		
יוכ]	2		
]ל[]○○	3	ל[	] 3

Notes on Readings

2 Olyan reads the last letter as a *yod*. The traces may also belong to a *bet*.

3 The editor offers no reading for this line (for either column).

Translation
1. man[

Frg. 58

ויֿת∘[1
]בכ [2

Notes on Readings
1 Olyan offers no reading for the first letter. According to PAM 43.466 this is a *waw* or a *yod*.

Frg. 60
The fragment most likely preserves a bottom margin.

]וֿכֿ[1
]יֿמ[2

Botto]m ma[rgin

Notes on Readings
1 Olyan offers no reading for the first letter. The vertical stroke with a hook-shaped top is a *waw* or a *yod* (PAM 43.466).

Frg. 61
The fragment may preserve a bottom margin.

] מֿ∘[

Frg. 63

]∘צ[

Notes on Readings
Olyan reads a *shin*. On PAM 43.466 a medial *ṣade* followed by a vertical stroke are visible.

Frg. 65

]יֳ [	1
]ֹם[	2

Frg. 66

]ובֹ ◦[	1
]כה[	2

Notes on Readings
1 Olyan reads]◦ה [. On PAM 43.466 an illegible trace of ink is visible. Next to it there is an interval, followed by a *waw/yod* and a *bet*.

Frg. 67

]רֹ יֹ◦[	1
]תכהֹ[	2
]◦◦[	3

Notes on Readings
1]רֹ יֹ◦]. The DJD edition reads] יֹ[. On PAM 43.466 an illegible trace of ink appears in the beginning of the line. Next comes a *waw/yod*. After an interval there is a *resh*, and not a *waw*, as is suggested by its concave upper bar.

Frg. 68

]תֹ[	1
]◦[	2
]◦[	3

Frg. 69

]◦◦[	1
]◦[	2
]◦[	3

Frg. 71
The fragment may preserve an upper margin.

]קִ֯[	1
]◦[	2

Frg. 72

]◦ו֯◦[	1
עֵ֯ל֯[	2

Translation
2.] on[

Frg. 73

]ה֯ [	1
]כ֯ [	2

Frg. 74

]ה ל֯◦[	1
]שׁ֯ ◦[	2
] ◦[	3
]וב֯[	4

Frg. 76

]קֻו֯◦[	1
]בכ֯[	2

Frg. 77
The fragment may preserve an upper margin.

]◦[	1
]עֻם[	2

Translation
2.]people/with[

Frg. 80

]יי [	1
]הֹ∘[	2
]יֹי [	3

Frg. 81

]∘[	1
]∘נות∘[	2
]∘ תה[	3

Frg. 83

]∘∘ל∘ב[	1
]למ∘ ∘[	2

2 Olyan reads]∘∘ כֹֹּל[. The concave upper bar of the first letter is characteristic of a *bet*. The second letter is illegible.

Frg. 84

]∘לֹ∘[

Frg. 85

]מֹנֹ[

Frg. 86

]ה מ∘[

Frg. 87

]בֹה[	1
]∘תֹ∘[	2
]∘[	3

Notes on Readings

1]בֹה[. Olyan reads the first letter as a medial *kaf*, yet the shape and the size indicate clearly that this is a *bet*.

2 The DJD edition has]o֯נ֯ת֯o[. What it reads as two letters seems to be one, a *taw* (see PAM 43.466).

Frg. 88
The fragment may preserve a top margin.

]o[	1
]ל֯[	2

Frg. 89

]oo[	1
]ה֯ו֯[	2
]oo[	3

Notes on Readings
2 The editor reads the first letter as an *alef*, yet on PAM 43.466 a vertical stroke with a hook-shaped top, as in *waw/yod*, is visible.

Frg. 90

]oo מד ו֯o[	1
]oo֯י֯ב֯מ ל֯[	2

Notes on Readings
1 Prior to the final *nun* there is a trace of another letter (absent from the DJD edition).

2 Olyan reads]מ֯כ֯ו֯ה֯[. The traces next to *yod* are illegible.

Frg. 91
The fragment may preserve a bottom margin.

]ת[

Frg. 92

]כ֯ז֯[

Frg. 93: See Appendix

Frg. 94
The fragment may contain a right inter-columnar margin.

]○	1
]הֹגֹ	2
]○○	3

Frg. 95
The fragment may preserve upper and right intercolumnar margins.

]○○	1
]○	2

Olyan assumes that there are five lines in this fragment, yet an inspection of the fragment and its photographs reveals traces of two lines only.

Frg. 97

]○[	1
]וֹשֹׁ[	2

Notes on Readings
There is a trace of ink above the *shin* (PAM 43.466; unnoted in the DJD edition).

Frg. 98: See Appendix

Frg. 99

]○[	1
]○עת[	2
]○○○[	3

Notes on Readings
There are traces of ink above and below]○עת[. These are the remains of lines 1 and 3 (unnoted by the editor).

Frg. 100

]∘∘[1

]בֿרֿ[2

Frg. 102

]∘[1

]כמו[2

]ה[3

Notes on Readings

2]כמו[. Olyan offers no reading for the first letter. On PAM 43.466 traces of a medial *kaf* are clearly visible.

Translation

2.   ]like[

Frg. 113

]ים מֿ∘[1

]פֿר כֿ[2

Notes on Readings

2]פֿר[. Olyan reads a medial *nun*, yet the shape of the top as visible on PAM 43.288; 43.467 is clearly that of a medial *pe* (Davis).

Frg. 120

]∘∘∘[1

]∘ ∘[2

Frg. 121

] הֿ[1

]∘רֿמֿ ∘[2

Notes on Readings

1 ‏הֿ[. Olyan sees no remains of ink besides those found in line 2. However on PAM 43.467 there are traces of a *he* in what seems to be line 1.

2]○מר ○[. The DJD edition reads]מֿרֿוֿ[. The reading of the last letter is difficult. There is a trace of an upper bar, which rules out Olyan's reading. Davis proposes a medial *pe*, yet this is also unsatisfactory.

Frg. 129

]תֿהֿ[	1
] מנ○[	2

Notes on Readings

2 מנ○[. Olyan reads]נֿמ[. According to PAM 43.288; 43.467 there is a trace of another letter before the medial *nun*. The last letter is clearly a final *mem*. Next to it there is a blank space (PAM 43.288), indicating that this is the last letter in this word.

Frg. 133

]○הֿ ויפ[	1
]○ב הֿ○[	2

Notes on Readings

1]○פיו. Olyan reads]וֿנֿפֿל[. The second letter has no base and thus can hardly be a medial *nun*. Perhaps it is a *waw* or a *yod*. The trace of the last letter is illegible.

2 ○ה[. The DJD edition has a *taw* in the beginning of the line, but the traces of ink are difficult to read.

Frg. 134

]○ מ○[

Frg. 136

]○מֿנו אֿוֿ[

Notes on Readings

מֹּגוּ[. The editor has ‏‎°ֹעׄי[. The diagonal and the base strokes visible in the beginning of the line belong most likely to a medial *mem* (PAM 43.290; 43.467).

אׄ‏°ֹ[. Olyan reads the final letter as a *resh*, but the reading is difficult.

Frg. 137

The fragment may preserve a left intercolumnar margin.

]‏הֹם‏°‏י[

Notes on Readings

Olyan assumes that there is an interval between the *yod* and the *he*, which is not supported by PAM 43.467.

Translation

]their   [

Frg. 148

]תח[

Olyan suggests] תוֹ°[. What he reads as two letters is, in fact, one letter, a *ḥet* (see PAM 43.467).

Frg. 149

[°כה וא°°°[

The traces of letters following the *alef* are illegible. Olyan suggests]°כה ואק°[.

Frg. 152

]ל ל°[

Discussion

One Literary Work or Several?
While accepting Strugnell's paleographic analysis, placing all the fragments studied above (except for frgs. 93, 98, 102 [see Appendix]) in one scroll, Olyan doubts the unity of the literary work emerging from 4Q382. Noting the generic diversity of its fragments, he concludes that this scroll contains at least two works. One is "a work recasting or quoting from the Elijah-Elisha stories in 1–2 Kings," while the "other fragments may be related to psalmic materials found elsewhere."[285] Two additional aspects of 4Q382 may strengthen Olyan's suggestion. First, there are very few (if any) verbal or thematic links between the fragments recasting 1–2 Kings and those containing speeches and prayers. Second, a closer look at the two fragments preserving superscriptions reminiscent of the Masoretic psalms (frgs. 15 and 46) suggests that the lines preceding the superscriptions also contain rhetorical materials. Frg. 15 1–4 features a 2nd person address, perhaps of a hortatory nature, whereas frg. 46 1–3 includes 1st and 2nd person speech. Thus, it appears that the two psalm-like compositions supplied with the superscriptions are not enclosed by a rewritten narrative, but are rather woven into a fabric of non-scriptural rhetorical embellishments.

While the concerns with 4Q382's literary unity should not be quickly dismissed, they ought to be weighed with other contemporaneous rewritten Scripture works. Indeed, this scroll contains diverse materials, including rewritten narrative from the Elijah-Elisha cycle, non-scriptural prayers, speeches, and even a fragment dealing with eschatological events. However, a similar "mix" of diverse materials is found in many rewritten Scripture texts. For instance, the scroll 4Q522, one of the Dead Sea Scrolls rewriting the book of Joshua, features, along with a reworked narrative, a non-scriptural 1st person address by Joshua, and Ps 122 with a superscription ascribing this psalm to David.[286] The absence of verbal and thematic links between the fragments recasting the Elijah-Elisha cycle and those with rhetorical content can be a result of the scroll's poor state of preservation. In fact, the attribution of one of those non-scriptural prayers to King Hezekiah (frg. 46) lends some support to the idea that other prayers and speeches found in this scroll might have also been put in the mouths of figures from Samuel-Kings. Finally, sequences of rhetorical materials, such as those exhibited in frgs. 15 and 46, are found in other rewritings, e.g., in LAB, which features multiple rhetorical expansions, including speeches, prayers, liturgy, and eschatology

---

285 Olyan, DJD 13:363.
286 See Feldman, *Rewritten Joshua Scrolls*, 151–152.

(cf. chapters 59–60 incorporating in its reworking of 1 Sam 16 two non-Masoretic psalms). Thus, while the highly fragmentary state of 4Q382 precludes any certain conclusions, it seems that in its present condition this scroll is best described as a single composition rewriting 1–2 Kings or, given the textual overlap with 4Q160, both Samuel and Kings (see Chapter 6).[287]

Scriptural Exegesis in 4Q382
If this assessment of 4Q382 is correct, this composition employs a variety of rewriting techniques, ranging from small modifications of the scriptural text to extensive embellishments thereof. In this way, its best preserved fragments concerned with figures and events from 1–2 Kings, frgs. 1+3, 9, and 11, feature a familiar fabric of quotations from 1 Kgs 18 and 2 Kgs 2 interspersed with a variety of additions, small and large. Frgs. 1+3, evoking Obadiah's hiding of the prophets, seems to refer to his fear of Jezebel and Ahab. Clearly, the queen is mentioned here first because, according to the biblical story, she was the main instigator of the persecution of the prophets and hence the primary object of Obadiah's distress. Frgs. 5 and 9 list names absent from the Elijah-Elisha cycle, which may reflect the well-attested tendency of the rewritten Scripture to name figures left anonymous in the biblical story. Expanding on the scriptural account of Elijah's ascent, frg. 9 introduces the phrase "and trustworthy is what has been decreed" (line 2). It seems to present the unfolding events as a part of the divine plan, perhaps responding, to the question left unanswered by 2 Kings, i.e., how did Elisha and the sons of the prophets, first in Bethel and then in Jericho, know of Elijah's being taking away? Another intriguing addition to the scroll's version of the latter's departure is the phrase "anyone who goes down into sil[ence" (frg. 9 10), alluding to Ps 115:117, "The dead cannot praise the Lord, nor any who go down into silence." Early Jewish writings reflect several views on the nature of Elijah's disappearance. In the Animal Apocalypse, Elijah is taken to "a high place," where Enoch dwells (1 En 89:51–52).[288] This "high place" stands for Paradise, located, according to the Enochic geography (shared also by 1QapGen II, 23 and Jub 4:23–26), at the northeast edge of the world.[289] In Philo's view, Elijah, following in the steps of

---

287 See also the arguments for 4Q382's literary unity marshalled by Davis, "Elijah," 11–16, though his classification of this work (which he compares to 4Q252) as a "periphrastic pesher" is questionable.
288 Cf. 1 Enoch 93:8, which states simply that during the sixth week "a man will ascend."
289 P. Tiller, *A Commentary on the Animal Apocalypse of 1 Enoch* (Atlanta, Georgia: Scholars Press, 1993), 249–250; G. W.E. Nickelsburg, *1 Enoch. A Commentary on the Book of 1 Enoch. Chapters 1–36; 81–108* (Hermeneia; Augsburg, Minneapolis: Fortress Press, 2001), 374, 544–45; D. Olson, *A New Reading of the Animal Apocalypse of 1 Enoch* (SVTP 24; Leiden: Brill, 2013), 157.

Enoch and Moses, ascends "on high from earth to heaven at the appearance of the divine countenance" (*QG* 1.86). Josephus's description of Elijah's departure is both succinct and vague: "Elijah disappeared from among men, and to this day no one knows his end … However, concerning Elijah and Enoch, who lived before the Flood, it is written in the sacred books that they became invisible, and no one knows of their death" (*Ant.* 9.28).[290] According to Pseudo-Philo, Elijah, who is none other than Phineas, was "raised up to the place where those who were before were raised up" (LAB 48:1).[291] Finally, 4 Ezra 6:26 places Elijah among those who "were taken up, who from their birth have not tasted death."[292] In light of these texts, the scroll's wording, broken as it is, seems to be yet another attestation of the belief in Elijah's continuous existence after his ascent.[293]

One of the larger embellishments found in 4Q382 is a description of eschatological events in frg. 31. Perhaps put into the mouth of one of the scriptural figures, it envisions an appearance of "the man of wond[er" which will take place "at the end." Although there are no verbal links between this fragment and the prophecy from Mal 3:23–24 (4:5–6), several scholars suggest that the scroll speaks here of Elijah's future return.[294] References to the future coming of Elijah are found in

---

On the location of Paradise in Second Temple writings, see P. S. Alexander, "Geography and the Bible (Early Jewish Geography)," *ABD* 2:977–88.

290 The English translation of Josephus's writings is quoted from the LCL edition. On this passage see further J. D. Tabor, "'Returning to the Divinity': Josephus's Portrayal of the Disappearances of Enoch, Elijah, and Moses," *JBL* 108 (1989): 225–238; L. H. Feldman, "Elijah," in idem, *Studies in Josephus' Rewritten Bible* (Leiden: Brill, 1998), 301–302; C. T. Begg, "Josephus' Portrayal of the Disappearances of Enoch, Elijah, and Moses': Some Observations," *JBL* 109 (1990): 691–693.

291 R. Hayward, "Phinehas-The Same as Elijah: The Origins of a Rabbinic Tradition," *JJS* 29 (1978): 22–34.

292 M. E. Stone, *Fourth Ezra* (Hermeneia; Minneapolis: Fortress Press, 1990), 172.

293 See further Davis, "Elijah," 105–106. Frg. 6 4 may also have a bearing on reconstructing 4Q382's view of Elijah's ascent. It reads, perhaps with reference to Elijah, "he we]nt up to the cloud[s (לשׁחק[ים])." The use of the Hebrew שחקים, standing for both "clouds" and "heaven," instead of שמים, as in 2 Kgs 2:1, 11, might be more than a stylistic preference. Some Second Temple sources seem to reflect an uneasiness with the notion of Elijah being taken to heaven, i.e., to God's presence. Thus the LXX 2 Kgs 2:1, 11 renders השמים as ὡς εἰς τὸν οὐρανόν ("as into heaven"; thus reads also 1 Macc 2:58; cf. Targum ad loc.: שמיא לציח, "toward the heaven"). Ben Sira 48:9 says that Elijah was taken מעלה, "up." Ginzberg, *Legends*, 999, observes that, while most of the rabbinic traditions assume that Elijah continues his existence in heaven or in Paradise (though the distinction between the two is blurred), there is also an opinion of R. Jose that neither Moses (when on Sinai) nor Elijah ascended to heaven (Mek. Baḥodesh 4 [ed. Horovitz-Rabin, 217]; b. Sukkah 5a).

294 Wise et al., *Dead Sea Scrolls*, 439; Davis, "Elijah," 163.

several Second Temple writings (e.g., 4Q558 51 4;[295] 4Q521 2 iii 2;[296] 1 En 90:31;[297] LAB 48:1; 4 Ezra 6:26).[298] Yet perhaps most relevant to this discussion is Ben Sira's description of Elijah's return in his Praise of the Fathers (48:9–11). According to him, Elijah, "who was recorded ready for the times," will return "to calm anger before wrath ... and to restore the tribes of Jacob (thus NETS rendering of Greek: καὶ καταστῆσαι φυλὰς Ιακωβ; Heb: ל[בטי ישרא]בטי ש[ולהבין] ש)." In frg. 31 the description of the appearance of "the man of wond[er" "at the end" is preceded and followed by references to Israel's being delivered into the hand of the nations, and to its dispersion. Still, given the paucity of the evidence, the identification of "the man of wond[er" with Elijah must remain a hypothetical one.

Of the many fragments containing liturgical embellishments, the best preserved one is the prayer in frg. 104 ii (parallel: 4Q160 2+6+10). Its beginning and end are lost. As a result, the identity of the speaker is unknown. The subject of the prayer is the people of Israel. It alludes to several biblical passages and deals with such topics as God's requirements for His chosen people (lines 1–2a), divine justice (line 2b), the election of Israel (line 3a), the father-son relationship between YHWH and Israel (line 3b), God's care for his people (lines 3c-4), abandonment of the commandments (line 7) and sin (line 8), and God's patience with Israel and readiness to forgive (line 9). These motifs are not unique to this prayer.[299]

---

295 É. Puech, DJD 27:216.
296 Of the voluminous bibliography on this scroll, see J. J. Collins, "The Works of the Messiah," DSD 1 (1994): 98–112; Å. Justnes, The Time of Salvation (Frankfurt: Peter Lang, 2009), 179–280.
297 The passage reads: "before the judgment took place" (Nickelsburg, Enoch, 1:402). Tiller, Apocalypse, 377, 379; Nickelsburg, ibid., 405, contend that the reference to the judgment is a textual corruption, a scribal gloss, or a misplacement of a verse. Olson, New Reading, 225–226, renders the verse differently: "unrelated to the judgment that had taken place." Less plausible is the suggestion of R. Nir, "The Appearance of Elijah and Enoch 'Before the Judgment Was Held' (1 Enoch 90:31): A Christian Tradition?" Henoch 33 (2011): 108–112, who argues that the entire notion of Elijah and Enoch's appearance is of Christian origin, and that the reference to the judgment should be viewed in light of the Christian tradition of these two appearing before the destruction of the Antichrist. On the traditions linking Enoch with Elijah, see M. Black, "The 'Two Witnesses' of Rev. 11:3 f. in Jewish and Christian Apocalyptic Tradition," in Donum Gentilicium (ed. E. Bammel et al.; Oxford: Clarendon Press, 1978), 227–237.
298 See further M. Öhler, Elia im Neuen Testament (BZNW 88; Berlin: de Gruyter, 1997); B. J. Shaver, "The Prophet Elijah in the Literature of the Second Temple Period: The Growth of a Tradition" (Ph.D. diss., University of Chicago, 2001).
299 For the motifs of election and divine justice in the liturgical texts from Qumran, see E. Chazon, "A Liturgical Document from Qumran and Its Implications (4QDibHam)" (PhD diss., Hebrew University, 1991), 105–106 (Hebrew); idem, "Tradition and Innovation in Sectarian Religious Poetry," in Prayer and Poetry in the Dead Sea Scrolls and Related Literature (STDJ 98; Leiden, Boston: Brill, 2012), 55–67. For references to the events of Israel's past in the Words of the Luminaries

Thus, several liturgical texts found among the Dead Sea Scrolls refer to a father-son relationship between God and His people. In these texts the notions of Israel being God's firstborn son and the divine discipline of his firstborn by means of the Torah intertwine (see 4Q369 1 ii 6, 10; 4Q504 XVI, 5–8).[300] It seems that the prayer in 4Q382 104 ii exhibits a variation on the same motif. While it does not refer to Israel as God's firstborn, it depicts God as Israel's father and highlights his loyalty to the people. Perhaps these serve as grounds for a plea for forgiveness, which, although not extant in the remaining text of the prayer, is implied in the confession of sins in line 8 and the mention of God's mercy in line 9. In addition to the links to the liturgy found at Qumran, the list of requirements from Israel in lines 1–2 displays an affinity with Jubilees 1:23–25, elaborating on what God will do once Israel repents and returns to Him. According to this passage, He will circumcise the foreskin of their hearts, create for them a new spirit, and purify them. As a result the people of Israel will observe God's commandments, and he will be their father and they will be his sons.[301]

Appendix: Unidentified Fragments

Frg. 93
The fragment preserves a right intercolumnar margin.

]○	1
]○	2

Notes on Readings
Olyan assumes that this fragment has 4 lines. The large interlinear spaces, which he counts as containing two lines each, may suggest that it belongs to another scroll, though the possibility that interlinear spaces in different sheets of papyrus comprising 4Q382 might have varied cannot be ruled out.

---

and in later Jewish prayer, see B. Nitzan, *Qumran Prayer and Religious Poetry* (STDJ 12; Leiden: Brill, 1994), 89–116.

300 See J. Kugel, "4Q369 "Prayer of Enosh" and Ancient Biblical Interpretation," *DSD* 5 (1999): 119–131.

301 As Prof. Kister pointed out to me in private communication. On this passage see further M. Kister, "Body and Sin: Romans and Colossians in Light of Qumranic and Rabbinic Texts," in *The Dead Sea Scrolls and Pauline Literature* (ed. J.-S. Rey; Leiden, Boston: Brill, 2014), 185–187.

Frg. 98

Olyan suggests that this fragment belongs to another scroll, since the hand is different (note especially the long upper stroke of *dalet*). The fragment seems to preserve a bottom margin.

```
1        ]○ בֿ[
         ]○ ׳ק]ו[חו
2        ]○ ודֹהֹ[
```

Notes on Readings

1 Olyan suggests that the last letter in this line is a *he*, yet the trace of ink is illegible.

2 What Olyan considers to be line 2 seems to be an interlinear addition. The DJD edition reads it as]קֹוֹשֹׁ[. On PAM 43.466 next to a *qof* a vertical stroke curving downwards at the top is visible. This is apparently a *waw* or a *yod*. Next to it a *waw/yod* is visible. Following, after a space, is a trace of ink unnoted by the editor

Translation

```
1    ].  .[
        ]his[ la]ws .[
2    ]give thanks .[
```

Frg. 103

Olyan suggests that this fragment does not belong to this scroll. Indeed, the shape of the *ayin* here differs from that of the *ayin* letters in the scroll.

```
1        ]○[
2        ]וע[
```

Olyan offers no reading for line 2. Yet on PAM 43.466 there are an *ayin* and a vertical stroke, perhaps a *waw*.

Chapter 4: 4Q481a

The scroll 4Q481a survives in three fragments. They are written in a late Has-monean hand with some features characteristic of Herodian script, and dated to 50–1 BCE.[302]

All the extant fragments of 4Q481a seem to deal with the aftermath of Eli-jah's ascent (2 Kgs 2). Frgs. 1 and 2 quote and paraphrase 2 Kgs 2:14–16, whereas frg. 3 may contain Elisha's lament for Elijah. Trebolle Barrera edited this scroll as 4QApocryphe d'Elisée.[303] A new edition of 4Q382 has been recently published by Qimron.[304]

Text and Commentary

Frg. 1

Top margin

1	וי[בְּקש לו להבֹּוֹת]
	וֹי°[
2	]°ֹל°° יֹ°[

Notes on Readings

1 [וי]בֹּקש. The DJD edition reads °שׂעו[. The upper bar of a *bet*, the top of a *qof*, and a *shin* are visible on PAM 43.174.

להבֹּוֹת[. The editor reads להנא[. Traces of a medial *kaf* (or a *bet*), followed by a *waw/yod* are visible on PAM 43.174. A trace of a vertical stroke next to the *waw* is consistent with the right vertical stroke of a *taw*.

2]°ֹל°° יֹ°[ ]°ֹי°. Traces of several letters, including a *lamed* and a *waw*, as well as an interlinear addition beginning with a *waw* and a *yod*, are visible on PAM 43.174 (unnoticed by the editor).

---

302 J. Trebolle Barrera, "Histoire du texte des livres historiques et histoire de la composition et de la rédaction deutéronomistes avec une publication préliminaire de 4Q481a, 'Apocryphe d'Elisée'," in *Congress Volume: Paris 1992* (ed. J. A. Emerton; VTSup 56; Leiden: Brill, 1995), 327–342; idem, DJD 22:305–309. See also his entries on "Elijah" and "Elisha" in EDSS, 1: 246–247.
303 Translated as "An Elisha Apocryphon" in Vermes, *The Complete Dead Sea Scrolls*, 590.
304 Qimron, *Hebrew Writings*, 3:221–222. He notes that frg. 1 contains a quotation from Isa 40:10–21 and therefore does not belong to this scroll. Qimron does not provide the text of the fragment or any further evidence corroborating this suggestion.

Translation

1   and](he) wanted to strike[

Comments

1 ‏יٜ[בֱ֖קש לו להֿבּ֑וֿתֿ]. This might be an allusion to the striking of the waters of the Jordan by either Elijah or Elisha (2 Kgs 2:8, 14; for the *dativus commodi*, ‏בֱּקש לו, cf. Isa 40:20).[305] If the fragment indeed refers to 2 Kgs 2:14, its wording may reflect an attempt to explain the double reference to Elisha's striking of the Jordan:

> ‏ויקח את אדרת אליהו אשר נפלה מעליו **ויכה את המים** ויאמר איה יהוה אלהי אליהו אף הוא **ויכה את המים**
> ‏ויחצו הנה והנה ויעבר אלישע
>
> Taking the mantle which had dropped from Elijah, **he struck the water** and said, "Where is the Lord, the God of Elijah?" As he also **struck the water**, it parted to the right and to the left, and Elisha crossed over.

The Greek adds after the first reference to the striking of the water καὶ οὐ διέστη ("and [they] did not part"). The Peshitta omits the clause ‏ויקח את אדרת אליהו אשר ‏נפלה מעליו ויכה את המים. With these in mind, the scroll's ‏וי[בֱּקש לו להֿבּ֑וֿתֿ] can be read as suggesting that the first striking is to be understood as merely an intent to do so, and not as the act itself.

Frg. 2

This fragment contains the left inter-columnar and bottom margins.

‏[יא כֿי	]1
‏אליֿ[שע	]2
‏[יעל אלישע ויראו	]3
‏[ס[	]4
‏עֱ[ויבאו לקרת	]4
‏[חמשים אנשים	]5
‏ה[הֿרٜ]ים	]6

Notes on Readings

4 On the photographs (especially on PAM 43.174) there is a vertical stroke above (and slightly to the right of) the *waw* of ‏ויבא (unnoticed in the DJD edition).

---

305 On *dativus commodi*, see Joüon-Muraoka, *Grammar*, 459.

Reconstruction with 2Kgs 2:14–16

[כי א'י   ] 1

[אלי'[שע ¹⁴ויואמר   ] 2

3 [איה יהוה אלהי אליהו אף הוא ויכה את המים ויחצו הנה והנה   ¹⁵וירא ו[יעל° אלישע

]○[

4 [אותו בני הנביאים אשר ביריחו מנגד ויואמרו נחה רוח אליהו על אליש[עֹ ויבאו לקרת

5 [אלישע וישתחוו לו ארצה ¹⁶ויואמרו אליו הנה נא יש עבדיך   חמשים אנשים[

6 [בני חיל ילכו נא ויבקשו את אדניך פן נשאו רוח יהוה וישלכהו באחד ה[הֹהֹ]ים או באחת]

Bottom margin

Translation

1. [   ].. for
2. [and Eli]sha [said,]
3. ["Where is YHWH, the God of Elijah?" As he too struck the water, it parted to the one side and to the other   and]Elisha [ca]me up.
4. [And the sons of the prophets at Jericho saw him over against (them) and they said, "The spirit of Elijah settled on Elish]a." And (they) came to meet
5. [Elisha and bowed low before him to the ground. And they said to him, "Behold now, your servants have   ]fifty
6. [able]men [with them. Let them go and look for your master; perhaps the spirit of YHWH has carried him off and cast him upon some mo]unt[ain or into some]

Comments

כי א'י[. As the editor observes, the wording of this line, absent from the extant versions of 2 Kgs 2, suggests that the fragment both quotes from the scriptural account and expands on it.

2–6 While it seems to be quite plausible that lines 2–6 quote 2 Kgs 2:14–16, the length of the lacunae in lines 3 and 5 indicate that the scroll contains a longer text than the one found in the MT, or those reflected in the ancient translations. Indeed, perusal of the extant text indicates that it contains three instances of a slightly longer text:

2 Kgs 2:14 (2) ויואמר אלי'[שע] ויאמר M

2 Kgs 2:14 (3) ו[יעל°] ויעבר M

M ויראהו [ויראו / אותו] (3) 2 Kgs 2:15

M לקראתו [לקרת / אלישע] (4) 2 Kgs 2:15

If frg. 11 indeed deals with 2 Kgs 2:14a, then frgs. 1 and 2 must have been located in close proximity to each other in the original scroll. Since frg. 1 preserves an upper margin and frg. 2 contains a bottom margin, one might suggest that this scroll had a relatively small writing block, perhaps of some 6–7 lines.[306] The physical data from frg. 3, partial as it is, may lead to the same conclusion.

Frg. 3

The fragment preserves the left inter-columnar and the bottom margins. It may also contain the upper margin.

[והוא ןֿ	] 1
[לנגדו	] 2
[בקינה ויואמר	] 3
א[ב ואדון ולוא	] 4
[שא ביהודה	] 5

Bottom margin

Notes on Readings

3 The editor reads a final *kaf* in the beginning of the line, yet the photographs leave it unclear whether there is a trace of a letter.

ויואמר. The DJD edition has וייאמר. *Waw* and *yod* are quite similar in this scroll. While the form וייאמרו (with a double *yod*) is otherwise unattested in the Dead Sea Scrolls, the proposed reading is frequent in these texts.

4 ב[. The DJD edition reads רֿב[. There are no traces of a *resh* on the extant photographs of the fragment.

---

306 The data pertaining to the Qumran scrolls with a small writing block are provided in Tov, *Scribal Practices*, 84–86.

Translation

1. [   ]. and he
2. [   ] before him
3. [   ] with the lament and said
4. [a fath]er and a master, and not
5. [   ].. in Judah

Comments

3 בקינה ויאמר [. The scroll might have read ויפתח] בקינה ויאמר (cf. Ps 78:2). The next line seems to indicate that the speaker is Elisha.

4 א[ב ואדון ולוא. The appellation א[ב ואדון may refer to Elijah. In 2 Kgs 2:12 Elisha addresses Elijah as אבי אבי. In the same chapter Elijah is several times referred to as Elisha's master (vv. 3, 5).

5 שא[ביהודה. The first word can be restored as a form of נשא, e.g., שא[נ, a 3ʳᵈ masc. sg. *qatal* in Nifal, "was taken," perhaps as a reference to Elijah's ascent (thus Trebolle Barrera). However, it may also be restored as a noun משא, "pronounce-ment," e.g., as a reference to Elijah's (or Elisha's) prophetic message. Hence the possible reconstruction: אשא/ישאו עליד/עליו מ[שא ביהודה.[307] In either case, the mention of Judah is somewhat puzzling, as in the biblical account Elijah (and Elisha) were active in the Northern Kingdom of Israel. One exception is the letter from Elijah to Jehoram, king of Judah, which arrives after the prophet's ascent (2 Chr 21:12–15).

---

307 HALOT, 639–640.

Chapter 5: 6Q9

The Manuscript
The scroll 6Q9 is preserved in some 72 fragments of papyrus. Based on paleo-graphic analysis, it is dated to the first half of the first century BCE. The attribu-tion of frgs. 67–72 to this scroll is uncertain.[308]

Contents
Two fragments of 6Q9 explicitly mention David, though the context is unclear (frgs. 22, 58). The king's visit to the King of Moab seems to be alluded to in frg. 33. Several fragments appear to rework 1 Sam 4 (frg. 32) and 17 (frgs. 26 and 30). Ref-erences to the exile (1, 2, 4?) lend some support to Baillet's assumption that this scroll deals with both Samuel and Kings, as indicated by the title he gave to 6Q9, "Un apocryphe de Samuel-Rois."[309] However, the extant text of the scroll yields no explicit references to figures and events from 1–2 Kings.

A number of fragments preserve a narrative (1, 2, 22?, 26, 29, 30–33, 44 i, 53, 57, 58). Among them are the fragments dealing with figures and events from Samuel. But there are also fragments that contain speeches (frgs. 21, 24, 27, 56, 59).

Editions of 6Q9
This fragmentary scroll has drawn very little scholarly attention. Qimron has recently re-edited ten fragments of 6Q9.[310] Still, the present study appears to be the first comprehensive attempt to revisit Baillet's *editio princeps*. For the reader's convenience most of the minute fragments of 6Q9 are presented last.

Text and Commentary

Frg. 1

אֿחת עשרא] [	1
וֹמה עד הגֹול]ה[	2

---

308 M. Baillet, DJD 3:119.
309 This scroll is frequently referred to as 6Qpap apocrSam-Kgs (e.g., García Martínez and Tig-chelaar, *Study Edition*, 2:1148; E. Tov, DJD 39:76).
310 Qimron, *Hebrew Writings*, 3:240–241. His readings and reconstructions are acknowledged below.

Translation
1.   ]eleven [
2.   ].... until the exil[e

Comments
1 אָ֯חת עשרא[. This might be a chronological note. The scroll's orthography, עשרא, reflects a weakening of the gutturals. Cf.]וגבורא in frg. 45 2.

2 עד הגולֹ]ה. The construction עד הגולֹ]ה occurs in 1 Chr 5:22: וישבו תחתיהם עד הגלה ("and they dwelt in their place until the exile").

Frg. 2

]○ ○[	1
]○צ ל רֹ[	2
]וֹהגלםֹ[	3
]ֹל[	4

Notes on Readings
2]○צל. Perhaps read לצי֯]ון.

3]וֹהגלםֹ[. The DJD edition offers no reading for the last letter. The vertical stroke projecting below the imaginary base line may belong to a final *mem*.

Translation
3.   ]and he exiled them[

Comments
3]וֹהגלםֹ[. The fragment may refer to the Assyrian and/or Babylonian exiles. This would confirm the editor's assumption that 6Q9 dealt with events related in both Samuel and Kings.

Frg. 3

]∘∘[1
[ע שכה]   2
]∘∘∘∘[3

Comments

2 שכה[. The extant letters can be variously read and reconstructed. In light of frg. 30, which paraphrases 1 Sam 17:52, a reading (with 1 Sam 17:1) of שכה as the toponym Socoh needs to be considered.

Frg. 4

י[בשבֿ]

Translation

]in captivit[y

Comments

With frgs. 1–2 in mind, the surviving three letters are restored here as referring to captivity (see, e.g., Jer 22:22).

Frgs. 5–14: See Minute Fragments

Frg. 15

[ב שילו]

Translation

]Shiloh in[

Comments

שילו[. While the remaining letters can be read as the toponym Shiloh (spelled as שלה and שילו in the MT; for the latter spelling see, e.g., Judg 21:21; 1 Sam 1:24), such reconstructions as המ[שילו (4Q301 3a–b 6) or הכ[שילו are equally possible.

Frg. 16: See Minute Fragments

Frg. 17

1   [עֲוֹ̇ן ∘∘]

2   [ודמו]

Translation
1.]iniquity [
2.]and his blood[

Frg. 18: See Minute Fragments

Frg. 19

1   [ ] [∘]

2   [הי̇ד̇]

Notes on Readings

2]הי̇ד̇[. The DJD edition reads the first letter as a *ḥet*, but offers no reading for the next two letters. According to PAM 42.942, the first letter is a *he*, which is followed by a *yod* and a *dalet*.

Translation

2]the hand[

Frg. 20: See Minute Fragments

Frg. 21

1   לשמו]עֲ בקולו ול]שמור את כל מצוותיו

2   לעשות [משפטו צ̇]דקה

3   ס]פ̇ר התור]ה

Notes on Readings

2 משפטוצ[דקה. The DJD edition reads]○ משפט[. The traces of the last letter as visible on PAM 42.944 may well belong to a medial *ṣade*. Hence, the reading suggested by García Martínez and Tigchelaar is followed here.[311]

Translation

1. to obe]y his voice and to[keep all his commandments
2. to do]justice and righteousness[
3. the bo]ok of the Tor[ah

Comments

1–2 לשמו[ע בקולו ול]שמור את כל מצוותיו. The reconstruction follows the recurring Deuteronomistic phraseology (e.g., Deut 13:19).

2 משפטוצ[דקה לעשות. For the proposed reconstruction compare, for instance, 2 Sam 8:15 (with reference to David) and 1 Kgs 10:9 (with reference to Solomon). The scribe left no blank space between the nouns משפט and וצדקה. Cf. frg. 26.

3 ס[פֿר התור]ה. This expression occurs several times in the Hebrew Bible, notably in 2 Kgs 22:8, 11 (relating the finding of the book of the Law in the days of King Josiah). Perhaps a form of כתב, e.g., ב- כבתוב, should be restored in the beginning of the line in accordance with the frequent biblical usage (cf. 2 Kgs 23:21).

Frg. 22

י עלי[ו]	1
[בכל דבֿ]רי	2
]בֿ ○[	3
[דוידֿ]	4
[עלי[ו]	5
[○○]	6

---

311 García Martínez, Tigchelaar, *Study Edition*, 2:1148.

Notes on Readings

1]עלי. The DJD edition offers no reading for the last letter. On the photographs a vertical stroke with a hook, as in a *waw* or a *yod*, is visible.

2 דּב[רי. The editor suggests no reading for the second letter. The vertical stroke and trace of a base are consistent with a *bet*.

3 The DJD transcription ignores an illegible letter in the beginning of the line.

Translation

1.]. upon[
2.]in all the wor[ds of
3.]. .[
4.] David[
5.] upon[

Comments

It is unclear whether the prepositions]עלי (lines 1 and 5) should be read as "upon me" or, more likely in light of the 3rd person narration elsewhere in this scroll, reconstructed with a 3rd person pronominal suffix.

Frg. 23

]◦ ◦[	1
[בכל מח]ן	2
] [	3
[ראוש]ר	4
[◦חא̊]	5
[ל̊]	6

Notes on Readings

5] ◦חא̊[. The DJD edition reads a *he*, whereas the shape of the letter is consistent with a *ḥet*. Next to it, traces of an *alef* are visible.

Translation

2]in all ..[
4]head[

Comments

Since frg. 30 appears to be concerned with 1 Sam 17:52, perhaps it is singnificant that the nouns מח]נה and]ראוש[occur in 1 Sam 17:53–54.

Frg. 24 i

ל̇ג̇דל̇ו̇[   ]   3

Translation

3   [   ]to magnify him

Frg. 24 ii

את]   1
כב̇ב̇]וד   2
ו̇°[3

Notes on Readings

3 The DJD edition reads a medial *pe*, yet the short space between the letters seems to indicate that this is a *waw*.

Translation

2.   gl[ory

Frg. 25

]°מ[1
וי[קו אל]   2
]ו ה̇[3

Translation

2.   and (he)]hoped for[

Frg. 26

[חֹרֹבֹש]לופה[

Translation

]d[rawn]sword[

Comments

The extant letters can be reconstructed with the phrase וחרבו שלופה, which occurs
in the Chronicler's account of David's combat with Goliath (1 Chr 21:16). The story
in 1 Sam 17:51 employs similar language: ויקח את חרבו וישלפה. Qimron suggests
[חֹרֹבֹש]אול (with 2 Sam 1:22). For another instance of writing without leaving a
space between the adjacent words, see frg. 21.

Frg. 27

[למען תֹ]חיה

Translation

] so that you[may live

Comments

This is Baillet's reconstruction (cf., e.g., Deut 16:20, 30:19).

Frg. 29

]שֹׁ∘∘[1
]∘∘הפ ∘[2
] וֹ]יֹרדפו   3

Notes on Readings

1 The editor read]שׁﬠׁﬢׁﬠׁ[. The traces of the first two letters can be variously construed. Hence, no reading is offered here.

2]∘∘הפ. The DJD edition reads הפנ[ם. Traces of the last two letters are difficult
to read.

Translation

2. and](they) pursued [

Comments

3 ‏ו̇ירדפו‎[ו‎. As do several other fragments of this scroll (e.g., frgs. 30, 32), this one seems to describe military activities. Given the use of the verb ‏וירדפו‎ in 1 Sam 17:52, which is reworked in frg. 30, perhaps this fragment also reworks this passage.

Frg. 30

ו‎[עד גת ועד ‎]עקרן‎   1
‎[הנופלים אשר ‎]   2

Translation

1. and]as far as Gath and [Ekron
2.] those who fell that [

Comments

1 ‏עקרן‎[עד גת ועד‎ו‎. The reconstruction (Baillet) follows 1 Sam 17:52: ‏וירדפו את הפלשתים עד בואך גיא ועד שערי עקרון ויפלו חללי פלשתים בדרך שערים ועד גת ועד עקרון‎ ("and they pursued the Philistines all the way to Gai and up to the gates of Ekron; the Philistines fell mortally wounded along the road to Shaarim up to Gath and Ekron").

2 ‏הנופלים‎. The editor suggested that ‏הנופלים‎ paraphrases ‏ויפלו חללי הפלשתים‎ of 1 Sam 17:52.

Frg. 31

‎[מ̇ ‎]   1
‎[ע̇[קרן ‎]◦‎   2

Notes on Readings

1 ‏מ̇‎[. The DJD edition offers no reading for the traces of the letter surviving in the first line. The bottom stroke and the two vertical strokes seem to be consistent with a final *mem*.

Translation

2   E]kron .[

Comments

Perhaps this fragment belongs with frgs. 29 and 30 (note the mention of Ekron in
1 Sam 17:52, which is cited or paraphrased in frg. 30).

Assuming that these three fragments, 29–31, are all part of a quotation from
1 Sam 17:52, the following combined text can be proposed:

[	]שׁ°°[ ]	1
[ויקמו אנשי ישראל ויהודה וירעו]	]°°הפ °[ ]	2
[ו]ירדפו [את הפלשתיי]ם [עד בואך גיא ועד שערי עקרן ויפלו חללי פלשתיים בדרך]		3
[	]שערים ו[עד גת ועד ע]קרן °[ ]	4
[	הנופלים אשר] [ ]	5

Frg. 32

מערכו[ת פלשתיּים °°		1
וימס]לבם ונגפו לפֹ֯נֹ֯יֹ֯]		2
לֹ֯וֹ֯ וֹ֯מֹ֯דֹים] קרעים[		3

Notes on Reading

3 לֹ֯וֹ֯[. The DJD edition offers no reading for the second letter. The vertical stroke
visible on PAM 42.944 may well be a *waw* or a *yod*. The editor read]לֹ֯וֹ֯מֹ֯דֹים[.

Translation

1.   forc]es of Philistines ..[
2.   and]their hearts [melted] and they were defeated before[
3.   ].. and garments[were rent

Comments

1 מערכו[ת פלשתיּים. The editor restored ת[א פלשתיּים. Yet in the absence of the
expected definite article, את הפלשתיים, it is suggested to reconstruct here with the
phrase attested in 1 Sam 23:3. For the orthography פלשתיּים (with a double *yod* vs.
פלשתים) see Amos 9:7.

2 וימס ‎[לבם ונגפו לפֿנֿיֿ]. The reconstruction follows a biblical idiom (cf. Josh 2:11). If the following line indeed depends on 1 Sam 4:12, this line may paraphrase 1 Sam 4:10: וילחמו פלשתים וינגף ישראל ("The Philistines fought; Israel was routed").

3 ‎[לֿ וֿמֿדֿיםֿ] קרעים. The proposed reconstruction follows 1 Sam 4:12: ויבא שלה ביום ההוא ומדיו קרעים ("and [a man of Benjamin] reached Shiloh the same day; his clothes were rent"). One wonders whether the beginning of the line could have read ויבא שיֿ[לֿוֿ. Shiloh is also mentioned in frg. 15.

Frg. 33

בי[דֿ֗ם]		1
]נתנוהו בידֿ[	]∘∘[ ]∘[	2
]וֿינוס משם אל מלך מואבֿ[		3
]מה[	]וֿל ו֗ש[	4

Notes on Readings

1 בי[דֿ֗ם. The first letter can be read either as a *dalet* or as a *resh* (Baillet).

Translation

1.   in]their [h]and[
2.   ].[ ]..[ ] they gave him into the hand[of
3.   ]and he fled from there to the king of Moab[

Comments

2]נתנוהו בידֿ[. Since the next line seems to allude to 1 Sam 22:3–4, it is likely that the 3rd masc. pl. form of נתן with a 3rd masc. sg. suffix is somehow linked to the preceding events, as described in 1 Sam 22:1–2. Perhaps restore ולא[נתנוהו.

3]וֿינוס משם אל מלך מואבֿ[. The fragment seems to deal with the episode recorded in 1 Sam 22:3–4. Unlike the biblical account, which depicts David's journey to the King of Moab using the verb הלך, the scroll utilizes a form of נוס, "to flee" (cf. the use of ברח to describe David's flight to Gath in 1 Sam 21:11).[312]

4]וֿל ו֗ש[ ]מה[. Qimron reads and restores with 1 Sam 22:6:]וישא[וֿל יש]ב בר[מה.

---

312 HALOT, 681.

Frg. 35

הת[פֿלשו לֹ]ֹ   1

]∘∘[2

Notes on Readings

1 הת[פֿלשו. The DJD edition reads the fourth letter as a *yod*, yet a *waw* is equally possible. There are traces of a *lamed* in the end of the line (see PAM 42.944; unnoticed by Baillet).

2 The DJD edition ignores the traces of ink visible under הת[פֿלשו.

Translation

2.   ](they) [rol]led in mourning .[

Comments

1 הת[פֿלשו. The Hitpael of פלש, "to roll about in mourning," is absent from the MT of Samuel-Kings.[313]

Frg. 36

]טֹ[1

ויד[עון כי כל]   2

]שֹתֹיֹ[3

Translation

2.   so that they may k]now for all[

3.   ]two[

---

313 HALOT, 935.

Comments

2 יד[עֻן. The 3rd pl. *yiqtol* forms with the ending וּ-, in this case a Qal form of ידע, occur, albeit rarely, in the Dead Sea Scrolls (e.g., 1QIsa^a XVI, 29; XXV, 27; 4Q464 5 ii 3).[314]

Frgs. 37–41: See Minute Fragments

Frg. 38

]○ ○[	1
מֹ והיא לֹו ח[	2

Translation

2   ]. to him and she .[

Frgs. 38–40: See Minute Fragments

Frg. 41

]○○[	1
]בני[	2

Translation

1.   ]sons of[

Frg. 42

יֹ[רושֹׁ]לים

---

314 See Joüon-Muraoka, *Grammar*, § 44e, pp. 136–137; Qimron, *Hebrew of the Dead Sea Scrolls*, 45.

Notes on Readings

The DJD edition reads]רוׄ ○[. According to PAM 42.944, the last letter can be read as a *shin*. The three letters seem to belong to the same word.

Translation

J]erusa[lem

Frg. 43: See Minute Fragments

Frg. 44 i

דׄ[	]1
וינ[גׄ]ף	]2
א֗בֹן[	]3
דׄ[]לׄ[	]4

Notes on Readings

3 א֗בֹן[. Baillet saw a trace of a letter before the *alef*. This trace seems to belong to a *lamed* written in the next line (PAM 41.735; 42.944).

Translation

2. [and (he) was] defeated

3. [ ]stone

Comments

3 א֗בֹן[. The context is unknown. Baillet points to the reference to a stone in 1 Sam 25:38, yet line 2, וינ[גׄ]ף, may suggest that the fragment deals with the war at Eben-ezer, אבן העזר (1 Sam 7:12; cf. also 4:1, 5:1). In 1 Sam 7:10 a form of נגף occurs.

Frg. 44 ii

]	1
]א	2
]בׄ	3
]○	4

Frg. 45

]מׄ[1
[וגבוראׄ]   2
]וׄרׄ[3

Translation
2.]and might[

Comments
2]וגבוראׄ[. The line could be restored with such biblical idioms as עצה וגבורה
(2 Kgs 18:20), משפט וגבורה (Micah 3:8), חכמה וגבורה (Job 12:13), הגדלה והגבורה
(1 Chr 29:11), or כח וגבורה (2 Chr 20:6). The scroll employs an *alef* as a *mater lectionis* for an 'a.' Cf. עשרא in frg. 1 1.

Frg. 46

]○[1
אלו[הים ○]   2
Bottom margin

Translation
2. Go]d .[

Frgs. 47–48: See Minute Fragments

Frg. 49

]בׄניׄ[

Translation
]sons of[

Frgs. 50–52: See Minute Fragments

Frg. 53

$$\text{]}\circ\text{ויך}[\quad 1$$
$$\text{]}\circ\circ[\quad 2$$

Notes on Readings
1 ויך[. The DJD edition offers no reading for the first letter. According to PAM 42.944 it is either a *waw* or a *yod*.

Translation
]and (he) smote .[

Frgs. 54–55: See Minute Fragments

Frg. 56

$$\text{[ממני הא]}$$

Translation
] from me ..[

Frg. 57

$$\text{א]ת הממלכֹהֹ]} \quad 1$$
$$\text{א]שֹר ידבֹרֹ]} \quad 2$$
$$\text{ות]קע נפֹש שניהֹם]} \quad 3$$

Notes on Readings
3]שניהֹם. The DJD edition has שניה[. However, on PAM 42.944 a trace of a vertical stroke is visible after the *he*. Its placement suits a final *mem*.

Translation

1.   ]. the kingdom[
2.   th]at (he) will speak[
3.   and]they both [be]came alienated[

Comments

3]קע נפֿש שניהֹם[ות. While several attempts have been made to read the first word as a form of תקע, "to blow" (see, e.g., the DJD edition), it is more likely that the scroll employs here a form of יקע, which in conjunction with the noun נפש denotes "to be torn away, alienated" (cf. Jer 6:8: פן תקע נפשי ממך).[315] It is unclear who the "two" referred to here are (David and Jonathan?).

Frg. 58

נ[שבעו]	1
אֿת[	
ושאול [ירא̇ד]ויד	2
י[שרא]ל	3
]ₒל̇ₒל̇[	4

Translation

1.   ](they) [s]wore[
2.   and Saul]was afraid of D[avid
3   I]srae[l

Comments

1]שבעו[נ. The reconstruction is by Qimron, who notes that the fragment may refer to David and Jonathan.

2 ושאול [ירא̊ת̊ד]ויד. This is Qimron's reconstruction.

---

315 BDB, 429.

Frg. 59

יִפֿדֿכמ]ה [	1
כ]יֿאֿ עֿוֿדֿנֿוֿ]	2

Translation
1.] he will redeem yo[u
2. f]or he still[

Comments
1 יִפֿדֿכמ]ה. The 3rd masc. sg. *yiqtol* of פדה, "to redeem,"[316] may have God as a subject.

2 כ]יֿאֿ עֿוֿדֿנֿוֿ]. The 3rd masc. sg. suffix in עֿוֿדֿנֿוֿ might also refer to God. If correct, the language of the fragment suits a prayer or an exhortation.

Frg. 60

]עֿ שֿ∘∘[	1
]תֿו נער]	2
]וֿבֿ לֿ]	3

Notes on Readings
3]וֿבֿ. The editor offered no reading for the first two letters.

Translation
2   ].. a youth [

Comments
2 נער. While the context of this fragment is unknown, one might note that David is referred to as נער in 1 Sam 17:58. Frgs. 26 and 30 may also deal with 1 Sam 17.

Frgs. 61–62: See Minute Fragments

Frg. 63

]תֿ רוחֿ[

Notes on Readings

The DJD edition disregards the space after the *taw*. It reads the last letter as a *he*, while a *ḥet* is equally possible.

Translation

]. spirit[

Comments

The extant wording can be variously reconstructed, e.g.,]תֿ רוחֿ[א, אפו]תֿ רוחֿ[מ נשמ (2 Sam 22:16).

Frg. 64

]אחרֿ[

Translation

]after[

Comment

The extant word may also be vocalized as]אַחֵרֿ[, "another."

Frg. 65: See Minute Fragments

Frg. 66

]בֿ[	1
כ]בוֿד[	2

Translation
2. g]lory[

Frgs. 67–72: See Minute Fragments

Minute Fragments

Frg. 5

]∘∘[	1
]לוֹה∘[	2

Frg. 6

]∘יֹ∘[	1
]∘א∘[	2

Frg. 7

]תֿ∘[	1
]∘ בֿה[	2

Notes on Readings
2 בֿה[. The right extremity of a base stroke before the *he* (left unread in the DJD) is, apparently, a *bet*.

Frg. 8

]יֿ∘∘[	1
]∘ תֿ[	2

Frg. 9

The fragment seems to preserve the left inter-columnar margin. It seems that there are traces of an interlinear addition in line 4 (see PAM 42.942).

○[	]	1
○[	]	2
○[	]	3
○○		
○[	]	4

Frg. 10

T]op m[argin

]כֹ̇○[1

Frg. 11

] קֿ[	1
]תֿ[	2
] יֿ○[	3

Frg. 12

] ל ○[

Frg. 13

]יֿ[	1
]○○[	2

Frg. 14

]○○○[

Frg. 16

]יוֹמֿ[

Notes on Readings

The DJD edition offers no reading for the first letter and reads the second one as a *yod*. The trace of a diagonal stroke in the beginning of the line may well be a *yod*, while the second letter can be read as a *waw*.

Comments

]יֹוֹמ[. This is, apparently, a form of the noun יום, "a day."

Frg. 18

]○	[	1
]○○○[		2

Frg. 20

]וֹ שֹׁ ת[

Frg. 28

]תֹ א לו [

Translation

] and not .[

Frg. 34

]○[	1
]תא[	2

Frg. 37

]○וֹ○[	1
]יֹ○[	2
]הֹ רֹבֹ[	3

Notes on Readings

1 The DJD edition reads the first letter as a *taw*, yet the reading is quite uncertain (e.g., a *bet* is likewise possible).

2 The last letter can also be a *ḥet*.

Frg. 39

ם[ ]◦[	] 1
ם[	] 2

Notes on Reading

The fragment may preserve a left inter-columnar margin.

Frg. 40

]שׁ ◦◦[	1
]◦ כֹל[	2

Frg. 43

]תֹה [	

This fragment may contain a left intercolumnar margin.

Frg. 47

]בֹה[	1
] וֹּנֹ◦[	2
]◦◦ל[	3

Frg. 48

]◦[	1
]◦נע[	2

Frg. 50

]◦ אֹהֹ[	1
]לֹֹ[	2

Notes on Readings
The trace of ink visible under the letter *he* (to the left) seems to belong to a letter *lamed* that was written in the next line.

Frg. 51

]∘כ∘[

Frg. 52

]ס֯[

Frg. 54

]שׁ֯∘[1
] ל֯[2

Notes on Readings
This fragment is not transcribed in the DJD edition.

Frg. 55

]∘ ∘[1
]∘∘[2

Notes on Readings
This fragment is not transcribed in the DJD edition.

Frg. 61

]ה֯תי[1
]∘מ∘[2

Translation
1.]rest[of

Frg. 62

]∘[	1
]ו גים וֹ[	2

Notes on Readings

2 ‫וֹגים‬[. The *DJD* edition suggests no reading for the first letter.

Frg. 65

]כה [	1
]∘∘[	2

Frg. 67

]∘	1
]∘∘וֹ	2
]∘אֹוֹ	3
]ומ	4

Frg. 68

∘[		][1
ים∘[		][2
∘∘∘∘∘∘[		][3

Frg. 69

לֹ[	1
ים∘[	2

Frg. 70

] ∘[	1
] תֹ∘[	2

Frg. 71

]ש [	1
] הוֹ∘[	2

Frg. 72

Top margin?

כי∘[	]1
ם[	]2

Notes on Readings

This fragment may contain a left intercolumnar margin.

Chapter 6: The Dead Sea Scrolls Rewriting Samuel and Kings

The Relationship between 4Q160 and 4Q382

A close scrutiny of the scroll 4Q160 led to the identification of a previously unnoticed overlap between this scroll and 4Q382. The overlapping text is a prayer:

4Q382 104 ii

1   מדבריך ולתמוך בבריתכה ולהיות לבבם [ל]ך̊ לקדשך̊ן] אותם ולהבר[

2   כפים למען יהיו לכה ואתה̊ להם ותצדק בֹ̊[ד]בֹ̊רֹ̊יכֹ̊הֹ [ותזכה בשפטכה]

3   כי אתה   למירֹ̊שֹ̊וֹנֹ̊ה̊ בעלתם והייתה להם לאב ולא̊א̊[לוהים ולוא]

4   עזבתם בידי מלכים̊] ולא [הֹ̊מֹשֹ̊לתה בֹ̊עמך̊ ○○ לֹ○ [ ] ○ [ ]○ ○[ ]   [

4Q160 2+6+10

1   אותם ולהבר כפים ל[מען יהיו]לכה ואתה תהיה להמה ותצ̊]דק בדבריכה]

2   [ותזכה בשפטכה   כ]יא אתה למרישונה בעֹ̊[לתם ו]הֹ̊ייתה לה̊[ם]

3   [לאב ולאלוהים ולוא עזבתם בידי מלכים ולוא המש]ל̊]תה בעמך   [

Along with the obvious similarities between the two texts, they also exhibit minor variations (underlined). First, the scroll 4Q160 2+6+10 1 reads תהיה להמה, while 4Q382 2 has להם. Second, the size of the lacuna in 4Q160 2+6+10 2 suggests that its wording might have been longer than that of the parallel section of 4Q382 2–3. This overlap allows for several possible scenarios:

a.   The scrolls 4Q160 and 4Q382 are copies of the same literary work.
b.   One of the two scrolls, perhaps 4Q160 as it yields a longer text, depends on the other.
c.   Both scrolls rely on an unknown written or oral source.

While recognizing that such a self-contained literary unit as a prayer is particularly prone to borrowing, the first scenario, i.e., that 4Q160 and 4Q382 are copies of the same composition, appears to be the simplest one. In this case, the addition of תהיה in להמה תהיה (4Q160) seems to be a clarification standing in parallel to the preceding יהיו לכה.

This putative literary work rewrites the following episodes from Samuel-Kings:

Samuel's prophetic call (1 Sam 3:14–18)	4Q160 1
Samuel's farewell address (1 Sam 12:2–3)	4Q160 7
Obadiah hides the prophets (1 Kgs 18:4, 6)	4Q382 1+3 (see also frgs. 2, 4, 5)
Elijah's ascent (2 Kgs 2:2–5)	4Q382 9, 11

The original scope of this composition remains unknown. Yet the reworking of Samuel's prophetic call (4Q160 1), the inclusion of a prayer by King Hezekiah (4Q382 46), and a possible reference to the Babylonian conquest (4Q382 39 7) indicate that it spanned the entire period of time covered in Samuel-Kings.

If this analysis is correct, the Dead Sea Scrolls yield at least three compositions rewriting Samuel and/or Kings. One is represented by the scrolls 4Q160 and 4Q382. The other two are 4Q481a, which deals with the events following Elijah's ascent, and 6Q9, which reworks several episodes from the book of Samuel and possibly from Kings, as the references to exile seem to suggest.

Scrolls Rewriting Samuel and Kings in their Literary and Exegetical Context
The attempt to place the scrolls rewriting Samuel-Kings within the Second Temple literature that is concerned with these books, especially other rewritings thereof, leads to several observations.

Dated before Josephus's *Jewish Antiquities* and, probably, LAB, these scrolls, along with the earlier Chronicles and the roughly contemporaneous work of Eupolemus, indicate that Samuel and Kings were the subject of considerable rewriting activity in Second Temple times, particularly in the last two centuries BCE.[317] On the other hand, unlike Chronicles, LAB and Josephus, which rewrite Samuel and Kings as a part of a larger literary project, the Dead Sea Scrolls studied here, at least in their present state of preservation, seem to focus on these books alone. While this might be accidental, the extant fragments of these scrolls rework passages excluded from the Chronicler's rewriting of Samuel and Kings. Whether these writings (or, at least, some of them) were meant to supplement the Chronicler's work in some way must remain unknown.[318] Similarly intriguing is the fact that at least two of the Qumran compositions, as we know them, focus on scriptural passages concerned with prophetic figures, Samuel, Elijah, and Elisha. To be sure, in the case of 4Q382 the references to Ahab and Jezebel, as well as the inclusion of Hezekiah's prayer (frg. 46), indicate a concern with royal figures too. Still, one wonders whether the main interest of these texts lies with the prophets.

Like other Second Temple rewritings of Samuel and Kings, the four Dead Sea Scrolls studied here extend the scriptural account with speeches, prayers, and psalms. Given their poor state of preservation, there is no way to estimate

---

317 It is with these scrolls in mind that the so-called "midrashic" features of the scroll 4QSam^a (see Chapter 1) ought to be studied, although, admittedly, the only exegetical concern this scroll may share with 4Q160 1 is the location of Samuel's sleep in 1 Sam 3.

318 A similar suggestion is often made with regard to LAB ending abruptly with the death of Saul, precisely the point where the Chronicler picks up in his reworking of Sam-Kgs.

the frequency and extent of these rhetorical and liturgical expansions in comparison to the sections that include a rewritten narrative. Yet one cannot fail to notice the sheer amount of fragments (especially in 4Q382) featuring rhetorical or liturgical content. The functions of these rhetorical and liturgical expansions might have been manifold, from a literary device, perhaps, even a literary convention following the example set by the Chronicler,[319] to a vehicle for the views of their authors,[320] to an implicit encouragement to pray.[321] This preponderance of speeches and liturgy and the paucity of narrative echo the impression gained from the overview of the Second Temple literature dealing with Samuel-Kings (Chapter 1).[322] This literature, including our scrolls, seems to have little interest in Samuel-Kings as a history (or historiography).[323]

As far as the textual history of Samuel and Kings in late Second Temple times is concerned, the foregoing study noted several cases where the wording of the four scrolls may reflect a Hebrew text diverging from the MT. Admittedly, these are very few and relatively minor, e.g., variations in prepositions and conjunctions, use of synonyms, and minor harmonizations. Still, they are a valuable addition to the "pool" of textual data garnered from other Second Temple texts.

---

319 On speeches and prayers in 1–2 Chr see, among others, M. A. Throntveit, *When Kings Speak: Royal Speech and Royal Prayer in Chronicles* (SBL Dissertation Series 93; Atlanta, Georgia: Scholars Press, 1987). On Josephus's use of speeches as a literary convention of Hellenistic historiography, see D. R. Runnalls, "The Rhetoric of Josephus," in *Handbook of Classical Rhetoric in the Hellenistic Period 330 B. C. – A. D. 400* (ed. S. E. Porter; Leiden, New York, Brill, 1997), 735–754.

320 On this aspect of the speeches and prayers embedded in Chronicles, see, for instance, R. Mason, *Preaching the Tradition: Homily and Hermeneutics after the Exile* (Cambridge: Cambridge University Press, 1990), 143; S. E. Balentine, "'You Can't Pray a Lie': Truth and Fiction in the Prayers of Chronicles," in *The Chronicler as Historian* (ed. M. P. Graham et al.; JSOTSup 238; Sheffield: Sheffield Academic Press, 1997), 246–267. For a discussion of the functions of the multiple prayers introduced by Josephus in his *Ant.*, see T. M. Jonquière, *Prayer in Josephus* (Ancient Judaism and Early Christianity 70; Leiden: Brill, 2007), 221–240.

321 Cf. a comment by D. Machiela regarding the didactic function of the prayers embedded in the Aramaic Dead Sea Scrolls in his "Prayer in the Aramaic Dead Sea Scrolls: A Catalogue and Overview," in *Prayer and Poetry in the Dead Sea Scrolls and Related Literature* (ed. J. Penner et al.; STDJ 98; Leiden, Boston: Brill, 2012), 305.

322 It is, perhaps, significant that the single fragment of 4Q118, considered by some to be the only Qumran copy of Chronicles, cites 2 Chr 28:27–29:3 (frg. 1 ii) alongside a 1st person speech unattested elsewhere (frg. 1 i). See further Brooke, "Books of Chronicles," 38–39.

323 See G. J. Brooke, "Types of Historiography in the Qumran Scrolls," in idem, *Reading the Dead Sea Scrolls: Essays in Method* (SBL Early Judaism and Its Literature 39; Atlanta: Society of Biblical Literature, 2013), 175–193, who points out the relative scarcity of the historical books, particularly Kings and Chronicles, among the Dead Sea Scrolls, as well as the paucity of quotations from or allusions to Samuel-Kings in the sectarian writings from Qumran. Compare similar comments by Davis, "4Q382," 93.

These scrolls have more to offer to the reconstruction of the Second Temple reception history of Samuel and Kings. They address passages that are rarely dealt with in detail in other contemporary writings (e.g., the events related in 1 Kgs 18, Elijah's ascent and its aftermath). Also, they reflect, albeit rarely, exegetical traditions unattested elsewhere (e.g., Samuel's sleep before Eli). Moreover, abundant with prayers and psalms, these scrolls enrich the already substantial body of liturgy pseudepigraphically ascribed to figures mentioned in Samuel-Kings (see Chapter 1). As is the case with the majority of this pseudonymous liturgy, the prayers embedded in these fragmentary scrolls are difficult to attribute to specific scriptural figures due to their lack of "biographical" links.

Though no effort was spared to offer the reader a comprehensive study of the Dead Sea Scrolls rewriting Samuel and Kings, this book, as any edition of the texts from Qumran, leaves ample room for further inquiry. New images and image enhancing techniques may help elucidate some of the obscure passages in the scrolls edited here. Also, as the scholarly debate over rewritten Scripture continues, more will need to be done in order to better situate these scrolls within this literature, as well as within Second Temple writings in general. To be sure, their poor state of preservation will always limit our ability to reconstruct their scriptural exegesis, scope, and *Tendenz*. Still, these four scrolls deserve to become an integral part of every inquiry into the early reception history of Samuel and Kings.

Bibliography

Aejmelaeus, A., "Hannah's Psalm in 4QSamᵃ," in *Archaeology of the Books of Samuel*. Edited by P. Hugo, A. Schenker. SVT 132; Leiden, Boston: Brill, 2010, 23–37.

Amara, D., "Psalm 151 from Qumran and its relation to Psalm 151 LXX," *Textus* 19 (1998): 1–35 (Hebrew).

Amir, Y., "Authority and Interpretation of Scripture in the Writings of Philo," in *Mikra*. Edited by M. Mulder. Peabody, Massachusetts: Hendrickson, 2004, 421–454.

Atkinson, K., *I Cried to the Lord*: *A Study of the Psalms of Solomon's Historical Background and Social Setting*. JSJSup 84; Leiden: Brill, 2004.

Attridge, H. W., *The Epistle to the Hebrews*. Hermeneia; Philadelphia: Fortress Press, 1989.

Balentine, S. E., "'You Can't Pray a Lie': Truth and Fiction in the Prayers of Chronicles," in *The Chronicler as Historian*. Edited by M. P. Graham et al.; JSOTSup 238; Sheffield: Sheffield Academic Press, 1997, 246–267.

Barthélemy, D., *Les devanciers d'Aquila*. SVT 10; Leiden: Brill, 1963.

Bartlett, J. R., *Jews in the Hellenistic World: Volume 1, Part 1: Josephus, Aristeas, The Sibylline Oracles, Eupolemus*. Cambridge Commentaries on Writings of the Jewish and Christian World; London: Cambridge University Press, 1985.

Barton, J., *Oracles of God*. New York, Oxford: Oxford University Press, 1988.

Bauckham, R. et al. (eds), *Old Testament Pseudepigrapha: More Non-Canonical Scriptures*. Grand Rapids, Michigan, Cambridge, UK: Eerdmans, 2013.

Baumgarten, J. M., *Studies in Qumran Law*. Leiden: Brill, 1977.

Idem, "A 'Scriptural' Citation in 4QFragments of the Damascus Document," *JJS* 43 (1992): 95–98.

Bearman, P. J. et al. (eds.), *The Encyclopedia of Islam*. Second Edition. Leiden: Brill, 1960–2005, 12 vols.

Beentjes, P. C., "'The Countries Marvelled at You': King Solomon in Ben Sira 47:12–22," in idem, *"Happy the One Who Meditates on Wisdom" (Sir. 14,20): Collected Essays on the Book of Ben Sira*. CBET 43; Leuven; Peeters, 2006, 135–144.

Begg, C. T., "Josephus' Portrayal of the Disappearances of Enoch, Elijah, and Moses: Some Observations," *JBL* 109 (1990): 691–693.

Idem, *Josephus' Account of the Early Divided Monarchy (AJ 8,212–420): Rewriting the Bible*. BETL 108; Leuven: Leuven University Press, 1993.

Idem, *Josephus' Story of the Later Monarchy (AJ 9.1–10.185)*. BETL 145; Leuven: Leuven University Press, 2000.

Begg, C. T., *Judean Antiquities 5–7*. Flavius Josephus: Translation and Commentary 4; Leiden: Brill, 2005.

Idem, Spilsbury, P., *Judean Antiquities 8–10*. Flavius Josephus: Translation and Commentary 5; Leiden: Brill, 2005.

Ben Zvi, E., *History, Literature and Theology in the Book of Chronicles*. London, Oakville: Equinox, 2006.

Bernstein, M. J., "4Q252: From the Re-Written Bible to Biblical Commentary," *JJS* 45 (1994): 1–27.

Idem, "The Employment and Interpretation of Scripture in 4QMMT: Preliminary Observations," in *Reading 4QMMT: New Perspectives on Qumran Law and History*. Edited by J. Kampen, M. J. Bernstein. Atlanta, Georgia: Scholars Press, 1996, 29–51.

Idem, "Review of Qumran Cave 4, VIII: Parabiblical Texts, Part 1, by H. Attridge, et al. Discoveries in the Judean Desert 13; Oxford: Clarendon Press, 1994," *DSD* 4 (1997): 102–112.

Idem, "Pseudepigraphy in the Qumran Scrolls: Categories and Functions," in *Pseudepigraphic Perspectives*. Edited by E. G. Chazon et al. STDJ 31; Leiden, Boston, Köln: Brill, 1999, 1–26.

Idem, Sh. A. Koyfman, "The Interpretation of Biblical Law in the Dead Sea Scrolls: Forms and Methods," in *Biblical Interpretation at Qumran*. Edited by M. Henze. Studies in the Dead Sea Scrolls and Related Literature; Grand Rapids: Eerdmans, 2005, 61–87.

Berthelot, K., "La notion de גר dans les textes de Qumrân," *RevQ* 19 (1999): 169–216.

Idem, "Guérison et exorcisme dans les textes de Qumrân et les évangiles," in *Guérisons du corps et de l'âme: Approches pluridisciplinaires*. Edited by P. Boulhol et al. Aix-en-Provence: Publications de l'Université de Provence, 2006, 135–148.

Black, M., "The 'Two Witnesses' of Rev. 11:3 f. in Jewish and Christian Apocalytic Tradition," in *Donum Gentilicium*. Edited by E. Bammel et al. Oxford: Clarendon Press, 1978, 227–237.

Bohak, G., "From Qumran to Cairo: The Lives and Times of a Jewish Exorcistic Formula (with an Appendix by Shaul Shaked)," in *Ritual Healing: Magic, Ritual and Medical Therapy from Antiquity until the Early Modern Period*. Edited by I. Csepregi, C. Burnett. Firenze: Sismel, Edizioni del Galuzzo, 2012, 31–52.

Bream, H. N., "Manasseh and His Prayer," *Lutheran Theological Seminary Bulletin* 66 (1986): 5–47.

Brenner, A., "מַרְאָה and מַרְאֶה," *Beth-Mikra* 25 (1980): 373–374 (Hebrew).

Brin, G., "The Bible as Reflected in the Temple Scroll," *Shnaton* 4 (1979–80): 182–225 (Hebrew).

Brooke, G. J., *Exegesis at Qumran: 4QFlorilegium in Its Jewish Context*. Sheffield: JSOT, 1985.

Idem, "The Significance of the Kings in 4QMMT," in *The Qumran Chronicle: Qumran Cave 4: Special Report: 4QMMT*. Edited by Z. J. Kapera. Krakow: Enigma Press, 1991, 109–113.

Idem, "Parabiblical Prophetic Narratives," in *The Dead Sea Scrolls after Fifty Years*. Edited by P. W. Flint, J. C. VanderKam. Leiden: Brill, 1998, 1:271–301.

Idem, "Some Remarks on 4Q252 and the Text of Genesis," *Textus* 19 (1998): 1–25.

Idem, *The Dead Sea Scrolls and the New Testament*. London: SPCK; Minneapolis: Fortress Press, 2005.

Idem, "The Books of Chronicles and the Scrolls from Qumran," in *Reflection and Refraction: Studies in Biblical Historiography in Honour of A. Graeme Auld*. Edited by R. Rezetko et al. SVT 113; Leiden, Boston: Brill, 2007, 35–48.

Idem, "From Florilegium or Midrash to Commentary: The Problem of Re-naming an Adopted Manuscript," in *The Mermaid and the Partridge*. Edited by G. J. Brooke, J. Høgenhaven. STDJ 96; Leiden, Boston: Brill, 2011, 129–150.

Idem, *Reading the Dead Sea Scrolls: Essays in Method*. SBL Early Judaism and Its Literature 39; Atlanta: Society of Biblical Literature, 2013.

Idem, "What Is a Variant Edition? Perspectives from the Qumran Scrolls," in *In the Footsteps of Sherlock Holmes: Studies in the Biblical Text in Honour of Anneli Aejmelaeus*. Edited by K. De Troyer et al. Leuven, Paris, Walpole, MA: Peeters, 2014, 607–622.

Idem, "Zedekiah and Covenant in the Scrolls from Qumran," in *On Warriors, Prophets, and Kings*. Edited by G. J. Brooke, A. Feldman. BZAW 470; Berlin: de Gruyter, forthcoming.

Brownlee, W. H., "The Significance of *David's Compositions*," *RevQ* 5 (1983–4): 569–74.

Camp, C., *Ben Sira and the Men Who Handle Books: Gender and the Rise of Canon-Consciousness*. Hebrew Bible Monographs 50; Sheffield: Sheffield Phoenix, 2013, 168–72.

Campbell, J. G., *The Exegetical Texts*. Companion to the Qumran Scrolls; London, New York: T & T Clark, 2004.

Charles, R. H. (ed.), *The Apocrypha and Pseudepigrapha of the Old Testament*. Oxford: Clarendon Press, 1913, 2 vols.

Chazon, E., "A Liturgical Document from Qumran and Its Implications (4QDibHam)." PhD diss., Hebrew University, 1991.

Idem, "Tradition and Innovation in Sectarian Religious Poetry," in *Prayer and Poetry in the Dead Sea Scrolls and Related Literature*. Edited by J. Penner et al. STDJ 98; Leiden, Boston: Brill, 2012, 55–67

Clancy, F., "Eupolemus the Chronographer and 141 BCE," *SJOT* 23 (2009): 274–281.

Clines, D. J.A. (ed.), *The Concise Dictionary of Classical Hebrew*. Sheffield: Sheffield Academic Press, 2009.

Cohen, N. G., *Philo's Scriptures: Citations from the Prophets and Writings*. JSJSup 123; Leiden: Brill, 2007.

Cohen, S. J.D., "False Prophets (4Q339), Netinim (4Q340), and Hellenism at Qumran," *JGRChJ* 1 (2000): 55–66.

Collins, J. J., "The Works of the Messiah," *DSD* 1 (1994): 98–112.

Collins, M. A., *The Use of Sobriquets in the Qumran Dead Sea Scrolls*. Library of Second Temple Studies 67; London: T&T Clark, 2009.

Conti, M. (ed.), *Ancient Christian Commentary on Scripture: Old Testament V: 1–2 Kings, 1–2 Chronicles, Ezra, Nehemiah, Esther*. Downers Grove, Illinois: InterVarsity Press, 2008.

Corley, J., van Grol, H. (eds.), *Rewriting Biblical History: Essays on Chronicles and Ben Sira*. Deuterocanonical and Cognate Literature Studies 7; Berlin/New York: de Gruyter, 2011.

Cross, F. M., Saley, R. J., "A Statistical Analysis of the Textual Character of 4QSamuelᵃ (4Q51)," *DSD* 13 (2006): 46–54.

Cross, F. M., Saley, R. J., "Singular Readings in 4QSamuelᵃ and the Question of Rewritten Scripture," *DSD* 20 (2013): 1–16.

Darshan, G., "The Long Additions in LXX 1 Kgs (3 Kgdms) 2 (35a-k; 46a-l) and their Importance for the Question of the Literary History of 1 Kgs 1–11," *Tarbiẕ* 75 (2006): 5–50 (Hebrew).

Davila, J. R., "Is the Prayer of Manasseh a Jewish Work?" in *Heavenly Tablets: Interpretation, Identity and Tradition in Ancient Judaism*. Edited by L. LiDonnici and A. Lieber. JSJSup 119; Leiden: Brill, 2007, 75–85.

Davis, K., "4Q481d frg. 3: A New Fragment of 4QApocryphon of Jeremiah C-b (4Q387)," *Semitica* 56 (2014): 213–230.

Idem, *The Cave 4 Apocryphon of Jeremiah and The Qumran Jeremianic Traditions*. STDJ 111; Leiden, Boston: Brill, 2014.

de Roo, J. C.R., "David's Deeds in the Dead Sea Scrolls," *DSD* 6 (1999): 44–65.

De Troyer, K., "The Septuagint and the New Testament: Another Look at the Samuel-Kings Quotations and Allusions in the New Testament," in *The Reception of the Hebrew Bible in the Septuagint and The New Testament*. Edited by D. J.A. Clines, J. C. Exum. Sheffield: Sheffield Phoenix Press, 2013, 49–55.

Debel, H., "'The Lord Looks at the Heart'" (1 Sam 16,7): 11QPsᵃ 151A–B as a 'Variant Literary Edition' of Ps 151 LXX," *RevQ* 23 (2008): 459–73.

Delamarter, S., *A Scripture Index to Charlesworth's The Old Testament Pseudepigrapha*. London: Sheffield Academic Press, 2002.

Dihi, H., "The Morphological and Lexical Innovations in the Book of Ben Sira," PhD diss., Ben-Gurion University of the Negev, 2004 (Hebrew).

Dimant, D., "Pseudonymity in the Wisdom of Solomon," in *La Septuaginta en la Investigacion Contemporanea*. Edited by N. Fernández-Marcos. Madrid: Instituto Arias Montano, 1985, 243–255.

Idem, "Use and Interpretation of Mikra in the Apocrypha and Pseudepigrapha," in *Mikra*. Edited by M. Mulder. Peabody, Massachusetts: Hendrickson, 2004, 379–419.

Idem, "Israel's Subjugation to the Gentiles as an Expression of Demonic Power in Qumran Documents and Related Literature," *RevQ* 22 (2006): 373–388.

Idem, "The Volunteers in the Rule of the Community: A Biblical Notion in Sectarian Garb," *RevQ* 23 (2007): 233–245.

Idem, *History, Ideology and Bible Interpretation in the Dead Sea Scrolls: Collected Studies*. FAT 90; Tübingen: Mohr Siebeck, 2014.

Doran, R. M., *2 Maccabees*. Hermeneia; Augsburg: Fortress Press, 2012.

Downing, F. G., "Redaction Criticism: Josephus' Antiquities and the Synoptic Gospels," *JSNT* 8 (1980): 46–65.

Egger-Wenzel, R., "The Testament of Mattathias to His Sons in 1 Macc 2:49–70: A Keyword Composition with the Aim of Justification," in *History and Identity: How Israel's Later Authors Viewed Its Earlier History*. Edited by N. Calduch-Benages, J. Liesen. Deuterocanonical and Cognate Literature Yearbook; Berlin: de Gruyter, 2006, 141–149.

Eshel, E., "Demonology in Palestine during the Second Temple Period," PhD diss., Hebrew University, 1999, 270–283 (Hebrew).

Eshel, H., "Non-Canonical Psalms from Qumran," in *The Qumran Scrolls and Their World*. Edited by M. Kister. Between Bible and Mishnah; Jerusalem: Yad Ben Zvi Press, 2009, 216–222 (Hebrew).

Feldman, A., *The Rewritten Joshua Scrolls from Qumran*. BZAW 438; Berlin: de Gruyter, 2014.

Idem, "An Unknown Prayer from 4Q160 and 4Q382," *Meghillot* 11 (2014), forthcoming.

Feldman, A., Goldman, L., *Scripture and Interpretation: Qumran Texts that Rework the Bible*. Edited by D. Dimant. BZAW 449; Berlin: de Gruyter, 2014.

Feldman, L. H., *Josephus's Interpretation of the Bible*. Berkeley: University of California Press, 1998.

Idem, *Studies in Josephus' Rewritten Bible*. Leiden: Brill, 1998.

Fernández-Marcos, N., "David the Adolescent: On Psalm 151," in *The Old Greek Psalter*. Edited by R. J.V. Hiebert et al. Sheffield: Sheffield Academic Press, 2001, 205–217.

Fidler, R., *'Dreams Speak Falsely'? Dream Theophanies in the Bible: Their Place in Ancient Israel Faith and Tradition*. Jerusalem: Magnes Press, 2005 (Hebrew).

Fiensy, D. A., *Prayers Alleged to Be Jewish: An Examination of the Constituones Apostolorum*. Chico, California: Scholars Press, 1985.

Flint, P. W., *The Dead Sea Psalms Scrolls and the Book of Psalms*. STDJ 17; Leiden: Brill: 1997.

Idem, "The Prophet David at Qumran," in *Biblical Interpretation at Qumran*. Edited by M. Henze. Studies in the Dead Sea Scrolls and Related Literature; Grand Rapids: Eerdmans, 2005, 158–167.

Franke, J. R. (ed.), *Ancient Christian Commentary on Scripture: Old Testament IV: Joshua, Judges, Ruth, 1–2 Samuel*. Downers Grove, Illinois: InterVarsity Press, 2005.

Fröhlich, I., "'Invoke at Any Time ...': Apotropaic Texts and Belief in Demons in the Literature of the Qumran Community," *BN* 137 (2008): 41–74.

Gilbert, M., "La figure de Solomon en Sg 7–9," in *Études sur le Judaïsme Helenistique*. Edited by R. Kuntzmann, J. Schlosser. Paris: Cerf, 1984, 225–249.

Ginzberg, L., *Legends of the Jews*. Philadelphia: The Jewish Publication Society, 2003, 2 vols.

Gnuse, R. K., *Dreams and Dream Reports in the Writings of Josephus: A Traditio-Historical Analysis*. AGJU 36. Leiden; Brill, 1996.

Goldman, L., "Biblical Exegesis and Pesher Interpretation in the Damascus Document." Ph.D. diss., University of Haifa, 2007 (Hebrew).

Goldstein, J. A., *1 Maccabees*. AB; Garden City, N. Y.: Doubleday, 1974.

Idem, *2 Maccabees*. AB; Garden City, N. Y.: Doubleday, 1983.

Gordley, M. E., *Teaching through Song in Antiquity*. WUNT 2 302; Tübingen, Mohr Siebeck, 2011.

Goshen-Gottstein, A., "Ben Sira's Praise of the Fathers: A Canon-Conscious Reading," in *Ben Sira's God*. Edited by R. Egger-Wenzel. Berlin: de Gruyter, 2002, 244–260.

Guttman, Y., *The Beginnings of Jewish Hellenistic Literature*. Jerusalem: Mosad Bialik, 1958–1963 (Hebrew).

Haran, M., "The Two Text-Forms of Ps 151," *JJS* 39 (1988): 171–82.

Harrington, D. J., "The Biblical Text of Pseudo-Philo's Liber Antiquitatum Biblicarum," *CBQ* 33 (1971): 1–17.

Hayward, R., "Phinehas-the Same is Elijah: The Origins of a Rabbinic Tradition," *JJS* 29 (1978): 22–34.

Hieke, T., "The Role of the 'Scripture' in the Last Words of Mattathias (1 Macc 2:49–70)," in *The Books of the Maccabees: History, Theology, Ideology*. Edited by G. Xeravits, J. Zsengellér. JSJSup 118; Leiden: Brill, 2007, 61–74.

Holladay, C. R., *Fragments from Hellenistic Jewish Authors, Vol. 1: Historians*. Atlanta: Scholars Press, 1983.

Hugo, P., "The History of the Book of Samuel: An Assessment of the Recent Research," in *Archaeology of the Books of Samuel*. Edited by P. Hugo, A. Schenker. SVT 132; Leiden, Boston: Brill, 2010, 1–22.

Hultgren, S., *From the Damascus Covenant to the Covenant of the Community*. STDJ 66; Leiden: Brill, 2007.

Hurowitz, V. A., "Eli's Adjuration of Samuel (1 Samuel III 17–18) in the Light of a "Diviner's Protocol" from Mari (AEM I/1, 1)," *VT* 44 (1994): 483–497.

Hurvitz, A., "The Linguistic Status of Ben Sira as a Link between the Biblical and the Mishnaic Hebrew: Lexicographical Aspects," in *The Hebrew of the Dead Sea Scrolls and Ben Sira*. Edited by T. Muraoka, J. F. Elwolde. STDJ 26; Leiden: Brill, 1997, 78–85.

Jackson, H. M., "Echoes and Demons in the Pseudo-Philonic *Liber Antiquitatum Biblicarum*," *JSJ* 27 (1996): 1–20.

Jacobson, H., "Samuel's Vision in Pseudo-Philo's Liber Antiquitatum Biblicarum," *JBL* 112 (1993): 310–311.

Idem, "Biblical Interpretation in *Liber Antiquitatum Biblicarum*," in *A Companion to Biblical Interpretation in Early Judaism*. Edited by M. Henze. Grand Rapids, Michigan/Cambridge, UK: Eerdmans, 2012, 180–199.

Japhet, S., *I & II Chronicles: A Commentary*. OTL; Louisville, Ky.: Westminster John Knox, 1993.

Jassen, A. P., "Intertextual Readings of the Psalms in the Dead Sea Scrolls: 4Q160 (Samuel Apocryphon) and Psalm 40," *RevQ* 22 (2006): 403–430.

Idem, *Mediating the Divine: Prophecy and Revelation in the Dead Sea Scrolls and Second Temple Literature*. STDJ 68; Leiden: Brill, 2007.

Idem, "Literary and Historical Studies in the Samuel Apocryphon (4Q160)," *JJS* 59 (2008): 21–38.

Idem, *Scripture and Law in the Dead Sea Scrolls*. Cambridge, MA: Cambridge University Press, 2014.

Justnes, Å., *The Time of Salvation*. Franfurt am Main: Peter Lang, 2009.

Kalimi, I., *The Retelling of Chronicles in Jewish Tradition and Literature: A Historical Journey*. Winona Lake, IN: Eisenbrauns, 2009.

Kappler, W., *Maccabaeorum liber I*. Göttingen: Vandenhoeck & Ruprecht, 1936.

Kedar, B., "The Latin Translations," in *Mikra*. Edited by M. Mulder. Peabody, Massachusetts: Hendrickson, 2004, 299–338.

Keddie, G. A., "Solomon to His Friends: The Role of Epistolarity in Eupolemos," *JSP* 22 (2013): 201–237.

Kister, M., "Ancient Material in Pirqe De-Rabbi Eli'ezer: Basilides, Qumran, The Book of Jubilees," in *"Go Out and Study the Land" (Judges 18:2): Archaeological, Historical and Textual Studies in Honor of Hanan Eshel*. Edited by A. M. Maeir et al. Leiden, Boston 2012, 69–93.

Idem, "Body and Sin: Romans and Colossians in Light of Qumranic and Rabbinic Texts," in *The Dead Sea Scrolls and Pauline Literature*. Edited by J.-S. Rey. Leiden, Boston: Brill, 2014, 171–207.

Knoppers, G. N., *1 Chronicles 1–9*. AB; New York: Doubleday, 2004, 2 vols.

Kugel, J. L., "David the Prophet," in *Poetry and Prophecy: The Beginnings of a Literary Tradition*. Edited by J. L. Kugel. Ithaca, NY: Cornell University Press, 1990, 45–55.

Idem, "4Q369 "Prayer of Enosh" and Ancient Biblical Interpretation," *DSD* 5 (1999): 119–131.

Kutscher, E. Y., *The Language and Linguistic Background of The Isaiah Scroll (1QIsaᵃ)*. Leiden: Brill, 1974.

LaCoste, N., "The Exemplary Sage: The Convergence of Hellenistic and Jewish Traditions in the Wisdom of Solomon," *The University of Toronto Journal for Jewish Thought* 1 (2010).

Lange, A., "'The False Prophets Who Arose Against Our God' (4Q339 1)," in *Aramaica Qumranica*. Edited by K. Berthelot, D. Stökl Ben Ezra. STDJ 94; Leiden, Boston: Brill, 2009, 205–224.

Idem, *Handbuch der Textfunde vom Toten Meer: Band 1: Die Handschriften biblischer Bücher von Qumran und den anderen Fundorten*. Tübingen: Mohr Siebeck, 2009.

Lange, A., Weigold, M., *Biblical Quotations and Allusions in Second Temple Jewish Literature*. JAJS 5; Göttingen: Vandenhoeck & Ruprecht, 2011.

Larson, E., "4Q470 and the Angelic Rehabilitation of King Zedekiah," *DSD* 1 (1994): 210–228.

Larson, E., Schiffman, L. H., Strugnell, J., "4Q470. Preliminary Publication of a Fragment Mentioning Zedekiah," *RevQ* 16 (1993–95): 335–349.

Leicht, R., "A Newly Discovered Hebrew Version of the Apocryphal 'Prayer of Manasseh'," *JSQ* 3 (1996): 359–73.

Machiela, D., "Once More, with Feeling: Rewritten Scripture in Ancient Judaism – A Review of Recent Developments," *JJS* 61 (2010): 308–320.

Idem, "Prayer in the Aramaic Dead Sea Scrolls: A Catalogue and Overview," in *Prayer and Poetry in the Dead Sea Scrolls and Related Literature*. Edited by J. Penner et al. STDJ 98; Leiden, Boston: Brill, 2012, 285–305.

Maori, Y., *The Peshitta Version of the Pentateuch and Early Jewish Exegesis*. Jerusalem: Magnes Press, 1995 (Hebrew).

McLain Carr, D., *From D to Q: A Study of Early Jewish Interpretations of Solomon's Dream at Gibeon*. SBL Monograph Series; Atlanta, Georgia: Scholars Press, 1991.

Mendels, D., *The Land of Israel as a Political Concept in Hasmonean Literature*. Tübingen: Mohr, 1987.

Milikowsky, Ch., "'Until Tzadoq Arose' in the Damascus Document: Tzadoq and His Appointment as High Priest in Early Jewish Interpretation," in *Shoshannat Yaakov: Jewish and Iranian Studies in Honor of Yaakov Elman*. Leiden, Boston: Brill, 2012, 285–299.

Mizrahi, N., "A Comparison of the List of David's Compositions" (11QPs^a 27:2–11) to the Characterization of David and Solomon in Kings and Chronicles," *Meghillot* 5–6 (2007): 167–196 (Hebrew).

Idem, "David's Compositions in 11QPs^a and the Semantics of נצח," *Studies in Language (Meḥkarim Balashon)* 11–12 (2008): 199–212 (Hebrew).

Idem, "'Kings' or 'Messengers' in 1 Sam 11:1? The Linguistic Background of the Masoretic Text," *Textus* 25 (2010): 13–36 (Hebrew).

Moore, C. A., *Daniel, Esther, and Jeremiah: The Additions*. AB; New York: Doubleday, 1977.

Morag, S., "'Light is Sown' (Psalms 97:11)," *Tarbiẕ* 33 (1964): 140–148 (Hebrew).

Idem, "'Well-Rooted Like a Robust Native Tree' (Psalms 37:35)," *Tarbiẕ* 41 (1971–72): 1–23 (Hebrew).

Muraoka, T., "Sir 51, 13–30: An Erotic Hymn to Wisdom?" *JSJ* 10 (1979): 166–78.

Murphy, F. J., *Pseudo-Philo: Rewriting the Bible*. New York: Oxford University Press, 1993.

Newman, J. H., "The Democratization of Kingship in Wisdom of Solomon," in *The Idea of Biblical Interpretation*. Edited by H. Najman, J. H. Newman. JSJSup 83; Leiden: Brill, 2004, 309–28.

Nickelsburg, G. W.E., *1 Enoch. A Commentary on the Book of 1 Enoch: Chapters 1–36; 81–108*. Hermeneia; Augsburg, Minneapolis: Fortress Press, 2001.

Nikiprowetzky, V., "Στείρα, Στερρα, Πολλη et l'exégèse de 1 Sam. 2, 5, ches Philon d'Alexandrie," *Sileno* 3 (1977): 149–185.

Nir, R., "The Appearance of Elijah and Enoch "Before the Judgement Was Held" (1 Enoch 90:31): A Christian Tradition?" *Henoch* 33 (2011): 108–112.

Nitzan, B., *Qumran Prayer and Religious Poetry*. STDJ 12. Leiden: Brill, 1994.

Idem, "4Q470 in Light of the Tradition of the Renewal of the Covenant between God and Israel," in *The Scrolls and Biblical Traditions: Proceedings of the Seventh Meeting of the IOQS in Helsinki*. Edited by G. J. Brooke et al. STDJ 103; Leiden: Brill, 2012, 163–176.

Noam, V., "The Origin of the List of David's Songs in 'David's Compositions'," *DSD* 13 (2006): 134–149.

Öhler, M., *Elia im Neuen Testament*. BZNW 88; Berlin: de Gruyter, 1997.

Olson, D., *A New Reading of the Animal Apocalypse of 1 Enoch*. SVTP 24; Leiden: Brill, 2013.

Olyan, S. M., *Social Inequality in the World of the Text: The Significance of Ritual and Social Distinctions in the Hebrew Bible*. JAJSup 4; Göttingen: Vandenhoeck & Ruprecht, 2011.

Pajunen, M. S., "The Prayer of Manasseh in 4Q381 and the Account of Manasseh in 2 Chronicles 33," in *The Scrolls and Biblical Traditions*. Edited by G. J. Brooke et al. STDJ 103; Leiden, Boston: Brill, 2012, 143–161.

Idem, *The Land to the Elect and Justice for All: Reading Psalms in the Dead Sea Scrolls in Light of 4Q381*. JAJSup; Göttingen: Vandenhoeck & Ruprecht, 2013.

Puech, É., "4QSamuel^a (4Q51): notes épigraphiques et nouvelles identifications," in *Florilegium Lovaniense: Studies in Septuagint and Textual Criticism in Honour of Florentino García Martínez*. Edited by H. Ausloos et al. BETL 224; Leuven: Peters, 2008, 373–386.

Qimron, E., "Improving the Editions of the Dead Sea Scrolls," *Meghillot* 1 (2003): 135–145 (Hebrew).

Rappaport, U., "A Note on the Use of the Bible in 1 Maccabees," in *Biblical Perspectives: Early Use and Interpretation of the Bible in Light of the Dead Sea Scrolls*. Edited by M. E. Stone. STDJ 28; Leiden: Brill, 1998, 175–179.

Reymond, E. D., *New Idioms Within Old: Poetry and Parallelism in the Non-Masoretic Poems of 11Q5(=11QPsª)*. Leiden, Boston: Brill, 2011.

Rodgers, Z., "Josephus' Biblical Interpretation," in *A Companion to Biblical Interpretation in Early Judaism*. Edited by M. Henze. Grand Rapids, Michigan/Cambridge, UK: Eerdmans, 2012, 279–307.

Rofé, A., "Midrashic Traits in 4Q51 (So-Called 4QSamª)," in *Archaeology of the Books of Samuel*. Edited by P. Hugo, A. Schenker. SVT 132; Leiden, Boston: Brill, 2010, 75–90.

Runnalls, D. R., "The Rhetoric of Josephus," in *Handbook of Classical Rhetoric in the Hellenistic Period 330 B. C.-A. D. 400*. Edited by S. E. Porter. Leiden, New York, Brill, 1997, 735–754.

Saukkonen, J., "The Story Behind the Text: Scriptural Interpretation in 4Q252." Ph.D. diss., University of Helsinki, 2005.

Schenker, A., "The Septuagint in the Text History of 1–2 Kings," in *The Books of Kings: Sources, Composition, Historiography and Reception*. Edited by A. Lemaire, B. Halpern. SVT 129; Leiden, Boston: Brill, 2010, 3–15.

Schiffman, L. H., *The Courtyards of the House of the Lord*. STDJ 75; Leiden: Brill, 2008, 505–517.

Schniedewind, W. M., "A Qumran Fragment of the Ancient 'Prayer of Manasseh'?" *ZAW* 108 (1996): 105–107.

Idem, *Society and the Promise to David*. New York: Oxford University Press, 1999.

Segal, M., "The Literary Development of Psalm 151: A New Look at the Septuagint Version," *Textus* 21 (2002): 159–174.

Segal, M. Z., *The Books of Samuel*. Jerusalem: Kiryat Sepher, 1956 (Hebrew).

Shaver, B. J., "The Prophet Elijah in the Literature of the Second Temple Period: The Growth of a Tradition." Ph.D. diss, University of Chicago, 2001.

Smith, M. S., "How to Write a Poem: The Case of Psalm 151 A (11QPsª 28.3–12)," in *The Hebrew of the Dead Sea Scrolls and Ben Sira*. Edited by T. Muraoka, J. F. Elwolde. STDJ 26; Leiden: Brill, 1997, 182–208.

Spiro, A., "Manners of Rewriting Biblical History from Chronicles to Pseudo-Philo." Ph.D. diss., Columbia University, 1953.

Stenhouse, P., "Samaritan Chronicles," in *The Samaritans*. Edited by A. D. Crown. Tübingen: J. C.B. Mohr, 1989, 219–264.

Stone, M. E., *Fourth Ezra*. Hermeneia; Minneapolis: Fortress Press, 1990.

Strugnell, J., "Notes en marge du volume V des "Discoveries in the Judaean Desert of Jordan," *RevQ* 7 (1970): 163–276.

Swanson, D., *The Temple Scroll and the Bible: The Methodology of 11QT*. STDJ 14; Leiden: E. J. Brill, 1995.

Tabor, J. D., "'Returning to the Divinity': Josephus' Portrayal of the Disappearances of Enoch, Elijah, and Moses," *JBL* 108 (1989): 225–238.

Talshir, Z., "Biblical Text from the Judaean Desert," in *The Qumran Scrolls and Their World*. Edited by M. Kister. Between Bible and Mishnah; Jerusalem: Yad Ben-Zvi, 2009, 1:109–141 (Hebrew).

Idem, "Textual Criticism at the Service of the Literary Criticism and the Question of an Eclectic Edition of the Hebrew Bible," in *After Qumran: Old and Modern Editions of the Biblical Texts – The Historical Books*. Edited by H. Ausloos et.al. BETL 246; Leuven, Paris, Walpole, MA: Peters, 2012, 34–60.

Idem, "The Miscellanies in 2 Reigns 2:35a-o, 46a-l and the Composition of the Book of Kings/
Reigns," in *XIV Congress of the International Organization for Septuagint and Cognate
Studies: Helsinki 2010.* Edited by M. K.H. Peters. Septuagint and Cognate Studies 59;
Atlanta: Society of Biblical Literature, 2013, 155–174.

Throntveit, M. A., *When Kings Speak: Royal Speech and Royal Prayer in Chronicles.* SBL
Dissertation Series 93; Atlanta, Georgia: Scholars Press, 1987.

Tigchelaar, E. J.C., "Lady Folly and Her House in Three Qumran Manuscripts: On the Relation
between 4Q425 15, 5Q16, and 4Q184 1," *RevQ* 23 (2008): 371–81.

Ibid., "Forms of Pseudepigraphy in the Dead Sea Scrolls," in *Pseudepigraphie und
Verfasserfiktion in frühchristlichen Briefen.* Edited. J. Frey et al. WUNT 246; Tübingen:
J. C.B. Mohr (Paul Siebeck), 2009, 85–101.

Idem, "Classifications of the Collection of Dead Sea Scrolls and the Case of Apocryphon of
Jeremiah C," *JSJ* 43 (2012): 519–550.

Tiller, P., *A Commentary on the Animal Apocalypse of 1 Enoch.* Atlanta, Georgia: Scholars Press,
1993.

Torijano, P., *Solomon the Esoteric King: From King to Magus: Development of a Tradition.* JSJSup
73; Leiden: Brill, 2002.

Tov, E., "The Temple Scroll and Old Testament Textual Criticism," *Eretz-Israel* 16 (1982): 100–111
(Hebrew).

Idem, *Hebrew Bible, Greek Bible and Qumran: Collected Essays.* TSAJ 121; Tübingen: Mohr
Siebeck, 2008.

Idem, "Reflections on the Septuagint with Special Attention Paid to the Post-Pentateuchal
Translations," in *Die Septuaginta—Texte, Theologien, Einflüsse.* Edited by W. Kraus,
M. Karrer. WUNT 252; Tübingen: Mohr Siebeck, 2010, 3–22.

Ibid., "The Aramaic, Syriac, and Latin Translations of Hebrew Scripture vis-à-vis the Masoretic
Text," in *Eukarpa, homage à Gilles Dorival.* Edited by M. Loubet, D. Pralon. Paris: Cerf,
2011, 173–185.

Ibid., *Textual Criticism of the Hebrew Bible: Third Edition Revised and Expanded.* Minneapolis:
Fortress Press, 2012.

Trebolle Barrera, J., "Histoire du texte des livres historiques et histoire de la composition et de
la rédaction deutéronomistes avec une publication préliminaire de 4Q481a, 'Apocryphe
d'Elisée'," in *Congress Volume: Paris 1992.* Edited by J. A. Emerton. VTSup 56. Leiden: Brill,
1995, 327–342.

Idem, "Samuel/Kings and Chronicles: Book Division and Text Composition," in *Studies in the
Hebrew Bible, Qumran, and the Septuagint.* Edited by P. W. Flint et al. SVT 101; Leiden,
Boston: Brill, 2006, 96–108.

Idem, "Qumran Fragments of the Books of Kings," in *The Books of Kings: Sources, Composition,
Historiography and Reception.* Edited by A. Lemaire, B. Halpern. SVT 129; Leiden, Boston:
Brill, 2010, 19–39.

Tromp, J., *The Assumption of Moses: A Critical Edition with Commentary.* Leiden: Brill, 1993.

van der Horst, P., Newman, J. H., *Early Jewish Prayers in Greek.* Commentaries on Early Jewish
Literature; Berlin: de Gruyter, 2008.

van Keulen, P. S.F., *Two Versions of the Solomon Narrative.* SVT 104; Leiden, Boston: Brill, 2005.

van Roy, H. F., *Studies on the Syriac Apocryphal Psalms.* JSSSup 7; Oxford: Oxford University
Press, 1999.

VanderKam, J. C., "Hanukkah: Its Timing and Significance according to 1 and 2 Maccabees," *JSP*
1 (1987): 23–40.

Ibid., "Studies on 'David's Composition' (11QPsᵃ 27:2–11)," *Eretz Israel* 26 (1999): 212*–220*.

Ibid., "The Wording of Biblical Citations in Some Rewritten Scriptural Works," in *The Bible as Book: The Hebrew Bible and the Judaean Desert Discoveries*. Edited by E. D. Herbert, E. Tov. London: British Library; New Castle, DE: Oak Knoll Press, 2002, 41–56.

Verheyden, J., *The Figure of Solomon in Jewish, Christian and Islamic Tradition: King, Sage and Architect*. Themes in Biblical Narrative; Leiden: Brill, 2013.

Vermes, G., *The Complete Dead Sea Scrolls in English*. London: Penguin, 2004.

von Weissenberg, H., *4QMMT: Reevaluating the Text, the Function, and the Meaning of the Epilogue*. STDJ 82; Leiden: Brill, 2009.

Wacholder, B.-Z., *Eupolemus: A Study of Judaeo-Greek Literature*. Cincinnati Hebrew Union College-Jewish Institute of Religion, 1974.

Wise, M., *Thunder in Gemini and Other Essays on the History, Language and Literature of Second Temple Palestine*. JSPSup 15; Sheffield: Sheffield Academic Press, 1994.

Idem, "4Q245 (PsDan Ar) and the High Priesthood of Judas Maccabaeus," *DSD* 12 (2005): 313–362.

Xeravitz, G., "The Figure of David in the Book of Ben Sira," *Henoch* 23 (2001): 27–38.

Yadin, Y., *The Temple Scroll*. Jerusalem: The Israel Exploration Society, 1983.

Zahn, M. M., "Genre and Rewritten Scripture: A Reassessment," *JBL* 131 (2012): 271–288.

Idem, "Talking about Rewritten Texts: Some Reflections on Terminology," in *Rewriting and Interpreting Authoritative Traditions in the Second Temple Period*. Edited by H. von Weissenberg et al. Berlin: de Gruyter, 2011, 93–119.

Zakovitz, Y., "'The Last Words of David': Studies in Psalm 151 from Qumran," in *On a Scroll of a Book*. Edited by L. Mazor. Jerusalem: Magnes, 1997, 73–84 (Hebrew).

Zetterholm, M., "The Books of Kings in the New Testament and the Apostolic Fathers," in *The Books of Kings: Sources, Composition, Historiography and Reception*. Edited A. Lemaire, B. Halpern; SVT 129; Leiden, Boston: Brill, 2010, 561–584.

Zsengellér, J., Gáspár, K. (eds.), *Rewritten Bible after Fifty Years: A Last Dialogue with Geza Vermes*. JSJSup 166; Leiden: Brill, 2014.

Index of Sources

Hebrew Bible

Jewish Apocrypha and Pseudepigrapha

New Testament

Index of Names and Subjects